NAXALISM

NAXALISM
How to Cope With

(Part II)

P.C. Joshi

ISBN : 978-93-5128-046-0
Price: ₹ 875

First Published 2014

Published by

Kalpaz Publications
C-30, Satyawati Nagar,
Delhi-110052
Ph. : 9212142040
E-mail: kalpaz@hotmail.com

Laser Typesetting : Shubham Printers, Delhi
Printed at : G. Print Process, Delhi

Cataloging in Publication Data—DK
Courtesy: D.K. Agencies (P) Ltd. <docinfo@dkagencies.com>

Joshi, P. C., 1941-
Naxalism : how to cope with / by P.C. Joshi.
v. 2 cm.
Includes bibliographical references.
ISBN 9789351280460

1. Naxalite movement. 2. Communism—India. 3. India—Politics and government. I. Title.

DDC 335.430954 23

Dedicated to

Shri M.K. Narayanan

Governor, West Bengal

This book is also in remembrance of :–

1. Shri Chaturvedi, Personal Senior Assistant to late Shri C.B. Gupta, the then chief minister of UP in late fifties and early sixties.
2. My B.Com. classfellow Shri Gyan Prakash Agarwal resident of 84, Raidopur, Baru Ram Bhawan, Azamgarh UP 276001 during 1958-60 at University of Allahabad.
3. Late Shri Purnanand Sanwal of Anand Niwas, Nainital and his daughter Late Smt. Ganga didi.
4. Late Shri B.D. Sanwal ICS who retired as the chief Secretary of UP.
5. Dr. R.K. Aggarwal D. Litt Assistant Professor in Commerce in late fifties and early sixties at University of Allahabad.
6. His (Dr. R.K. Aggarwal's) mother who was more than a mother for me.
7. Late Shri Rama Shankar Sanwal of Lucknow.
8. Late Shri Chandra Bhanu Gupta, the then chief minister of UP.
9. Late Shri Lalta Prasad Gupta of Karkhana Bazar, ALMORA my B.Com classfellow in 1958.
10. Late Jagdish Prasad Marwari, my B.Com classfellow at University of Allahabad in 1958-60.
11. Late Shri Shyam Bihari Tiwari, Tehsildar resident of village Aihar, in RAE BARELI district of UP, his late parents and wife Mrs. Shyama Tiwari.
12. Major Dewak Ram, Officer Commanding of 8 UP Battery, NCC, University of Allahabad in 58-61. He got NCC 'C' certificate examination postponed by one day when I was selected for a commission in Army in 1960 since the date was clashing with SSB interview. Major S.N. Sharma (in 1960) who had come down to Allahabad from Ranchi for taking my 'C' certificate exam had kindly agreed to such postponement simply to make my career in Army. I express

my gratitudes to them. Such were the officers of yesteryears-kind, honest, straightforward and helping.

13. Ms. S. Nisha who sustained me when I found myself in financial doldrums. It was not possible for me to re-pay her debt. I only express my respectful gratitudes and say I am beholden for the help. Karl Marx would not have been Karl Marx had Engles not come to his rescue financially.

14. Late Professor Shri J.K. Mehta, the then Head of Economics department of University of Allahabad in Sixties.

15. Shri P.N. Bhargava retired Assistant Director of Ministry of Home Affairs with gratitude.

P.C. Joshi

(A grateful person)

"If you wish to know where you are going to go in the future, you must first know where you have come from."

–An old African proverb

Contents

Preface

The book has to be read after the reader had gone through the first part of it–"Naxalism - at a glance." Though it is 'at a glance', it depicts almost the entire picture of Naxalism - now called Maoism-in India right from its inception to this date.

This part of the book is primarily on the measures to be adopted for containing Naxalism from the country altogether. Maoism is deepening its roots and widening its scope, spreading in more and more states with the ultimate aim of engulfing the whole of India. Naxalites will never abjure violence and arms. More or less it is a challenge for the security forces and the Intelligence Bureau which possesses intelligence collection capability. Perhaps, 'blow hot and blow cold' is the policy to be adopted by the Security Forces depending upon the ground situation of a particular area. In order to put a spanner in the Naxal movement, the grievances of tribals must be answered by including implementation of land ceiling laws and protecting them from exploitation. Funds allocated for their developmental projects must be spent on them and for their all round development. Funds should not simply evaporate to make the handlers rich. The aim of SF/local police has to be two-pronged-one minimising their own casualties and destroying the insurgents. The problem has to be taken up seriously and not as routine ritual. It has to be dealt with today and now. It is a dangerous trend that the Maoists have developed relations with People's Liberation Army, insurgents of North East, procuring arms from some of the foreign countries and seeking guidance and training from them. Even a few arms dealers inside India have been supplying ammunition, etc., to Naxalites. Naxals are elated by the success of Maoists in Nepal, most of whom have been recruited in the Nepal Army and some of them have been given officer's rank. All this shows that the Maoists have carved out a future for themselves in India as well.

Since the Maoists would never give up violence, India has to be prepared for the consequences. It has to be taken note of what Charu Mazumdar stated during his hey-days "militant struggle must be carried on not for land, crop etc., but for the seizure of the state power". And it can never be achieved unless violence is perpetrated all round.

In order to make the reading light and interesting, I have tried to mention a few true tit bits here and there.

December 2013 **P.C. Joshi**
New Delhi

1
The Beginning

In October 1920 Communist Party was formed in Tashkent by Ambani Mukherjee and Manvendra Nath Roy (M.N. Roy). In India it was founded in Kanpur (UP) under the banner of Communist Party of India (CPI). In 1964 a split occurred between CPI workers-one group supported by USSR retained the nomenclature of CPI and the other supported by China came to be known as Communist Party of India (Marxist) CPI-M. There was exodus from CPI (M) also in 1967. When in November 67 All India Coordination Committee for Communist Revolutionaries, (AI CCCR) was formed, which ultimately resulted in the formation of CPI (ML) in 1969.

In West Bengal state there arose a peasant's uprising engineered by Charu Mazumdar, Kanu Sanyal and Jangal Santhal in the village of Naxalbari. The work Naxal or 'Naxal wadi' is derived from the name of this village in 1967. Presently Naxalites call themselves as Maoists deriving the name from Mao-Tse-Tung of China. In November 1967 on the occassion of Lenins birth anniversary, radical revolutionaries opted out of CPI (M). It was caused since Charu Mazumdar, Kanu Sanyal and Jangal Santhal primarily desired to adopt armed struggle by peasants against landlord's atrocities on poor peasants, forced labour and not giving them their full share in crop produced by them with their toil and distribution of land to the landless. Jangal Santhal who was president of Siliguri Kisan Sabha declared such intentions on May 18, 1967 that they were ready to launch such a struggle against landlords. Alarmed and agitated over this announcement and subsequent developments, Landlord's men thrashed a share cropper within 5-6 days of this incident and the police was summoned to arrest peasants leaders. Police party was ambushed by a group of tribals led by Jangal Santhal. A police inspector was killed on May 23, 1967 many tribals joined the movement attacking the landlords. Charu Mazumdar who advocated the idea was inspired by Mao-Tse-Tujs ideology and thoughts to overthrow the government and elite classes by force. He wrote "historic eight documents" which influenced a lot of persons and were basis of Naxalite ideology. People were definitely inspired and impressed. In their estimation it was the right time for revolution and indeed they jumped into revolutionary violence.

In the year 1946 when the 'Tebhaga' movement began in Bengal it was, mainly for share in the produce. The movements, demand was to reduce the share of landlord from one half to one third. The movement was not for land, it was only to take greater share in the produced crops. But the move fizzled out.

In Telengana the movement was based on economic issues, exploitation and forced labour. Telengana movement (1946-51) had to be withdrawn by Communist Party when about 4000 people died in the struggle.

In 1967 the Naxalbari uprising was by Agriculture labour for foodgrains. Land Reforms Act of 1955 in West Bengal fixed land ceiling and the land owners (called Jotedars) started Transferring the land on the name of different people, of course, mostly on paper only and ultimately uprising in Naxalbari, Khairbari and Phansidewa resulted in the birth of Naxalism. Communist cadres who took inspiration from China's upheavels inspired, rather instigated, agriculture labourer and Tea plantation workers, etc., to unite and raise voice against the land owners (Jotedars). This uprising was led by Charu Mazumdar, Kanu Sanyal and Jangal Santhal, etc. Ultimately all this resulted in the formation of Communist Party of India (Marxist-Leninist) in April 1969. Explotation of peasants seemed to be one of the main causes of its birth.

In Srikakulam in 1968, the uprising of peasants again was based on agricultural produce, land and poor labourers. Tribals known as Girijans in Andhra Pradesh were a suppressed lot - exploited by the rich landlords. According to the Act no land was to be transferred from a Girijan to others with the permission of

Deputy Commissioner. Since most of the Girijans were under debt, they were compelled to alienate their land. Otherwise also two - third of their produce was to be given to the landlords. Vempatapu Satyanarayan united Girijans and started the movement which showed remarkably favorable results to them. He used to hold meeting of these poor tribals/agriculture labouress to make them awakened from the exploitation and the small groups which were attending such meetings were named as 'Dalams' which with the passage of time became agitated and violent. Landlords also became concerned and afraid of the violent Girijans/tribals. On October 31, 1967 landlords shot dead two tribals which was similar to throwing oil on the fire. Charu Mazumdar also paid a visit to Srikakulam. The landlords and money lenders were exploiting peasants. After being organised many peasants and tribals tried them, i.e., the culprits and then punished. Thereafter a well organised movement followed in Medinapore district of West Bengal, Bihar and Orissa during 1967-71. Tribals belonging to Santhal, Oron and Lodha tribes were mostly landless and cultivated Jotedars land under the 'Berga' system. It was tough handling the situation by the government when tribal groups used arrow and spears to attack landlords, looted cash and burnt all land deeds. Thus, slowly the movement died down in this area.

UP and Bihar also saw Naxal uprising in 1967-70 again on harvests by peasants. They seized the land at place and at time forcibly used to harvest crop. Zamindari abolition action by the government saw more and more land grabbing. In Bihar there was a fight for land which was achieved by adopting violent means. CPI (M) cadres saw an opportunity and encouraged such activities ultimately setting them branded as Naxalites.

In UP, Kheri-Lakhimpur district was also affected. Hunger to grab big chunks of land, particularly in Indians, exists even today. Operation 'Steeplechase' that surrounded Naxalites areas and action taken by local police was launched. They were provided outer security cordon by Army and this led Naxalites to disarray.

Meanwhile the leadership of the movement also developed differences of opinion/ideology and the main pillar of Naxalism, Charu Mazumdar died which was a great impediment for Naxal movement, at least for sometime to come. After lying low for sometime Charu's friends Kondapalli Seetharamaiah, K.G. Satyamurthy and Suniti Kumar Ghosh took over the leadership and formed a Central Organising Committee COC-ML in 1972. Earlier in 1969 when AICCCR was formed 'Dakshin Desh' and 'T. Nagi Reddy Group' came into existence. Dakshin Desh later on became Maoist Communist Centre. Kondapalli Seetharamiah prompted his group to go for 'money action', i.e., the focus shifted to looting money instead of concentrating on snatching land or land grabbing or forcible occupation of land. He formed People's War Group (PWG) after separating from COC-ML on April 20, 1980 whose main aim was to stop peasants/labourers/tribals from exploitation by the landlords/money lenders in Andhra Pradesh. Landlords were known in AP as Dora (Lord).

Land Ceiling Act was not enforced by the state government and PWG forcibly occupied the land of big landlords and passed it on to poor tribals/peasants. Party workers also got the wages of these people increased forcibly. They even occupied the forest land and distributed among the poor which resulted in branding Naxals as "Gorakala Doras" (Lords of the bushes).

Ideological differences led to the formation of Provisional Central Committee-Marxist Leninist (PCC CPI-ML). They also split into SN Singh group and Chandra Pulla Reddy group. SN died in Vishkhapatnam on October 21, 1984 and CP Reddy at Calcutta on November 4, 1984.

During Emergency period a number of Naxals were jailed. Exhibiting a sympathetic attitude a number of jailed prisoners were released by the Congress government, in 1989. Naxals took advantage and started extorting money, slapping levy and establishing People's Of this lenient attitude, courts. On May 8, 1992 PWG was banned but by next year they indulged in more violence. Next step Naxals took was to sneak into tribal district of Bastar in erstwhile Madhya Pradesh and launched an agitation for increased wage for Tendu leaf to labourer by the contractor, punished the corrupt officers which enhanced their prestige in the eyes of poor villagers. The tribals of Gadchiroli district in Maharashtra were also impressed with the movement since the forest officers had almost vacated the forest land after being afraid of Naxals. Today there is a nexus between mine managers and Maoists. They obtain levy, tax and explosives from mining companies and thrive on mineral rich districts of different states. In Latehar alone there are twenty coal blocks, eight of which are in the private sector. Naxalites are making mineral rich areas their habitat and not allowing any political interference or intrusion by the security forces. These areas are gold mines and private companies do not want government to step in.

In Bihar three groups of Naxalites namely, the Maoist Communist Centre (MCC), CPI-ML (Anti Lin Biao) formed by Vinod Mishra in December 1993 and Party Unity CPI-ML, formed by COC CPI-ML of Andhra and Unity Organisation of CPI-ML. West Bengal in 1982. The Naxal group 'Dakshin Desh', formed on Oct 20, 1969 did not join any group and it was led by Kanai Chatterjee and Amulya Sen. But later on it merged with Revolutionary Communist Centre (RCCI) in 2003. In Bihar the Naxal movement had cast-based bias and Yadavs, belonging to MCC Billed 42 Rajputs (upper caste villagers) on May 29, 1987 of Baghaura, Dalechak villages of Aurangabad district. MCC also ventured to bill 37 land owning 'Bhumihars' in Bara village of Gaya district. Later on in the year 2004 when CPI (Maoist) was founded a document was adopted on "strategy and tactics" which stated that "by following the tactics of sudden attack and annihilation, it is absolutely possible to defeat the enemy and achieve victory for the people in single battles".

Three districts of Bihar - Gaya, Jamui and Aurangabad account for 60 per cent of Maoist violence according to Home Ministry. It further opines that the contribution of anti-Maoist forces is not visible. MHA wrote to the Bihar, Ashok Kumar Sinha that the Revolutionary Democratic Front, alleged to be a Maoist front enjoyed a free run, it organised a rally under the banner of Janata Par Yudh Virodhi Manch allowed by the state though the central government was against it. A top CRPF official in this connection said, "the event was meant to showcase the organisational capabilities of the North Bihar unit of CPI (Maoist). It was aimed at conducting mass mobilisation which needs to be viewed seriously by the state Administrations.[1]

Forcible occupation of the property is one of the prominent tactics in Bihar. In Nangla (Jehanabad) Bihar former Pakistan Prime Minister (Aug 27, 2004 to November 15, 2007) Shaukab Aziz's wife Mrs. Rukhsana's ancestral home was forcibly occupied by Naxalites of People's War Group hoisting a red flag over the lavish building. The 'Haveli' is now in shambles and around 40 bighas of agricultural land belonging to Rukhsana's parents is under the control of Naxalites[2]. Ultras in Bihar are a real menace. They surround police building and cause indiscriminate firing to scare away people (Khudwa village in Aurangabad on August 4, 2013) disrupting trains, blowing up railway lines, attacking police

Rukhsana Aziz's Ancestral *Haveli* in Nagla is in a Dilapidated State.

jawans etc., is theirs ritual. Vexed with these problems Bihar BJP chief and former state Deputy Chief Minister Sushil Kumar Modi had asked Nitish Kumar, the Chief Minister to take tough action against Naxals and that they would fully support such action by Nitish government.

Naxals demand price for allowing road projects in Bihar. They have even bargained for upto 20 per cent levy of the cost of the project. Several Area Commanders arrested in Aurangabad and Gaya have admitted to charging levy of upto 7-10 per cent of the project cost. A CPI (Maoist) politburo member arrested recently in Gaya, Jagdish Yadav reportedly told the police that he had collected at least Rs. five crores as levy in Aurangabad and Gaya Jungles. Forty central government road projects are under way in areas hit by Left wing Extremism (LWE) in Bihar-since 2009.

In Gaya	15
In Jamui	14
In Aurangabad	6
Jehanabad	5

The cumulative project cost worked out to Rs. 497.94 crore to build 468 km of road. Till May 27, 2011 work was finished on 220.4 km. The Asian Development Bank (ADB) is funding state highways worth nearly Rs. 700 crore in Gaya, Aurangabad and Jehanabad.[3]

Tendu leaves and illegal mining is the real game plan in Naxal heartland. Both of them are thriving source of income for extremists in the Karbandia hills in Rohtas.

To counter the central government's efforts of consolidation by way of forming a joint coordination committee consisting of police chiefs of Naxal-effected states, People's War (STET) attempted to bring together all revolutionary parties that followed Marxist-Leninist-Maoist ideology. Resultantly, by July 2001 nine left-wing extremists agreed to form an umbrella organisation not only in India but Bangladesh, Nepal and Sri Lanka as well. The organisation was named, The Coordination Committees of Maoist

Parties and Organisation of South Asia (CCOMPOSA) which consisted of–

1. CPI-ML People's War
2. The Maoist Communist Centre (MCC)
3. The Revolutionary Communists Centre of India (MLM)
4. The Purba Bengal Sarbohara Party (Maoist) (Punargathan Kendra)
5. The Bangladesh Samyawadi Party (ML)
6. The Communist Party of Nepal (Maoist)
7. The Revolutionary Communist Centre of India Maoist
8. The Purba Bangla Sarbohara Party
9. The Communist Party of Ceylon (Maoist)

(article by K. Srinivas Reddy in the Front line).[4]

The Director General of Police, Jharkhand has stated that the Maoists are receiving support from outside India. Union Home Ministry found that the Sweden-based author Jan Myrdal son of Noble Laureate couple Gunar and Alva Myrdal had attended pro-Naxal conventions in Kolkata, Hyderabad, Ludhiana and Delhi in early 2012 and allegedly expressed support to the CPI (Maoist) ideology of armed struggle against the state. "Jan Myrdal during his stay in India advised CPI (Maoist) to garner support from the middle class in India by focussing on propaganda against security forces and highlighting human rights issues."[5] In one of his books *"India Waits"* Jan Myrdal has mentioned that India awaits a Marxian inspired people's movement emanating from rural India, parallel to the Chinese Communist revolution. About three years ago, Myrdal had visited Bastar and met CPI (Maoist) leaders including Mupalla Laxman Rao alias Ganpathy.[6]

A Hindi daily "Hari Bhumi" on June 3, 2013 ran a report that Myrdal had reportedly visited Chhattisgarh last year with tips for Naxals about their movements. The report mentioned a recently seized letter written by senior Maoist Katkam Sudarshan with details of foreign help. Myrdal did visit Bastar a few years ago and interviewed CPI (Maoist) Supreme Commander Ganpathy[7].

Five Germans entered Balangir district in Odisha without seeking permission from the state/central authorities on May 6, 2012 and stayed for a week at Turla. They were taken into custody from premises of an NGO.

The Bihar government ousted 'French Tourists' from Nawada (Bihar) for violating Visa Rules on April 23, 2012. The government suspected the tourists working for a 'Maoist sympathasiers' voluntary group claiming to be working for rights of the landless people. The tourist entered Nawada from Jamui on April 21, 2013. It seems that the Communist regimes of yesteryears deeply support Maoists in India.

Recently, on January 16, 2013 Nepali Congress leader Sushil Koirala warned in Kathmandu that if the Maoist's bid to capture state power "by hook or crook" succeeds in Nepal, the country would become a fertile ground for Indian Naxalites which would not be in the interest of India.

Thus together, i.e., Indian and Nepali Maoist may connive to capture state power together in Nepal as well as in India. As it is, Nepali Maoists are already in touch with Indian Naxals and vice versa.

Even Nepali Congress leader Sushil Koirala has given a hint of trying to capture state power together in Nepal as well as in India. As it is, he say, Nepali Maoists are already in touch with Indian Naxals and vice versa.

On June 3, 2013 the Communist Party of Nepal-Maoist (CPN-Maoist) chairman Kiran announced a renewal of the bonding with the South Asian Marxist Leninist-Maoists (MLM) parties with special emphasis on Indian Maoists.[8]

However, Naxal movement is expanding quietly.

A document from central committee meeting of Maoists in Saranda forest in Jharkhand in February 2011 shows that the Maoists have decided to set up four (4) guerrilla bases in Jungle Mahal in the next two years. The transfers of several officials after Mamata government took over disturbed their plans to some extent as Maoists had contacts within the administration at the grassroots. Since then, sources close to CPI (Maoists) say they have been able to regroup at least 17 squads in West Midnapore district alone in the past two months (Aug-Sept 2011). – The Indian Express, Oct 14, 2011.

Maoists are trying to spread their presence/influence in Assam. Even the Assam state government declared that the Maoist activities are growing in at least seven (7) districts of the state, particularly the tea-belt. On April 26, 2013, two Maoist cadre identified as Aklanta Rabha and Siraj Rabha who were on their way to Meghalaya to spread Maoist idealogy in some Khasi village(s) were captured.

A Constitution Bench led by Justice Patnaik of the Supreme Court of India, emphasising on validation of rights of tribals and forest-dwellers over the forest lands, said that Naxalism was a result of an oversight of constitutional provisions relating to administration of schedule areas and tribes of the country "Nobody looks at Schedules V and VI of the Constitution and the result is Naxalism. These provisions apply to states like Andhra Pradesh, Jharkhand, Gujarat, Himachal Pradesh, Maharashtra, Madhya Pradesh, Chhattisgarh, Orissa, Rajasthan and North-Eastern states such as Assam, Meghalaya, Tripura and Mizoram.[9]

In November 2010 a couple of 'miscreants' threw chilli powder at some of the jawans of 19 Assam Rifles Battalion of Rajgarh in Assam's Dibrugarh district and snatched two AK-47 rifles. Later on it came to the notice that the 'miscreants' were Maoist elements. In the first week of May 2013 Assam state police saw first encounter leading to the death of left wing extremists.

In 2010 Aditya Bora said to be topmost leader of Assam unit was arrested on the Jharkhand-Orissa border which gave the inkling of the presence of Maoists.

The first ever CPI (ML) member to the Lok Sabha, Jayanta Rongpi was elected to the Lok Sabha for four consecutive terms since 1991. For the first three times he won as a leader of Autonomous State Demand Committee (ASDC) and in the 4th time he declared himself a CPI-ML (Liberation) candidate.

Maoists in Assam have targeted Assamese speaking population including Ahom community. The four Maoists killed on May 9, 2012 in Sadiya were from Ahom community. Maoists are believed to have two frontal groups :

(i) Upper Assam Leading Committee

(ii) Assam Students Youth Organisation.

CPI (Maoist) are so well-entrenched in Bastar Abhujmad area that CRPF launched "Operation Hakka" in 2012 to clear the Abhujmad area of Naxal concentration but it tailed and the operation had to be abandoned.[10]

Besides, it should be taken note of the fact that Naxals have sufficient arms and ammunition. On February 6, 2004, 500 rifles were looted from District Police Armoury in Koraput (Orissa), on November 11, 2006, 185 rifles looted from Home Guards Training Centre ; on March 15, 2007, 55 policemen were killed and 48 rifles looted in Chhattisgarh; on April 6, 2010, 75 CRPF men were killed in an ambush and 82 weapons were looted from them. Recently on July 30, 2013 National Investigation Agency (NIA) declared that M-16 rifles seized from a Maoist courier Anil Kumar in Hazaribag (Bihar) on August 29, 2012 was that of an American military. Yet another weapon in the hands of Maoist is explosives. They plant landmines on the road and when any vehicle of security forces passes through it, "it explodes and then Maoist ambush the patrol party which causes considerable damage. Shri K.P.S. Gill former Punjab Police Chief says "The anti-Naxal strategy is a flop. Someone picked up the strategy from some book and forced it down the throats of the paramilitary forces".

Charu Mazumdar had exhorted Naxal cadres saying "Militant struggles must be carried on not for land, crops, etc. but for the seizure of state power." Of late, there is a small change in the approach of some individual Naxals who have bifurcated from the original ideology and have taken to extortion, levy etc. But Maoists of the stature of Ganpathy and Kishanda have toed the line of Charu Mazumdar. Their line is "She immediate aim and programme of the Maoist Party is to carry on and complete the already ongoing and advancing New Democratic Revolution. The revolution will be carried out and completed through protracted People's War with the armed seizure of power remaining as its central and principal task."

However, a recent report that appeared in the *Indian Express* filed by Ashutosh Bharadwaj says "Maoists admit Support down, strength and weapons depleted." It says an 11-page resolution was passed by CPI (Maoist)'s Central Committee in its fourth meeting earlier this year-the 4th after merger of PWG and MCC in September 2004. The resolution says:–

1. Present status of the party:–
   (a) Setbacks in all zones and divisions across the country. North Regional Bureau completely damaged.
   (b) Urban movement weakend middle class and intellectual support ended.
   (c) Central Weapon manufacturing and supply unit damaged.
   (d) Movement facing critical situation.
2. Future Plan–
   (a) Abduction of 'political prisioners' has limitations, to be used selectively.
   (b) 'Preserve' top leadership, develop 'Secondary leadership leadership at all levels.
   (c) Strengthen party ideology and politically defeat 'revisionist' and 'post modernist' theories.
   (d) Recently non 'proletariat trends' in the party intensify guerrilla war.

The Resolution describes about :–

1. Dandakaranya Special Zonal Committee–mass base and PLGA recruitment decreased.
2. North Telangana (NT)

3. Andhra-Orissa Border (AOB). Both is in ebb.
4. Gondia division–continues in weak condition. Since a series of arrests took place in the past few years, the Maharashtra movement is facing setback.
5. Orissa movement–weakened because of Sabyasachi Panda and enemy onslaught.
6. Bihar-Jharkhand (BJ) Movement suffered setback due to decrease in mass base.
7. The Paschim Bang Movement-Lalgarh movement and in 'Asom' (Assam) The movement weakened because of encounter of the state committee's secretary and arrest of other comrades.
8. North Regional Bureau-was completely damaged and movements of various states weakened a lot.
9. Tamil Nadu and Karnataka movement, the political and organisation weaknesses led to the weakening of movement in these states. It worsened by the arrest of three state committee members in Tamil Nadu and two in Karnataka and some cadres at various levels.

The Resolution admitted–"Between 2009 and 2012, the enemy damaged our central weapon and manufacturing and supply, departments, the political and military peoples intelligence departments, the central magazine department, Central Sub-committee on Mass Organisations (SUCOMO) and the international department."

It further said "Since the third central committee meeting, four central committee members Bhupesh, Amber, Sukant and Jaspal–had been arrested and politburo member Kishanji had been killed."

The resolution also decided to "intensify political agitation for the unconditional release of senior party leaders Narayan Sanyal, Sheela Di (Sheela Marandi), Kobal Gandhy and Amberda (Purnendu Shekhar)". "Defence Committee" will be formed and an office opened in Delhi for the purpose.

Yet the party's Central Committee is sure to succeed. It says "Once again we can create favourable subjective situation and advance for the fulfillment of the tasks given by the Unity Congress (of September 2004)"[11]. Material conditions are more ripe than earlier. The movement will recover"[12].

Make no mistake to understand Maoist conflict with the sovereign state power of India as inscribed in the Constitution of the CPI (Maoist) itself which says "The ultimate aim or maximum programme of the party is the establishment of a communist society. This New Democratic Revolution will be carried out and completed through armed agrarian revolutionary war, i.e., Protracted People's War with area-wise seizure of power remaining as its central task"[13]. CPI Maoist is already working fast on these lines as set for the party by the their constitution. They are already carrying out area-wise war by way of Protracted Peoples War to achieve the goal of seizure of state power.

Attached are a few maps of Naxal affected states of India depicting districts where Maoists have 'established' themselves and are trying to spread their influence. Unless we use effective and radical remedy Maoism is here in India to stay.

References

1. The *Indian Express*, March 6, 2013 report by Rahul Tripathi.
2. Story by Faizan Ahmad TNN (Times News Network).
3. The *Indian Express*, August 2, 2011 Report by Santosh Singh.
4. http://www.frontline on net.com/fi2021/stories/20031.24003602000.htm.
5. Statement by Jitendra Singh, Minister of State in Rajya Sabha.
6. The *Decan Herald*, May 21, 2012,
7. The *Indian Express*, June 6, 2013.
8. *Times of India*, Kolkata edition at July 6, 2013. Report by Ceaser Mandal.
9. The *Indian Express*, October 3, 2011.

10. *Ibid.*
11. The *Indian Express* of September 19, 2013 Report by Ashutosh Bharadwaj.
12. *Ibid*-statement by Leftist ideologue Varavara Rao.
13. Party's constitution. Also available on line.

Bihar

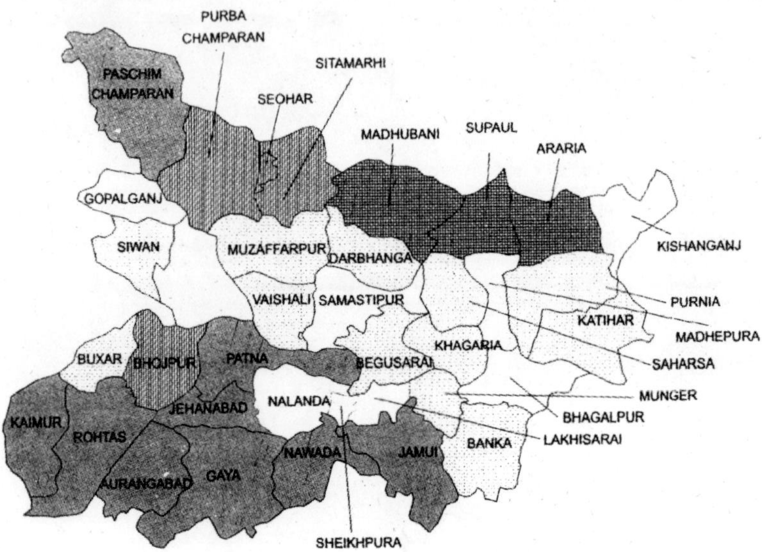

Naxal Affected Areas with Maoists Influence.

West Bengal

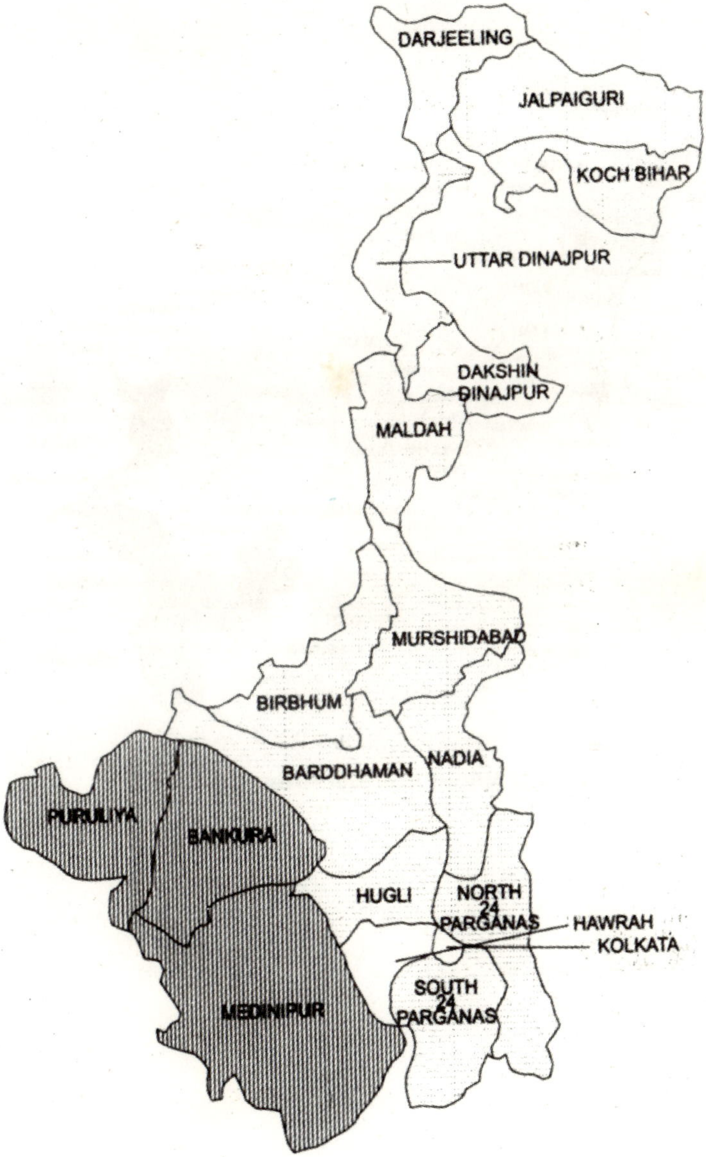

Naxual Affected Area with Maoists Influence.

Uttar Pradesh

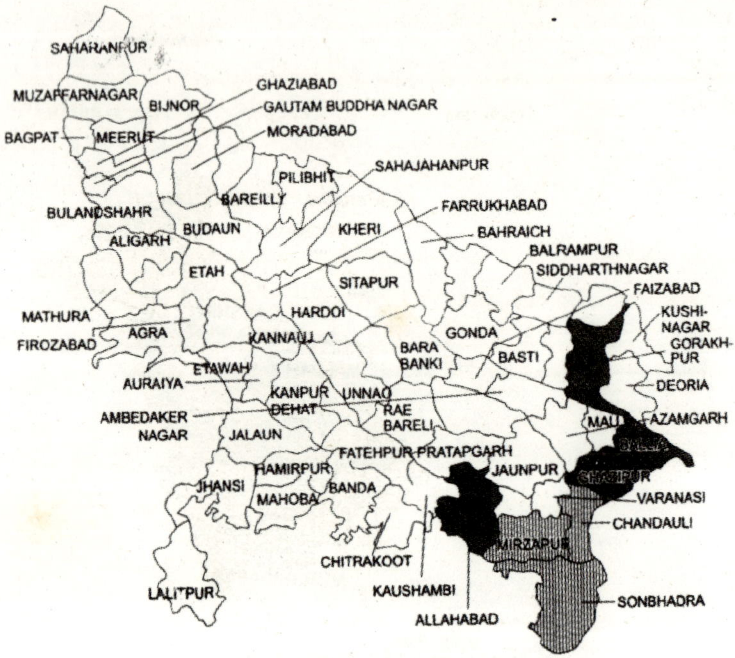

Naxual Affected Areas with Maoists Influence.

Uttaranchal

Naxual Affected Area with Maoists Influence.

Maharashtra

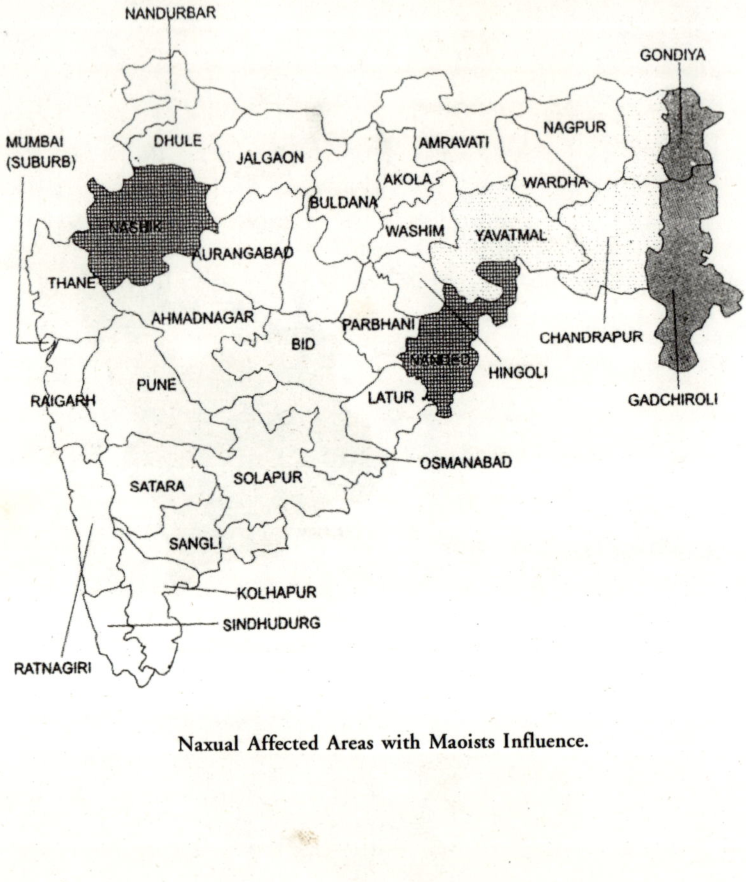

Naxual Affected Areas with Maoists Influence.

Karnataka

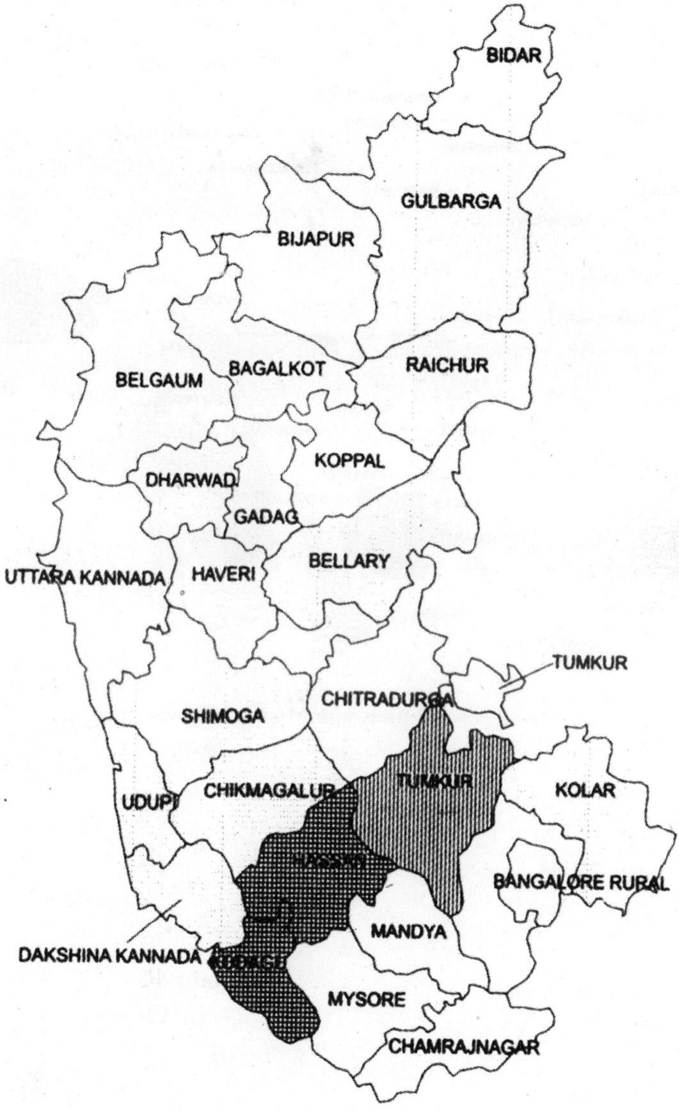

Naxual Affected Areas with Maoists Influence.

Madhya Pradesh

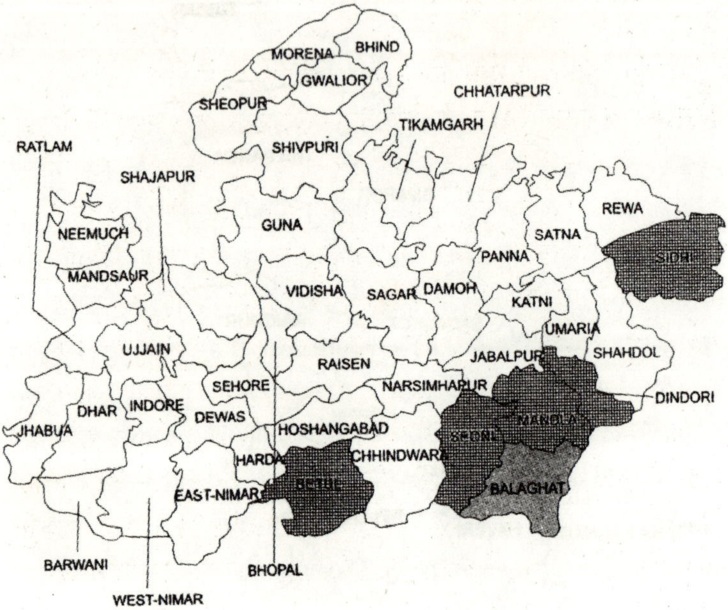

Naxual Affected Areas with Maoists Influence.

Tamil Nadu

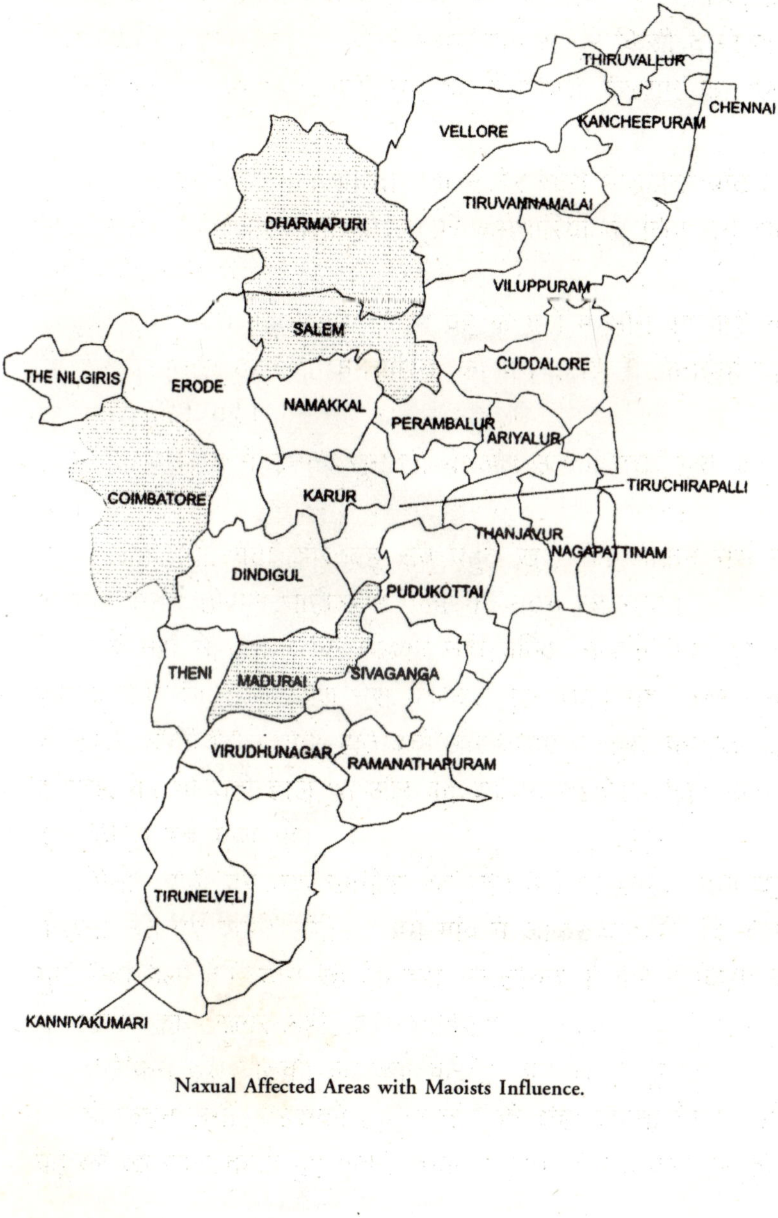

Naxual Affected Areas with Maoists Influence.

Kerala

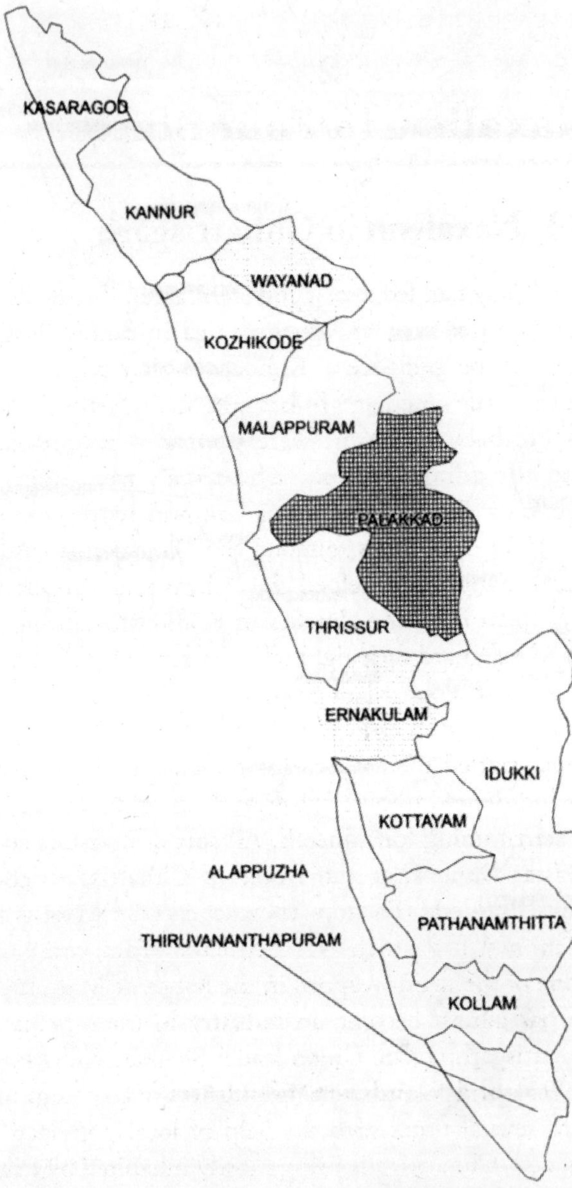

Naxual Affected Areas with Maoists Influence.

2
Naxalism in Four States

1. Naxalism in Chhattisgarh

Because of heavy handedness of and stern action by the Andhra Police, Maoists shifted to Dandakarnya area in South Bastar of Chattisgarh under the guidance of Kondapalli Sitar a maiyah who chose this area as a safe sanctuary. In late eighties in Andhra Pradesh the Adivasis (Tribals) of Bastar were poor and suppressed by landlords and the administration. The tribals were doing the collection work of Tendu leaves and bamboo works for their livelihood. In 1989 the Naxals founded the Dandakarnya Adivasi Mazdoor Kissan Sangh and helped the Adivasis in various ways like protecting them from the clutches of landlords, fighting with forest officials to safeguard their right to forest etc., which ultimately made Naxals popular. Poor tribals considered them as their saviour. Soon after or better said in early nineties the capitalists, companies and government started their search for minerals in these areas of Chhattisgarh and desired to oust tribals with the aim of occupying their land to start mining for minerals. All sort of investors started rushing to Bastar Dantewada and whole of Chhattisgarh then a part of Madhya Prasdesh. To stop 'encroachers' the Maoists used land mines, money for which was extracted from companies. Extortion is one of the main weapons in the hands of Maoists now. This practice has almost become an industry in the sanctuary of Naxals in Chhattisgarh. Trade Union leader Shankar Guha Niyogi (killed in 1991) and Gondwana Gantantra Party organised demonstrations several times with the help of local populace. But nothing happened. Chhattisgarh being mostly inhabited by tribals–about 32 per cent of the population of state–are poor and almost 55 per cent of rural tribals live below poverty line. Because of state repression, some tribals left their villages and went to Orissa, Andhra and Jharkhand.

Gradually Naxals grew in strength in Bastar, primarily because of three factors:–

1. It fought alongside the Adivasis against the local contractors and ensured that the contractors paid the Adivasis the minimum wages for Tendu leaf collection–the main source of income for Adivasis. Naxals CPI-(Maoist) helped people out of exploitative Maalik–Makbuja bonded labour system in timber felling.
2. It organised people against the excesses of forest officials who took them for a ride, and
3. Through force, it distributed the land of *malguzars* (feudal lords) to landless adivasis.[1]

Salwa Judum (Movement for peace) was founded by Mahendra Karma on June 5, 2005 to save villagers from Naxal menace. Slowly it turned into a militant force and started uprooting villagers/tribals. Their huts/house were burnt. About 5000 tribals were displaced, their womenfolk disrespected. Some of the villagers were made special police officers (SPO) who were responsible for rape, killing and depriving the villagers of their houses, etc., and uprooting them. Ultimately it was disbanded by the Supreme Court of India which branded Salwa Judum as an organisation. "Illegal and unconstitutional". Mahendra Karma, who was a founder member of Salwa Judum, himself was killed in a road block cum ambush on May 25, 2013 by Maoist in which 27 people mostly Congress men were killed at Jeeram Ghati on South Bastar.

Many civil rights groups had opposed "Salwa Judum". The state government used it to its advantage. After the ambush/attack a press note issued by the CPI (Maoists) declared Nand Kumar Patel and Vidya Charan Shukla as "Peoples enemies". It justified the killing stating with this action we have taken revenge of over a thousand Adivasis who were brutally murdered in the hands of Salwa Judum goons and government armed forces. We have also taken revenge on behalf of those hundreds of mothers and sisters who were subjected to cruelest forms of violene, humiliation and sexual assault. We have taken revenge on behalf of the thousands of Bastarites who lost their homes, cattle, chickens, goats, pottery, clothing, grain, crops...everything and were forced to live a miserable life in subhuman conditions"[2]

Around mid-2000 Tatas also stepped in Chhattisgarh state with a view to start their own business ventures which was disliked by Maoists.

CPI (Maoist) run a tax-based parallel government called 'Janatana Sarkar" in the area of Abujhmad (inaccessible hilly forest) that is spread from Central Bastar to Gadchiroli and Bijapur. They formed Dandakaranaya Special Zonal Committee (DKSZC) whose secretary is Comrade Ravula Srinivas who replaiced Comrade Khosa. CPI (Maoist) have control over 70 per cent of the area and claim it to be "liberated zone".

There were Naxalite excesses in Chhattisgarh and a rebellion against them was shaped up in mid-2005. People and the government together started a movement to counter Naxal menace and the movement was named as Salwa-Judum. Naxalites got alarmed and considered it as threat to them. Salwa Judum means "All together". Mahendra Karma led the movement. But it failed. The Chhattisgarh government submitted before the Supreme Court on January 18, 2011 that Salwa Judum has turned into a bad "movement" and it is extinct since 2006. Mahendra Karma was killed by Maoists on May 25, 2013.

The Cabinet Committee on Security has, for this purpose proposed an outlay during 12th plan ciyusgt if Rs. 280 crore by the centre and Rs. 56 crore by the states to raise specialised forces in 4 Naxal-hit states of Bihar, Jharkhand, Chhattisgarh and Orissa. It was decided by the committee on April 2, 2013. But the condition is "that, the special force of the state has to be upgraded as per approved guidelines of Greyhounds. Only states that give such an undertaking will be considered for funding" as stated by the authorities.

In Chattisgarh the state govt as a special action plan for the construction of the roads approved a sum of Rs. 2719.63 crore. The roads would mainly be in Sarguja, Rajnandgaon, North Bastar (Kanker), Narayanpur, Baster (Jagdalpur), South Bastar (Dantewada) and Bijapur. The state govt. proposed to Central Government to upgrade total of 16 roads measuring 629.65 km in Sarguja district, Rajnandgaon district measuring 54.50 km, five roads in North Bastar (Kanker) measuring 210.40 km, three roads in Narayanpur district measuring 152 km, three roads in Bastar (Jagdalpur district) measuring 32.10 km, four roads in South Bastar (Dantewada) measuring 188 km, Seven made in Bijapur district measuring 349.50 km and four roads in sukma district measuring 324.93 km.

The centre started developmental schemes to hold Left–Wing hit areas. They got Rs. 25 crore each. They would also receive special funds for security and infrastructure related expenditure (SRE). The centre also decided to provide more helicopters to Naxal-hit areas. After a battle of 13 long years against Naxal attacks, an imposing 315 meter long, 8. meter tall, 9 span bridge was ready for inaugration in July 2011.[3]

Bastar district of Chhattisgarh, though governed by Vth Schedule of the Constitution of India wants to move to sixth schedule that covers areas close to North Eastern states bordering Tibet and Myanmar. The main reason for such a move is that sixth schedule gives tribals inhabitants of Assam, Tripura, Mizoram and Meghalaya considerable autonomy and gives a special status to directly govern themselves.

A trend of declining population was noticed in Six Left Wing Extremist (LWE) affected districts of Koriya, Dakshin Bastar, Dantewada, Bijapur, Sukma, Jashpur and Kanker as reflected in the Provisional census 2011. This matter was also to be taken up at the National Human Rights Commission (NHRC) full commission sitting at Raipur on April 11 and 12 when it would take up 28 other cases of human rights violations including unethical removal of wombs to claim money under the Rashtriya Swasthya Bima Yojna. In Bijapur district the decadal population growth rate is 8.76 per cent, in Dantewada it is 11.9 per cent, Sukma–a new district carved out of Dantewada–has growth rate of just 8.0 per cent, Koriya, it is 12.40 per cent, Jashpur's population is growing at 14.65 per cent while it is highest in Kanker at 15.01 per cent.[4]

Chhattisgarh's Jails are overcrowded. National Crime Reports Bureau (till 2011) had stated that for every 100 prisoners, it has to accommodate 250 prisoners. In 2011 it had 256 whereas in 2010, Chhattisgarh jails had 237 prisoners, In Jagdalpur Central Jail, of 546 prisoners accused of being Maoist or Maoist supporters, 512 are tribals, 53 of them women, as disclosed to the activist Swami Agnivesh on his RTI application. In Dantewada jail, the response said 372 tribals are among 377 prisoners. In Kanker jail, tribals amount for 134 out of 144.

The highest number of undertrials booked on Maoist-related charges are in Jagdalpur jail. In a March 23, 2013 statement, Maoist leader Ganesh Uike said "Jail officers make prisoners work as bonded labourers".

The *Indian Express* of April 8, 2013
report by Ashutosh Bhardwaj

Tribals of a Bastar Village in a Rally for Prisoners' Rights.
Photo from the Indian Express, April 8, 2013.

Maoists observed a "Prisoner's rights week" by tribals in the interior villages of Bastar, accusing the government of going back on an agreement to expedite the release of their comrades and innocent villagers in exchange of Sukma collector Alex Paul Menon's freedom nearly a year ago. But only release has been of Raipur-based Raja Dhruva (22) on May 9, 2012.

On May 25, 2013 a convoy of Congress leaders ambushed in Darba Ghaati (35 km, away from Jagdalpur in Chhattisgarh in which 27 persons were killed and 40 injured. The security forces did not seem to have taken note of the warning on May 13, 2013 through displayed banners that Maoists would kill atleast half a dozen important Congress and BJP leaders. Maoists in a precision move executed their plan within 10-11 days but the local security forces did not bother to take the warning seriously. With such an attitude of indifference, security forces can not take on Maoists. This sort of mindset has to be changed and the challenge accepted. They should be alert round the clock.

National Investigation Agency (NIA) and the Intelligence Bureau's conclusion was that the attack was led by Sudarshan Katakam alias Anand alias Mohan alias Birenderji, a politburo member of CPI (Maoists) who has been working in Bastar area. He hails from Adilabad and carries Rs. 12 lakh reward on his head. Earlier he was with People's War Group which later merged with MCC.

Maoist insurgents took away 15 lakhs of rupees as well as ornaments found on the dead bodies. Insurgents also looted ? Rifles 500 rounds of live cartridges from the sight of attack from security guards.

A 3-page statement dated May 28, 2013 written in Telugu, English and Hindi signed by party's spokesperson Gudsa Usendi in Chhattisgarh, apologising for the death of "innocent people" in the attack stated. "The Dandakarnya Special Zone Committee of CPI (Maoist) regrets this and expresses condolences and sympathies to the families." The ambush was only to eliminate Mahendra Karma and other Congress leaders. It congratulated the PLA on the ambush. The outlawed party identified Nand Kumar Patel, Mahendra Karma and Vidya Charan Shukla as 'People's enemy'. Karma was branded as notorious 'Tyrant' and 'Murderer' who was involved in a series of 'anti-tribal campaigns and was responsible for foiling a massive movement in 1996 to demand implementation of Sixth Schedule of the Indian Constitution and took bitter stand against that movement. In 1999 Karma's name was linked to a big timber scam called "Malik Makbuja". The statement appealed to 'people' to call off Operation Green Hunt, repeal various Special Acts, strict lesislation, like Unlawful Activities Prevention Act, Chhattisgarh Special People Security Act and 'cancel' all memoranda of understanding with corporates to exploit natural resources, take back all security forces in Bastar region in the name of training and all leaders languishing in Jails should be immediately released. The attack was revenge for Salwa Judum, Green Hunt.

A delegation led by Union Home Secretary R.K. Singh and Intelligence Bureau Director S.A. Ibrahim dashed to Chhattisgarh on May 28, 2013. They advised the state government to hold regular political rallies and not be afraid of future attacks. They concluded that the attack was an act of 'Desperation'. They want to create fear in the mind of the political class and disturb the democratic process.

Air Chief Marshal N.A.K. Browne stated (May 28, 2013) that the technology is the key to eleminating the Naxal problem and stated that the new equipment is being bought by the centre to improve its survelliance capabilities in the affected area and additional choppers will be deployed in operation.

National Human Rights Commission said (May 28, 2013) the Maoists have now made it impossible for authorities to take social welfare programmes to the most needy.

Former Director General of Police of Chhattisgarh state Vishwaranjan stressed the use of force against Maoists. He opines that there is no point in holding talks with them as they do not want to come on common ground. They want to replace the democratic system. But if the government and administration, recognise tribal's rights *'Jal, Jangal* and *Zameen'* things would subside to a great extent.

However, Chhattisgarh Chief Minister Raman Singh favouring the tribals scolded the state - run corporation N M D C (National Mineral Development Corporation) for allegedly, "ignoring" the needs of the tribals 'in the states' Naxal - hit Bastar district by denying them promised employment and spending paltry money for their welfare.[4A]

On June 10, 2013, Prime Minister Man Mohan Singh urged the state governments and the centre to adopt "the Two-pronged strategy of sustained operations to clear the areas of Maoist influence and pursue the objectives of effective governance and rapid development and to use all legitimate means to defend the security of the country and its institutions and quell armed insurgency and violence." The statement was issued in the wake of Chhattisgarh carnage of May 25, 2013 when 26 Congress activists were killed by Maoists. He further said that it was a frontal attack on democratic foundations of the nation. The strength and robustness of the democratic forces in our country would suffer if the space for political activity gets restricted because of the fear of terror. It was an attack on democracy, freedom, and free speech and expression. Nothing can be more dangerous to our Republic than the insurgency of the CPI (Maoist) in pursuit of its misguided goal of overthrowing parliamentary democracy and the Constitution of India through violent means. The Indian state cannot and will not accept the pernicious Maoist doctrine."

Ms. Arundhati Roy opines that the Centre's war against Maoists is to rob tribals of the only dignity left with them–their land. And hand it over to big corporate sharks. She also writes "even if the ideologues of the Maoist movements are fighting to eventually overthrow the Indian state, right now even they know that their ragged, malnutrioned army, the bulk of whose soldiers have never seen a train or a bus or even a small town, are fighting for survival."[6]

Chhattisgarh Special Public Security Act 2005 (CSPSC) prevents journalists to have access to the Maoists and publish their views whereas Press Council of India (PCI) dictates otherwise. PCI opines that journalists should make public the views of Maoists without any threat. PCI says "While journalists are threatened with CSPSC, they are also asked to negotiate with the Maoists during a crisis and this is clear double speak on the part of the government.

In Chhattisgarh state, during a The Hindu-CNN-IBN Election Tracker Survey 2013 conducted by the Centre for the Study of Development Societies (CSDS) Delhi, 24 per cent of the respondents believed that 'maximum force' should be used to deal with the rebels (Naxals). In contrast, 46 per cent believed that the tribal grievances ought to be addressed and justice be provided while 15 per cent favoured the idea of a ceasefire and talks with Maoist.[7] The aim of Maoists is to spread Communism by taking over the Sovereign power and furling the red flag over the Red Fort. So any amount of soft paddling or talks or mitigating grievances would not eliminate Naxals altogether. It might slow down the process of tribal villagers joining the Naxal movement.

Recent Activities

On February 28, 2006, 55 civilians were killed 40 injured and 125 kidnapped in Dantewada in (Chhattisgarh State).

On March 15, 2007, 55 killed in an attack and bombing at Bijapur.

On April 6, 2010, 76 CRPF personnel were massacred in Dantewada.

On May 17, 2010, Naxals blew up a bus on Dantewada-Sukhma road in Chhattisgarh killing 15 policemen and 20 civilians.

On June 29, 2010, 26 CRPF personnel were killed in Narayanpur district of Chhattisgarh.

On September 19, 2010, Maoists abducted 8 policemen from Bhopal Patnam area of Bijapur, Four of them were killed while rest were freed after concerted efforts. Naxals demanded to stop a proposed Army Training School in Narayanpur district. In total, they came up with 11 demands. The five security men were kept in the custody of East Bastar Divisional Committee led by Com. Nitu.

On January 25, 2011, Maoists abducted six persons including five police officers belonging to Chhattisgarh Armed Forces in Narayanpur district in Bastar region of Chhattisgarh.

On February 11, 2011 Maoists freed police hostages in the presence of Swami Agnivesh. (They had been abducted on Jan 25, 2011).

In February 2011, when Supreme Court of India asked the Chhattisgarh government to shift villagers from Relief camps., it expressed its inability stating that it is difficult to shift them, under the time frame as directed by the Supreme Court, because of the Maoist reprisals who were blocking their shift.

On July 5, 2011, Supreme Court declared Salwa Judum illegal and directed Chhattisgarh to disarm special police officers and proble their alleged crimes.

—**The Hindu,** July 6, 2011

With the result, 5267 SPO's were to be confined to Camps in Chhattisgarh.

References

1. Frontline, June 28, 2013 issue article "The war in Bastar" by Ajoy Ashirwad Mahaprashasta.
2. Frontline, June 28, 2013 issue.
3. The Indian Express, July 5, 2011.
4. The Hindu, April 1, 2013.

4A. The Indian Express of September 13, 2013 Report by Priyadarshi Siddhanta.

5. Outlook, November 9, 2009 issue, "Mr. Chidambaram's War" by Arundhati Roy.
6. *Ibid.*
7. The Hindu, dated July 25, 2013 article, "A rejection of the 'Maximum-force' approach" by Prashant Jha.

Chhattisgarh

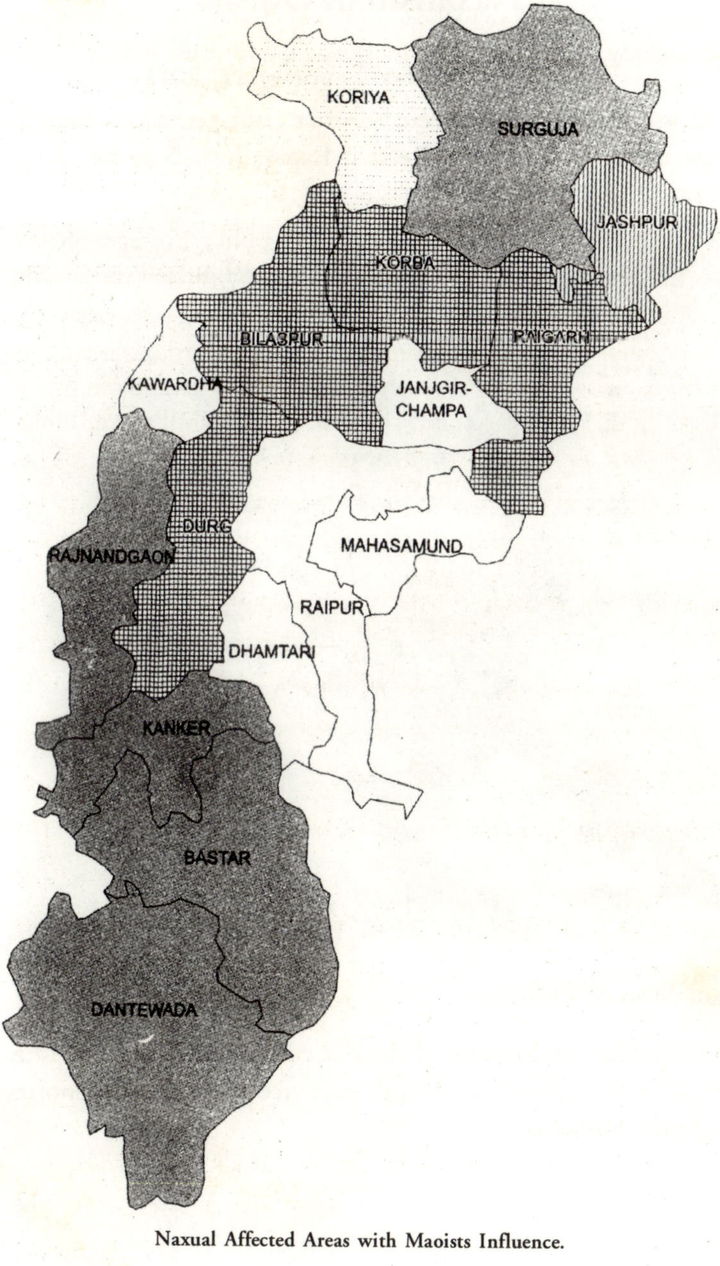

Naxual Affected Areas with Maoists Influence.

2. Naxalism in Odisha

The Indian Express, February 27, 2011

Orissa has 19 Naxal-affected districts, but gets funds from the Centre under the 'Security Related Expenditure Scheme' for 15 districts.

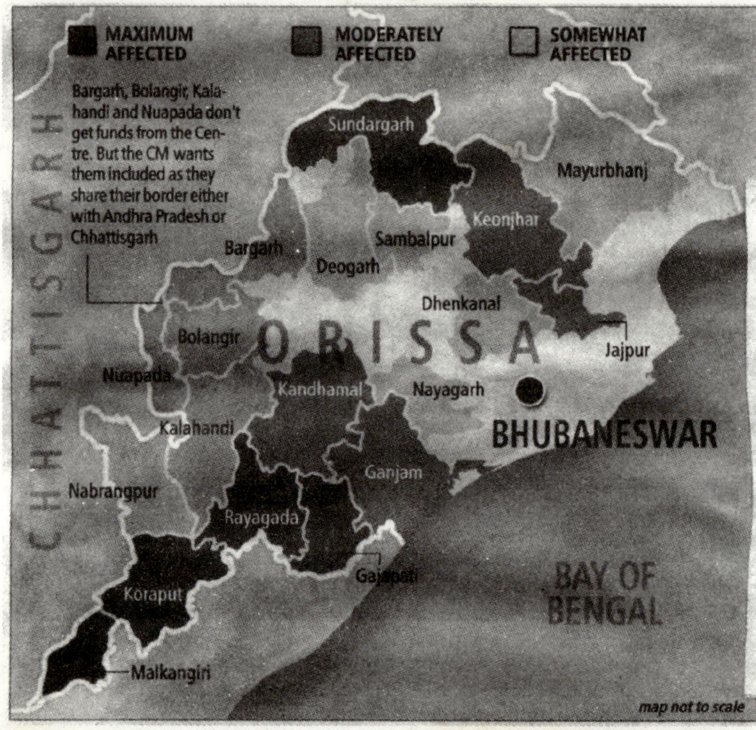

Naxal Map of Odisha

The abduction of Malkangiri district collector R Vineel Krishna highlights the spreading Naxal presence in Odisha, reported Debabrata Mohanty

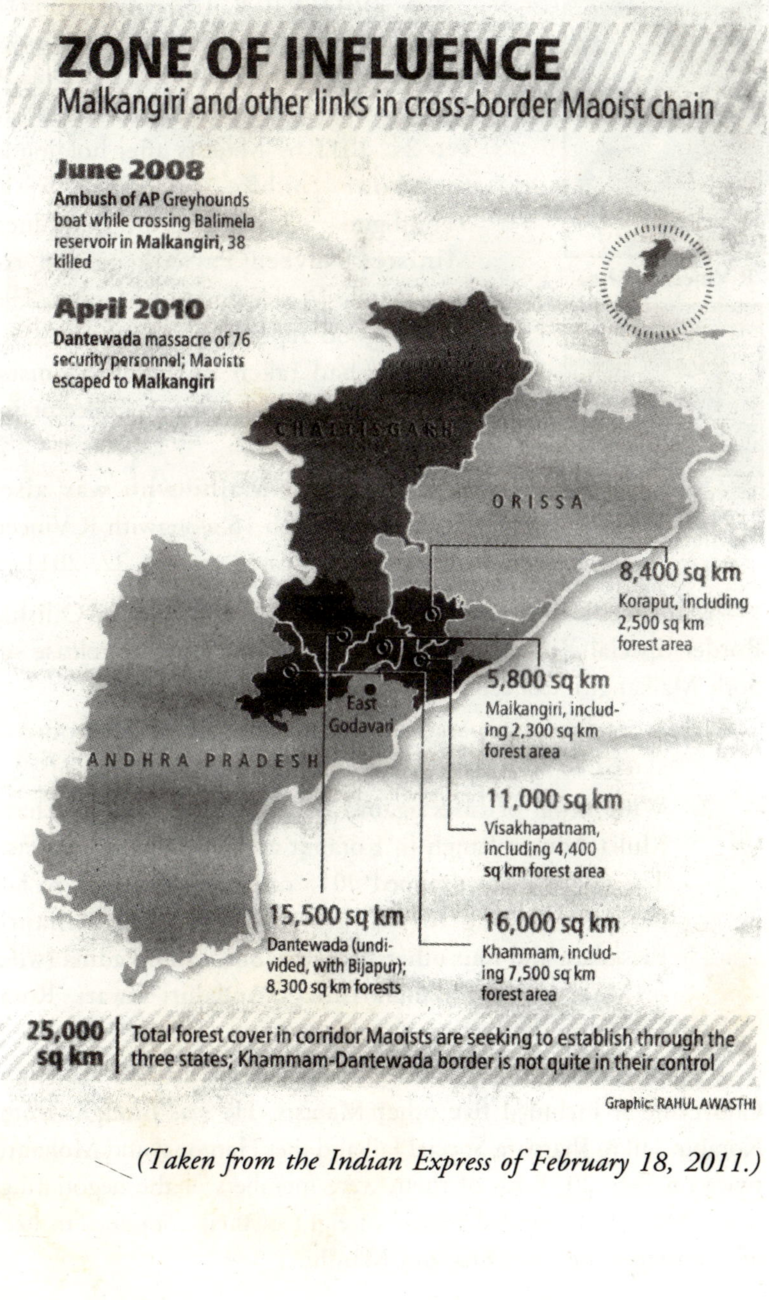

(Taken from the Indian Express of February 18, 2011.)

R Vineel Krishna

A 2005 batch IAS, Malkangiri Collector Shri. R. Vineel Krishna was abducted on February 16, 2011 at a place near Jantapai village. He was released on Feb 24, 2011 by Maoists after holding a four-hour public meeting with Tentuliguda villagers and Odisha Chief Minister Naveen Patnaik agreed to concede all 14 demands of Maoists. He carried good reputation among welfare since he had taken up many Maoists schemes after taking over as Collector in 2010.

Junior Engineer Pabitra Majhi

JE Pabitra Majhi who was also kidnapped on Feb 16 alongwith R.Vineel Krishna was released on Feb 22, 2011.

Maoist (Bhaskar, Secretary of CPI Maoist Andhra-Odisha Border Special Zonal Committee) put conditions for release of both Malkangiri Collector and the Junior Engineer.

1. Stoppage of Operation Green Hunt. The government agreed to stop Anti-Maoist operations.
2. Withdrawal of cases against tribals and workers of Chasi Mulia Adivasi Sangh in Koraput and Malkangiri districts. The government dropped 9015 cases against tribals so far besides agreeing to withdraw a case against Ghanti Prasadam and four others-Kandula Sirisa alias Padma (wife of Maoist leader Ramakrishna), Andaluri Iswari, Rosa Mandangi and driver Gokul Kuldipia.

Ghanti Prasadam had been granted bail by the Odisha High Court and it included five other Maoists. He was brought from Koraput Jail to Jharpara Special Jail and met Hargopal and Mohanti twice on Feb. 20. Both of them were members of the negotiating team. Maoists demanded release of eight of their comrades in lieu of 2 hostages, i.e., Krishna and Manjhi.

Talks for the release of hostages started on Feb 20 which finally yielded results on Feb 22, 2011 and Collector Vineel Krishna and Junior Engineer. Pabitra Mohan Manjhi were released after 7 days's captivity.

The Indian Express, Feb 21, 2011

Bio-data by Debabrata Mohanty IE Correspondent

8 for 2, The Maoist wish-list

Abductors of the Malkangiri district collector and a junior engineer have demanded release of eight Maoists. Debabrata Mohanty profiles them.

1. **Shriramula Srinivas, 41**

Chief of Revolutionary Writers' Association, member of the Andhra-Orissa Border Special Zone Committee. Suspected to be involved in an attempt on the life of former AP Chief Minister N Chandrababu Naidu in 2003. Arrested in Malkangiri in July 2007. Tried (and acquitted) in six cases in the last four years.

2. **Ganti Prasadam, 55**

Close aide of top Maoist leader Ramakrishna alias RK. Central committee member, state president of Martyrs' Friends and Relatives Committee, and "political tutor" to Naxals. Arrested by Koraput police in November 2010. Hails from Bobbili in Vizianagaram district, known as "Bobbili hero". One of the six accused in the "Aurangabad conspiracy" of May 2005. Brother of Ganti Ramesh alias Rajanna, Srikakulam division secretary who was among 11 Naxals killed in Kopardung encounter in 1998.

3. **Padma**

Alias Sirisha alias Nirmala, Ramakrishna's wife. Carrying a reward of Rs. two lakh, arrested from forests of Koraput while allegedly trying to meet her Maoist son Prithvi in a conspiracy to blow up mobile towers and a bridge. In Koraput jail since November 2010. Maoists deny allegations against her; say she only runs an orphange in Hyderabad.

A rally seeking collector's release

4. Buduni Munda

Alias Sobha alias Sheela-Budhini. Founding member and president of Nari Mukti Sangh, a Maoist front organisation that is active in four states. A tribal from Jharkhand, joined Marxist-Leninist movement in Bihar and built up a strong women's organisation of tribal, rural women. In Rourkela jail since September 2006.

5. Gananath Patra, 71

Adviser of Chasi Mulia Adivasi Sangh in Narayanpatna. Till arrest, had been fighting for tribal land rights in poverty-ridden southern Orissa for over two decades, persistently demanding implementation of Scheduled Area (Scheduled Tribe) Land Transfer Regulation of 1956 that prohibits transfer of land from a tribal to a non-tribal person. Chased by police since November 2009 when, during a protest against bauxite mining from Deomali Hill, two tribals were killed in police firing at Narayanpatna police station. Arrested in Bhubaneswar, in Koraput jail since January 2010.

6. Motilal Soren, 41

Alias Ashutosh. Born in Jharkhand. One of the 21 members of the CPI (Maoist) Central Committee as well as and one of seven in the Central Military Commission. Said to be involved in the conspiracies to murder VHP leader Laxmanananda Saraswati in

Kandhamal in August 2008 and former Jharkhand Chief Minister Babulal Marandi's son Anup in October 2007. Arrested in March 2009 from Rourkela, in Bhubaneswar jail since then.

7. Ishwari Anduluri

Padma's cousin, hails from Visakhapatnam, AP. Arrested by Koraput police along with Padma in November 2010. Was supposed to join as the central regional commander of Narayanpatna Dalam. In Koraput jail since November 2010.

8. Tapan Mishra, 42

Civil rights activist in Narayanpatna and leader of Chasi Mulia Adivasi Sangh. Once a member of All India Democratic Students Organisation (student wing of SUCI) and president of Ravenshaw College Students' Union. Later joined CP (ML-Liberation) and was part of a movement with forest dwellers. Was councillor of Athamallik NAC in Dhenkanal district and also contested the last Assembly elections. Arrested in November 2009 when he was about to board a train to Narayanpatna from Parvatipuram. In Koraput jail.

Feb 23, 2011 The Indian Express

The Peace Brokers in the abduction of Malkangiri collector Shri R. Vineel Krishna and Junior Engineer Pavitra Mohan Majhi.

The mediators hand-picked by Maoists for holding talks with the government.

G HARAGOPAL, 66

The man who led the team is well-versed in the art of negotiations. A political science Professor in Central University, Hyderabad, Haragopal had brokered a deal during the 1993 abduction of Congress MLA from Visakhapatnam P Balaraju in exchange of release of top Maoist leader Kranti Ranadev. In 2002, when the Naidu government was getting ready for talks with erstwhile PWG leaders, he was the negotiator. The talks didn't take off as the state government refused to lift the ban on PWG. Again in 2004, when the YSR government declared cease-fire against the Moaists, he was among the negotiators.

R SOMESHWAR RAO, 75

Though ailing, it was his vast experience in tribal issues that the Maoists wanted to exploit for articulating their demands. A retired professor of economics from Sambalpur University, Rao is currently based in Hyderabad. Rao was also associated with the Sarvodaya Movement. His friends say his knowledge in the economics of displacement due to developmental projects like mining and hydel projects is tremendous. Having started his career in the Deccan Institute of Pune, he moved to Sambalpur where he did extensive studies on displacement due to Hirakud Dam project.

DANDAPANI MOHANTY, 71

A graduate from Khallikote College in Berhampur, Mohanty is a trade union activist and has a long record in activism for marginal workers, tribals and displaced. A close associate of former CPI (M-L) (Liberation) leader Nag Bhushan Patnaik since 1967 and general secretary of the Orissa Forest Mazdoor Union, Mohanty was once the head of Daman Pratirodh Manch that was banned by the Orissa government in June 2006. Mohanty later rechristened it Jana Adhikaar Manch. But it is his avatar as convener of the Political Prisoners Release Committee that endeared him to the Maoists. Police sources say Mohanty knows the region of Malkangiri and Koraput inside out.

Negotiations with Maoists were held on February 22, 2011. Talks had started on Feb 20.

The Sunday Express, February 27, 2011

Maoist Ideologue Ghanti Prasadam

Some Important Strikes by Maoists in Orissa

1. **Koraput Arms loot (February 6, 2004)**–Over 200 Naxals looted 2000 guns, killed 4 policemen after storming major police installations in Koraput.
2. **Gavapati (R Udaygiri) Jail Break (March 24, 2006)**–Over 500 Maoists attacked Orissa State Armed Police (OSAP) camp, sub-jail, police station and treasury. Kidnapped OC of R Udaygiri Police Station and Superintendent of the local sub-jail. They also set 40 prisoners free.
3. **Nayagarh armoury Loot (February 15, 2008)**–Maoists killed 14 policemen and one civilian, set Police Training School on fire, looted district police armoury. Police also killed 20 Maoists in combing operations thereafter.
4. **Malkangiri Greyhound Drowning (June 29, 2008)**–Naxals sunk a boat carrying 61 anti-Maoist Greyhound Policemen of Andhra Pradesh. 38 of them drowned.
5. **Malkangiri Landmine Blast (16 July 2008)**–Naxals killed 17 personnel of Special Operations Group (SOG) in a land-mine blast on Kaliamela Motu road in Malkangiri.
6. **Kandhmal Vishwa Hindu Parishad (VHP) leader killing (August 29, 2008)**–Swami Laxmanand and his 4 disciples were killed in an attack on an Ashram at Jalespata.
7. **Koraput Bauxite Mines Attack (April 12, 2009)**–Eleven CISF personnel were killed in an attack on the warehouse of Nation Aluminium Company at Panchpatmali Hills near Damanyodi.
8. **Narayanpatna Landmine Blast (June 2009)**–Eight Orissa Special Security Force Jawans were killed when Maoists triggered several landmines in Narayanpatna Block.
9. **Koraput Blast (April 2010)**–Eleven SOG policemen killed and eight others injured when Naxals triggered a landmine blast targeting a mini bus in which they were travelling.

10. **Kandhamal Ambulance Blast (November 2010)** – Mistaking an ambulance for a police vehicle, Naxals killed 5 people including a 3-year old girl.

(The Sunday Story of the Sunday Express – Indian Express, dtd Feb 27, 2011)

On January 25, 2010, CITU leader Thomas Munda was abducted during an attack on SAIL-owned Kalta mines in Sundargarh district. His body was found in Renjda forest four days later.

On July 7, 2010, Asstt Sub Inspector Umesh Chandra Marandi was abducted from Keonjhar. He was ultimately released on July 18 on 'humanitarian grounds'.

On September 29 2010 'Sarpanch' of Gram Panchayat abducted in Koraput.

On February 7, 2011 Maoists fired at Rourkela-Kiriburu train (between Chandipur and Patashi Railway Station in Sundargarh district during 'Bharat Bandh'.

On Feb 8, Maoist leader Samir Khalko who was involved in killing of a sub inspector and bombing of Railway Station was killed by the security forces in an encounter in Mundatola forest.

Activities of the Chasi Mulia Adivasi Sangh (CMAS) headed by Nachika Linga. (A Maoist Frontal Organisation in Orissa)

CMAS became prominent in 2006 when Ryot Kuli Sangham a banned organisation based in Parvatipuram of Andhra Pradesh came together to form CMAS in 2006. "The CMAS and Nachika Linga showed their violent face in 2008, when he declared himself the organisation's convener. With CMAS members, Linga formed Ghenua Bahini–men wearing red shirts and armed with traditional tribal weapons like bows and arrows," said a government official in Koraput. "He started an armed movement against people who opposed him and those who did not join in the Sangh. They forcibly encroached their land, snatched their valuables and left many of them homeless. They did not even spare tribals who opposed them."

Of the 5,500 people who lost their homes in Naryanpatna between 2008 and 2010, those most affected were in Podapadar gram panchayat where eight upper caste families, 264 Dalit families ad 35 tribal families had to flee their homes. A hundred Dalit families in Balipeta gram panchayat, 105 Dalit and tribal families in Narayanapatna gram panchayat, 121 Dalit and tribal families in Kumbhari, 200 Dalit families in Talagumandi, 215 dalit and tribal families in Bijaghati and 45 Dalit families in Tentulipadar, too, were driven away.

Here are some examples of the violence unleashed :

August 9, 2010. Arjun Kendruka, a CDMA leader fallen out of favour, is shot dead in Bondhugaon while riding a bicycle with his wife Rama Kendruka. He had opposed violence and contested the 2009 Assembly Elections on a CPM ticket.

August 15, 2010. Maoists kill Ghasi Kendruka, a teaching assistant in Narayanpatna's Dumsil village. Kendruka too opposed CMAS and Maoist violence. Some 50 armed men accompanied by about 150 CMAS dragged him out of his house and slit his throat in front of his wife.

August 23, 2010. Five Maoists abduct Sikunu Meleka, a former Linga aide, from his house in Tentulipadar village of Narayanpatna along with 11 other persons. Maoists slit his throat; the others are released.

August 29, 2010, Maoists shoot dead Anand Kirsani, 38, zilla parishad member, Congress leader, and working president of Shanti Committee, at Dhusura village, Semiliguda, Kirsani, a Dalit, had opposed CMAS violence.

September 18, 2010, Maoists kill Kapur Khora and his son Disha, slitting their throats at a public meeting in Lachhamani village.

September 27, 2010. Maoists slit the throat of Mishra Turuk alias Khosla, a disabled person of Talagumandi village in Narayanpatna block, accusing him of being a police informer.

November 23, 2011. Biswanath Kartasia, 60, survives after attackers slash at his throat in the market in Bikrampur village, Narayanpatna block. "I was gasping for breath. My wife took me to hospital where I stayed 21 days," says Kartasia, who now lives in Laxmipur block headquarters. He had resisted a CMAS invitation to join.

Nachika Linga : government at his mercy

–*The Indian Express,* April 17, 2012

Report by Debabrata Mohanty from Narayanpatna

Filmmaker Deba Ranjan as Sarangi who belongs to a Bangalore-based group Pedestrian Pictures and also an anti-mining activist is to provide an insight into the situation in Southern Odisha through a documentary Film *"At the Crossroads"* about which he says "The Nehruvian era made the common man, especially Adivasis and the Dalits lose their lands, forests and streams for the greater common good. Besides not enjoying the fruits of development they are deprived of basic necessities. While being the victims of injustice, they are being labelled anti-development and Maoists and Naxalite when they resist corporate land-grab for mining and industrialisation. This banding provided the state a licence to kill them with impurity. This resulted in the CPI (Maoist) consolidating its presence in southern Odisha in the recent past..."

At present Odisha has two prominent Naxal outfits/fronts. (1) Special Zonal Committee of the CPI (Maoist)–AOB (Andhra Orissa Border) (2) Chhattisgarh Orissa Border (COB).

Odisha

Naxual Map of Odisha.

3. Naxalism in Jharkhand

Maoists cropped up in Jharkhand–South Bihar in early nineties (1990). The Maoist Communist Centre (MCC) was most dominant Naxal group that time though CPI ML (Liberation), Party Units groups also existed and were active. They split into several splinter groups on ideological issues. Later on in Jharkhand, Caste and ethnicity played important role-more than the ideology itself. The Maoist movement in Jharkhand has taken place of criminalisation. Kidnapping and extortion, demanding ransom etc., has almost replaced the old ideology on which the movement was running its show. To some extent, they did flourish since they were protecting poor and helpless peasants and tribals against the atrocities of 'Zamindars' (landlords) and other officials particularly that of Forest department. But now greed and personal interest of the leaders of Naxal group has taken over everything. The movement is no longer based on giving vent to grievances of poor peasants and tribal inhabitants.

Around a dozen and half (in fact 19) Naxal groups operate in the state of Jharkhand. The Jharkhand Liberation Tigers Front (JLT), the CPI (Maoists), The Tritiya Prastuti Committee (TPC), and the People's Liberation Front of India (PLFI) are active. In a way, these groups could be called breakaway factions of CPI (Maoist). Swatantra Jharkhand Prastuti Committee (SJPC) and Jharkhand Prastuti Committee (JPC) Jharkhand Jannukti Parishad (JJP), also exist and play their role. All the groups keep on harbouring grudge against each other and resist other groups interference in their area of influence. They even oppose the action taken by other factions, e.g., on December 28, 2012 when CPI (Maoist) called Jharkhand bandh to protest the Operation Anaconda-II in Saranda forest by the security forces against the Naxals, it was opposed by Jharkhand Liberation Front (JLF) Non-CPI (Maoist) Naxals have taken recourse to criminal activities like kidnapping for ransom and collection of levies. This has eroded the popularity of Naxals and their movement. A bandh was called on February 23-24 in Latehar and Palamu district by PLFI. On 23rd February 2013 night, PLFI attacked and set fire to a hotel near NH-75 in Latehar, attacked its owner and burnt down vehicles. After CPI (Maoist) ambushed CRPF on January 7, 2013, Tritiya Prastuti Committee fired on SP's convoy on February 5 to make their presence felt. Eleven CRPF personnel were killed as a result of January 7 incident though there were no casualties on February 5. However, PLFI has active presence in 3 of Jharkhand 24 district–Gumla, Simdega and Khunti.

Jharkhand police has prepared a web portal which depicts 16,000 Maoists and 19 Naxal and splinter groups active in the state.

Operation ANACONDA–I was launched in August 2011 deep inside the Saranda forest at Thalkobad area to liberate it alongwith 24 other villages and destroy the CPI (Maoist) Eastern Regional Bureau and a number of training camps inside Sarand sal forest. CPI (Maoist) had declared it as "liberated zone" which lies in Jharkand's West Singhbhum district along with the Odisha border. In the operation, 37 persons were arrested and more than 100 were detained. Twelve large mining companies including that of Steel Authority of India, JSW steel owned by Sajjan Jindal, Jindal Steel and Power (JSPL) of Naveen Jindal, Rungta Mines etc. operate in this area of 200 sq km of 800 sq km forest. Ho adivasis living in the forest first launched "Lal Pani Andolan" against the pollution of these mining concerns. Resultantly the health of the tribal inhabitants suffers and it is bound to culminate in violent protest in times to come.

Extortion is one of the main weapons in the hands of 'Maoists in Jharkhand where the Naxal rebel outfits have their bases. Together these outfits extort Rs 50 crore from 'industries and construction companies. According to an estimate given by Jharkhand police spokesperson S.N. Pradhan, the extremists' extortion revenue is worth Rs. 150-200 crores nationally. In Jharkhand alone about 100 industrial units are based. In the last week of July 2013, Maoists beheaded three contractors in Gumla district when they refused to pay extortion money.

In the year 2000 the only Naxal group existing in Jharkhand was Maoist Communist Centre (MCC) and today 19 groups exist. This is how they are expanding and prospering. In the year 2002 a new group was formed after parting ways with MCC and it was named as Tritiya Sammelan Prastuti Committee (TPC) headed by Panda. In the year 2004 MCC joined the group of Kindapalli Sitaramaiyah of People's War and later MCC parted ways and formed People's Liberation Front of India (PLFI). But this Front also passed into oblivion.

Jharkhand Prastuti Committee was formed around 2005 whose founding partner was one Prashant also known as Jagannath Sao who was arrested by Hazaribag police on August 28, 2013 for murder of Tapeshwar Prasad, 'Mukhia' of Shahpur village who was killed an August 19, 2013. JPC has mostly taken to extortion. Prasant was recruited as a constable-driver in District police in August 2010 after surrendering but he maintained secret contacts with JPC. It has a cadre of about 45 persons and don't wear the black dress. It hoists national flag inverted and is opposite to Tritiya Prastuti Committee.[1]

Displacement of tribals is in vogue in Jharkhand as well. Anti-displacement activities of Vishthapan Virodhi Jan Vikas Andolan (VVJVA) (an umbrella organisation of Maoist in Jharkhand affiliated to CPI (Maoists)) could control little so far. Two of its members Vishvanath Singh Khairwar and Utpal Vaska (a cultural activist) were arrested on August 31, 2013 with Maoist literature from the organisation's office in Ranchi. Both of them were anti-displacement activists opposing forcible land acquisition in Jharkhand.[2]

Jharkhand Chief Minister Hemant Soren has taken good steps by offering to hold talks with Maoists and other extremists. He also laid online foundation for welfare projects to the tune of Rs. 135 crore in Khunti district.[3]

Information and Technology wing has uploaded information about 2759 Naxal cadre alongwith details of 4227 individuals of considered supporters or sympathisers to the Maoist cause and even data on 810 police weapons looted by them i.e. by Left Wing Extremist organisations stands uploaded. Because of this data 262 of the looted arms have been tracked down. It has also uploaded 4896 LWE related incidents in Jharkhand state. The Open Group of E-governance (OGE) would animate 50 Major LWE incidents of Jharkhand and make it available / accessible to the police personnel for training purposes.[4]

Some Important Activitics

On April 8, 2004, 19 Jharkhand Armed police personnel and 1 CRPF man killed in landmine blast at Chaibasa in Jharkhand.

On September 30, 2009 Special Branch Inspector Francis Induwar was kidnapped near Kunti. His beheaded body was later found in Ranchi after a week.

On February 13, 2010 Block Development Officer kidnapped from near his office at Dalb Hungarh. He was released after 8 days.

On January 28, 2011 in an hour-long gun battle with Jharkhand Police in Luhur jungle of Latehar district, 9 Maoists were killed. Zonal Commander Basant Yadav was commanding Koel Sankh Zone of CPI Maoist.

February 2, 2011-Maoists of Jharkhand Regional Committee (JRC), a militant wing of CPI (Maoist) held a meeting of its Commanders at Marangburu under Arki Police Station. Maoist leaders Annalda, chief of JRC, Kundan Pahan Zonal Commander of South Chota Nagpur Zonal Committee, Prasadji, Sub Zonal Commander of Podahat sub Zonal Committee, Navin Manjhi Zonal Commander and many others participated in the meeting which discussed the military strategy for Jharkhand for the year 2011. (*The Pioneer,* Feb 28, 2011)

February 7, 2011 Maoists blasted Railway Tracks at Ramgarh district. Another stretch of trains track was blasted between Dania station in Bokaro district and Bihar's Jageshwar station.

(*The Indian Express,* Feb 8, 2011)

References

1. *The Indian Express*, September 4, 2013. Report by Deepu Sebastion Edmond.
2. *The Hindu*, September 10, 2013. Report by Anumeha Yadav.
3. *The India Express*, Sept. 14, 2013
4. *The Indian Express* Sept. 15, 2013 article by Deepu Sebastian Edmond "Jharkhands Digital Leap".

Jharkhand

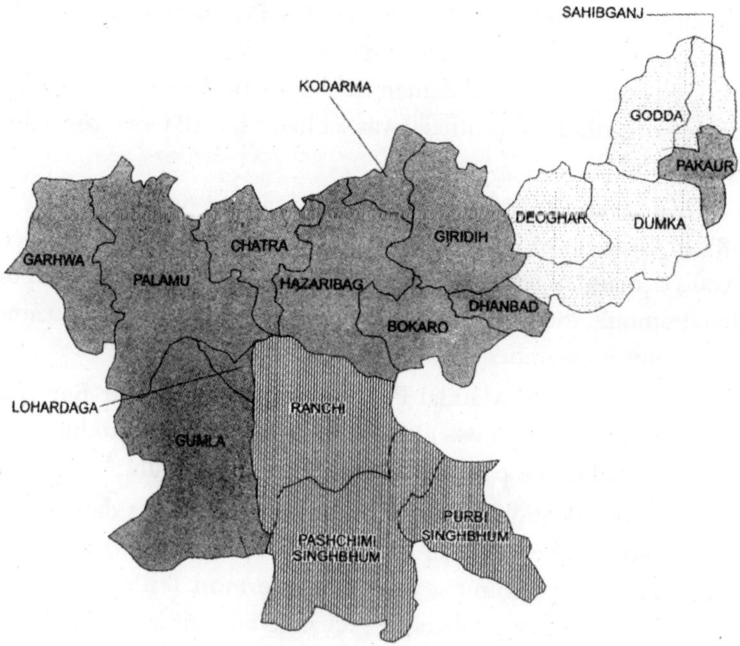

Naxual Map of Jharkhand.

4. Naxalism in Andhra Pradesh

Naxals normally adopt the kidnapping tactics but, by and large, it seems to have not succeeded on expected lines. The first kidnapping in Andhra Pradesh was reported on September 6, 1984 when Naxals took away a senior revenue official at Addateegala of East Godavari district and demanded release of Perumalla Devudu, a central organiser.[1] The official was set free after AP Govt. conceded the demand.

Then seven (7) IAS officers were kidnapped on December 27, 1987 in Gurtedu of East Godavari districts. Again Govt. conceded Naxal's demand of releasing of jailed Naxalites including Wadkapur Chandramouli, then a division committee secretary who later became a polit bureau member and killed in 2006.[2]

In June 1989, a Mandal Parishad President Malhar Rao was abducted and shot dead when the government failed to produce two missing Naxalites-Gopagani Ilaiah and Burra Ramulu.[3]

Legislator P. Sudhir Kumar was kidnapped after a daring raid on his house in the centre of Hyderabad. To get him released, the Channa Reddy government released seniormost leader Nemaluri Bhaskara Rao and two others in exchange of Sudhir Kumar.[4]

In 1993, tribal lagislator P. Balarau and IAS officer Srinisulu were abducted in the Viskhapatnam agency area and a Naxal leader Kranti Ranadeo was released in exchange.[5]

As the kidnaps continued and vexed with the Government soft attitude towards Naxals, police did act on their own in August 1989. When two policemen were abducted in Karimnagar the police organised a counter-kidnap of civil rights activist Balgopal by a supposedly civil vigilante group "Praja Bandhu". Naxalites released the constables and Balgopal was let off.[6]

Government proscribed the People's War Group (PWG) on May 20, 1992 and the police unleashed reign of terror and there was not even a murmur of protest from people even when those arrested were shot dead in full public view which later came to be known as "encounters".[7]

Kidnappings are done mainly to get their own Naxal colleagues, who stand arrested by police, released and demoralising the state machinery including its security forces.

Asim Chatterjee "Kaka", the Naxalite intellectual opines that heavy deployment of armed forces can bring occasional successes but more the deployment of men in uniform, more the risk of bloodshed and alienation from the tribal people.

Even on Telangana issue People's War Group of CPI-ML had raised its demand for a separate state through Gummadi Vithal Rao popularly known as Gaddar who was associated with the party's cultural front Jan Natya Mandali. He went to the extent of forming Telangana Praja Front as an alternative to Telengana Rahtra Samiti (TRS) in 2010.

References

1. *The Hindu*, May 7, 2012 kidnaps could be a failed experiment for Maoists. Article by K. Srinivas Reddy.
2. *Ibid.*
3. *Ibid.*
4. *Ibid.*
5. *Ibid.*
6. *Ibid.*
7. *Ibid.*

Andhra Pradesh

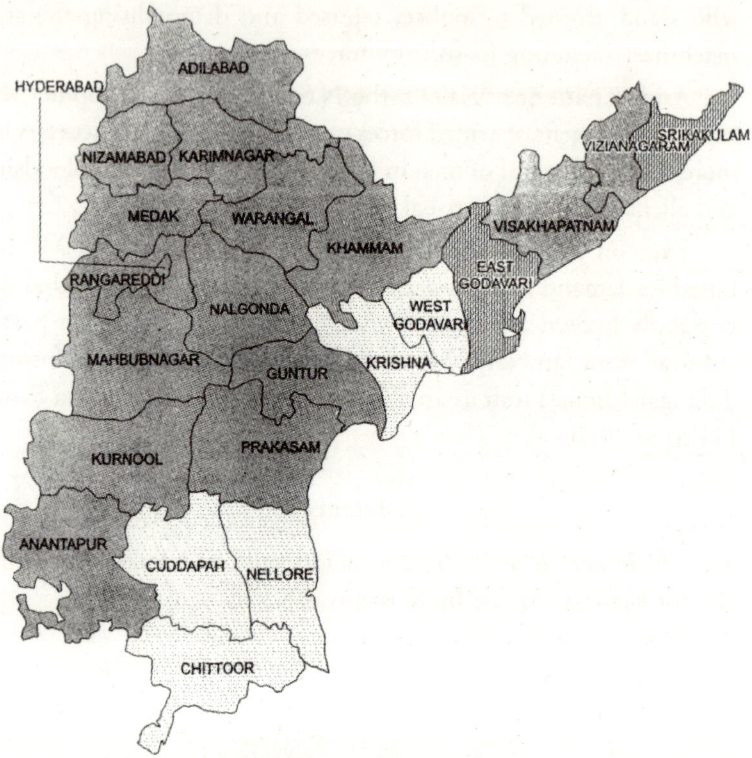

Naxual Map of Andhra Pradesh.

3
How to Cope with Naxalism

Naxalism, in a way, can be branded as insurgency. Shri E.N. Rammohan former DG of BSF draws a parallel between Maoist insurgency and the HUK insurgency of Phillipines and goes on to explain as to how President Magsaysay tackled it by amending the tenancy laws of his country once he came to power. Naxals, now known as Maoists, consider the land reforms, as a means and a step only towards achieving their main aim which is to snatch state power by revolutionary means. In the beginning, in mid-sixties in fact, tea plantation workers were a suppressed lot in West Bengal. Their agitation spread to include the agricultural-labour share cropper who used to work in the fields of Jotedars (landlords) and share one-third of the agricultural produce. They started demanding larger share of the crop produced by them. This agitation was mainly confined to Dinajpur and Rangpur. Big landlords were not willing to give more share in the crop and tried to put down the agitation with the help of the police. Bloody clashes was the outcome of the uprising by the peasants. Meanwhile the members of the Communist Party of India–Marxist (CPI-M) grabbed the opportunity and sided the peasants and labourers. CPI-M was running Krisan Sabhas to look after or take peasants into their fold. In 1946, this sort of agitation that was quietly simmering was known as 'Tebhage' Movement. Repression was let loose and for the time being the peasants remained dormant. But when their strength increased, their leadership was taken over by Charu Mazumar, Kanu Sanyal, Jangal Santhal, etc., and in the year 1967 a sort of revolt was staged in Naxalbari, Kharibari and Phansideva. The movement was joined by about 65-70 per cent of 'Baghchashis' who were exploited by big landlords and moneylenders. These moneylenders aimed to grab the land of poor labourers / peasants who took loans from them. With the passage of time, many things changed. Land Reforms Act was passed in West Bengal in 1955 restricting the land holding. Jotedars started transferring their land which enraged the Santhal inhabitants. But, of late, many Naxals have given up the old ideological path to achieve their goal and instead have taken over the recourse of looting, kidnapping, extracting money, snatching arms from security forces personnel after killing them, collecting levy and taxes, extortion etc. Many such Naxals have thrived in Bihar, Jharkhand and Chhattisgarh particularly. Maoism in India is NOT solely for land reforms as was the only demand of Huk guerrillas. They have wider aspirations of bringing the Communist rule after revolutionary overthrow of the democratically elected government.

Land reforms, of course, strikes at the root of Naxalism but they adopt many other methods also. K Srinivas Reddy, a brilliant correspondent of 'the *Hindu*' writes "however Rammohan's proposition that security forces should be involved in enforcing land reforms" is not only unimplemented but frought with risks.[1] Professor Rabindra Ray places the roots of Maoist phenomenon 'not in poverty of labouring rural population but the psychological traumas of the urban educated youth".[2]

Naxalism is war against the state whereas the Huk uprising was for land. In Phillipines, the insurgency dried up once the land reforms were introduced but Maoists would not rest in peace until they drive out the State Government and take over the government. The word Naxalism gained currency with the passage of time after the uprising took place in a village called Naxalbari in West Bengal in 1967. Now they hold Kangaroo Courts, demand right to forest land staging 'Dharna' and holding demonstrations. Earlier they had adopted the weapon of physical liquidation or annihilation of landowning class or money lenders but now they have given up this practice to a great extent.

Jairam Ramesh, Minister for Rural Development said (Sept. 8, 2013) forcible land acquisition by Public Sector Undertakings (PSU) led to the Naxal problem. "Land Acquisition is the root of the Maoist issue. If you have a humane, sensitive and responsible land acquisition policy, lot of your problems relating to Naxalism would go. Tribals will be with you. It is a fact that many of the tribals have been displaced and they have not got proper compensation, they have not got rehabilitation and resettlement... Particularly in mining of coal and irrigation projects." he said. Parliament passed the Right to Fair Compensation and Transparency in Land Acquisition, Rehabilition and Resettlement Bill 2013 to mitigate the problems of Tribals. Ramesh opined that old Land Acquisition Act 1894 has played an important role in encouraging Maoist activities in Odisha, Chattisgarh Jharkhand, parts of tribal Maharashtra and tribal areas of Andhra Pradesh. But when the government knows that acquisition of tribal land makes tribals disgruntled and prone to adopt Naxalism, why go for such activities. PSUs can be established elsewhere also where conditions are favourable for setting up public sector undertakings. Why disturb the tribals who have been living in their areas for ages and ages. They don't love money or compensation. They do not want to be uprooted from their land where they have been living for generations. Once they are displaced, nobody would bother for them. If we want to curb the Naxalism, let us not do that. Or else, the major portion of ownership of such PSUs if established in tribal areas should be given to them only. In all circumstances the interests of tribals must be protected. Their land in forest or tribal area must neither be taken over by the government nor be given to capitalists. You can defeat the Naxalism or reduce its impact by way of establishing suitable industries / industrial houses in tribal areas by giving its ownership to them.

Naxalism does not include poor people's misery in its entirety. Today there are rich and influential persons occupying reasonably fair positions in all walks of life with left leanings and Maoist bands have become rich. A Hindi newspaper "*Patrika*" of May 29, 2013 described that the attack by Maoist on May 25, 2013 on Congress convoy showed how rich the Naxals have become. It said Maoists drank Rs. 50 a litre mineral water, Lassi etc. to beat the dehydration at Bastar's Darbha Valley while attacking the Congress convoy. It further said around 500 bottles were found at the spot of Darbha attack. One bottle's cost was Rs. 50 and empty lassi containers were found." Such is the state of Naxals today. These days the ideology on which Naxalism started and thrived had been left behind and terrorism has taken over in most of the Naxal affected places. Naxals have killed many a poor tribal villagers to spread terror. They move in the strength of 100-200 in the jungles trying to escape the eye of the security forces and resorting to guerrilla techniques and ambushes for snatching their arms etc. There is change in the tactics also now. They organise more and more agitations on various pleas, take up the issue of land of the forest which they claim to have a right to forest for all the tribals. These forests have gold mines, coal, mineral etc. They want the government and other multinational companies, etc., to stop mining in tribal areas, apply Schedule V of the Indian Constitution, enforce land ceiling, stop police excesses etc. in order to expand their base. Schedule V of the Constitution provides protection to the Adivasis and disallows alienation of their land. For tribals, the forest land of Central India - Chhattisgarh, Jharkhand, Bihar etc. is the matter of their life and death. In fact the minerals deep down the earth in those areas belong to them only and should not be encroached upon by industrial houses. Maoists are not in mood to forgive or give up this sort of encroachment either by Industrial Houses or security forces or even the government itself.

In the name of uplifting the tribals, many 'high thinking' 'rich' people, cry beyond their strength that if tribals are to be developed, bring them out of forest, let them shed their primitiveness and backwardness to join the urban atmosphere and modern education with the main aim of resettling them elsewhere.

This is resented by the Tribals. But this plea to oust them from their abode is very cleverly contrived one. The main purpose behind such a move is to snatch their land, occupy the forests where tribals lived for ages and generations. If they are comfortable with their lives in jungles let them live peacefully there and the way they want to. Yes, the Administration can provide them with the schools, dispensaries and good roads, electricity and employment to their womenfolk by establishing some small scale industries according to the produce of the particular area. Tribals had been demanding schools to be located in their villages where teachers should be regular to teach the children, dispensaries attended by full time doctor and equipped with necessary medicines and equipment, good roads connecting their abode with the cities so that they could transport their produce and buy the necessities of life. If we do not deprive them of their land and forest, provide schools, hospitals etc., certainly tribals would not lean towards Maoism. Maoists enter into the picture only when we cleverly want to deprive tribals of their land and ignore to provide them basic necessities. Maoists side and sympathaise the tribals who think that they are the real and only saviours and emancipators and join the left extremist bands. Union Minister of State for Human Resources, Shashi Tharoor had suggested (November 2, 2012) good quality education and its need for universalisation. In his opinion, making education relevant for all, alongwith access would prevent the youth from taking to Naxalism and other violent activities. But it must be taken note of that even most educated and learned persons had joined Naxal movement. Asim Chatterjee @ Kaka, Nagbhushan Patnaik, Dr. Binayak Sen, Professor Rabindra Ray, Muppala Lakshman Rao @ Ganapati (a science graduate), Kobad Ghandy (a Chartered Accountant in UK left his job and emerged as ideologue) are a few names who joined Naxals and nurtured it.

Jairam Ramesh, Union Minister for Rural Development and Drinking Water and Sanitation while delivering Sardar Patel Memorial lecture organised by Prasar Bharti, New Delhi on October

11, 2011 said, "In devising our approach we must recognise the unique characteristics that define the 60 districts across seven states, identified by the Union government as effected by LWE. When you look at these districts - 15 in Orissa, 14 in Jharkhand, 10 in Chhattisgarh, 8 in MP, 7 in Bihar, 2 each in Maharashtra and Andhra Pradesh and one each in West Bengal and Uttar Pradesh - on a map of India, five characteristics stand out, each calling for a policy response :

1. First, an overwhelming majority of these districts have a substantial population of Tribal communities.
2. Second, an overwhelming majority of the districts have a significant area under good quality forest cover.
3. Third, a large number of these districts are rich in minerals like coal, bauxite and iron ore.
4. Fourth, in a number of states, these districts are remote from the seat of power and have large administrative units.
5. Fifth, a large number of districts are located in tri-junction areas of different states.

In a letter addressed to Odisha Chief Minister Naveen Patnaik; in June 2013 Jairam Ramesh requested to address the problem of village leaders to combat left wing extremism. He stated "that my belief has always been that local body elections are an essential first step in the process of political dialogue, reconciliation and settlement as far as the Maoist issue is concerned. He was referring to the conditions prevalent in Malkangiri district and complaints received therefrom.

True, addressing the genuine problems of the inhabitants would certainly lesson if not altogether mitigate the problem of Maoism anywhere in Indian states. Odihsa is one of most Naxal effected state where dialogues, reconciliation and settlement of problems are required. Some members of Chasi Mulia Adivasi Sangh (A Maoist Front in Orissa) have surrendered and leaders like Golla Ramullu alias Madhav were killed. Sabyasachi Panda separated his group from CPI (Maoist) and named it as Tritiya Prastuti

Committee. It is suspected that he got some Naxals killed by police in an encounter. NHRC is also probing an 'encounter' with Maoists by Orissa Police. Thus, Maoists are under pressure in the state of Orissa.

At present Naxal groups are spread well over 20 states of India in about 223 districts having an estimated strength of around 30,000. Their strength is ever increasing because Naxals claim they fight against the administration or state for their action in displacing the tribals and poor governance, land alienation, unemployment and giving their tribal land to multi-nationals, corruption etc. They fight against injustice caused by Administrative officials against poor tribals.

Naxals all over are certainly in an advantageous position. Yet they took time in spreading fast all over the country because of internal differences within various groups based on ideology. Various Naxal leaders wanted to capture states power by adopting different ways. Initially they never liked the idea of participating in parliamentary process but now some of them are adopting electoral process. The smaller the Naxal group, the advantage would go to security forces either in eliminating them or become friendly and winning them over to surrender as it happened in Odisha in case of Tritiya Prastuti Committee which was established in the year 2002. It would also be easy to set one Naxal group against the other and obtain information about their plans, movement, etc., in advance. But to achieve this, dedicated and trained teams of intelligence staff are required. Knowledgeable staff, expert in human behaviour, is certainly helpful in obtaining advance information of the presence or movement of the Naxal group, their thinking, planning and future moves. This way the Maoist leaders can be caught and the group made rudderless. In order to create such a selected and dedicated team(s), the head of such a force should himself be taking interest. This writer knows a highly placed very senior officer (since retired) who personally used to induct officers in a particular unit working directly under his command, train them on the subject by holding classes and monitoring progress inspite of occupying a position laden with responsibilities of the country. Having a wonderful memory he was a very learned, kind and considerate, helpful, welfare oriented officer. He personally knew almost all the staff personnel of his time numbering in hundreds. He even got maximum number of stagnating staff of his organisation promoted and they were called from their homes to come to office to submit the joining report on promotion. He commanded respect from them. Government of India rewarded him by assigning responsibilities of yet another high office of National Security Advisor and later on made him Governor of West Bengal state. Recently some Communist leaders had remarked that Shri M.K. Narayanan may be this or that but he does not know how the politburo functions. The gentleman who made such comments did not know that Shri Narayanan knows which intestine of which Communist organisation moved, which side, when and how long it remained at that position and why did it move with what effects etc. Shri Narayanan is a master of communism. Such an officer with above qualities is required to command the forces who are to deal with Naxalism in the country.

A recent example is that of Director General of Police of Jharkhand State, Shri Rajiv Kumar who personally led an ongoing operation against the Maoists in the jungles of Latehar district on March 14, 2013. A few other officers of guts like DIG Ravindra Kadam who was well versed in Anti-Naxal operations and a young superintendent of police Sauvez Haq were responsible for successful Naxal fight in Gadchiroli. Shri Prakash Mishra, DG of Police camped in a nearby location when Police carried on anti-Maoist operations to review the progress in Malkangiri district on May 2, 2013.

Poor quality of arms, gear, etc., is a great impediment in the battle against the Maoist which must immediately be redressed. Even CRPF DG Pranay Sahay stated on June 14, 2013 that the state of weaponary and protection gear and quality of food and water given to Jawans is very poor. He said the helmets provided to CRPF Jawans can not withstand rifle bullets while food packets are so heavy that they force foot soldiers to decide between carrying enough bullets and enough food. Government should forthwith take care of these needs of our Jawans. Government should also provide a fixed amount of Rs. five lakh to be paid to those who operate in Naxal areas on completion of their postings. In case of any casualty, govt. should take care of the education, money for his wife and children besides a, compensaton of Rs. 50 lakhs which should be given to the Jawans wife and parents as well. parents should be given money separately. The new chief of CRPF Mr. Dilip Trivedi would like to do it during his tennure. Jawans should be provided with weapons of international standard.

In the year 2007, 294 Maoists were recorded killed in Police action. In 2010, the number came down to 170. In the year 2005, 150 police and 281 civilians were killed whereas in 2010 the number was 277 and 626.[3] In the year 2011, the number of casualties in Naxal violence had dipped. In 2010, violence claimed 1005 lives and in 2011 it claimed 611.4 The Maoist violence recorded a new low in the year 2012 in the last six year period. In 2012, there were 1365 incidents of violence by Maoists in nine (9) states. Maoist Guerrillas killed 409 persons–296 civilians and 113 security personnel.

MHA says Jharkhand has overtaken Chattisgarh in Maoist killings in 2012. Out of total 409 killings last year Jharkhand accounted for 160 deaths followed by Chhattisgarh (107), Odisha (45), Bihar (43), Maharashtra (41) and Andhra Pradesh (13).

Casualty Count

Year	*Civilians*	*Security Personnnel Killed*	*Naxals Killed*	*Arrested*	*Surrendered*
2008	490	231	199	1743	400
2009	591	317	220	1981	150
2010	720	285	172	2916	266
2011	469	142	99	2030	394
2012	301	114	74	1903	440
2013*	95	43	43	585	116

State by State

State	*2008*	*2009*	*2010*	*2011*	*2012*	*2013**
Andhra	46	18	24	9	13	5
Bihar	73	72	97	63	44	21
Chhattisgarh	242	290	343	204	109	33
Jharkhand	207	208	157	182	163	67
Maharashtra	22	93	45	54	41	5
Odisha	101	67	79	53	45	7
West Bengal	26	158	258	45	-	-

*Till March in both Charts.

Central and State governments in consultation with each other and the chief of security agencies, security forces should sit together once a fortnight to decide the areas which require soft paddling or stern action by the security forces. Weak spots should be identified after discussing threadbare who are willing to negotiate with the state government either for surrender or for observing peace for a given period. Meanwhile the intelligence outfits should keep on breaking the movement from within. Dialogue may be in the spirit of give and take. For example, the government may agree to let the tribals have their rights of habitat in Jungles or enforce Schedule V of the Constitution and stop mining in the tribal inhabitated areas. Or else if the govt. decides to deal with Maoists with stern hands, as was done by Andhra government's police; it would also be an answer to the rebel's uprising, albeit temporarily. In Andhra, the iron-hand dealing with Naxals by the police saw all Naxals ousted from the state but now again they are sneaking or taking shelter there. But it should be ensured that there are no fake encounters. A helpful attitude towards tribals would definitely pay dividends. The main problem today is 'corruption'. Whatever funds the central or state governments give for developing the tribal areas or for their welfare does not reach them and instead it is pocketed by the authorities/administration for their own personal welfare after retirement in making lavish bungalows or buying land at various places. Most of them particularly in Naxal effected states had not been paying any heed to the grievances of tribals or caring for their welfare. They never bothered to find a friendly solution to their problems which has resulted in their agitation and killing of security forces members.

Ill treatment and injustice towards Naxals must be stopped forthwith. During a drive named "Manomilan" (meeting of hearts) in the April 2013 the Gadchiroli Supdt of Police and the deputy Inspector General observed that some kind of injustice and ill-treatment drove Naxals to join the Naxal 'dalams'. They often visited the families of Naxals with gifts, etc., and as a result 28 Naxals surrendered on June 11, 2013.

Soothing and sincere words and actions by the state security forces or the government goes a long way to win over the Naxals. Karnataka Home Minister K.J. George while retorting reports in some sections of media stated "We have not declared war against Naxals – who said so ?" On 15th June, 2013 he clarified at the Police Commissioner Bangalore's office that he was unhappy with the reports that spoke of the state government declaring war against left-wing extremists. "They are our people. We will deal with them within the democratic framework." Government wanted to recruit young tribal boys and girls in the police force. Luring these young trirbals and recruiting them in police force that would provide them jobs would certainly be helpful in curbing Naxal uprising.

Rural Development Ministry has in June 2013 announced a plan "Aajeevika" for LWE effected 82 districts of Indian Union. A part of "Aajeevika" programme is "Roshni" which is mainly directed to skill development programme which would ensure the placement of trainee villages. From Andhra Pradesh, Chattisgarh, Bihar, Jharkhand, Madhya Pradesh, Maharashtra, Orissa, Uttar Pradesh and West Bengal for the time being or to begin with 27 districts have been chosen for this scheme which would also empower women folk in these areas, to be started from November 1, 2013. In the next three years, the centre plans to train 50,000 youth under "Roshni" scheme at a cost of Rs. 100 crore.[6] Indeed, it is a good step in reducing unemployment, restricting youth from joining Naxal ranks and increasing a number of trained hands who would be given on the job training as well as salary. All the 82 Naxal effected districts should be covered simultaneously under this scheme.

Statistics given by the media for three year's is[7]–

	3–year Report Card		
	2011	*2012*	*2013*
Encounters	161	145	100
Naxal deaths	72	50	63
CRPF deaths	26	37	14
Arms recovered	156	213	76

Rural employment schemes, facilities for children to go to school, medical care and housing, etc., are a few amenities that should be provided to the tribals. Modern agriculture development and animal husbandary are the basic needs one requires in undeveloped or under developed areas. Then schemes should be envisaged whereby the rural youth get employment. They should be encouraged to settle for producing handicrafts, local produce of the available grains, fruits, develop the places of tourism in the tribal areas. Local small scale industries should be started with the help of locals so that they are engaged in these activities and are not lured by Maoists. But all the agencies of Govt.–may be agriculture / education / health, etc., should ensure that they are not encroaching upon the privacy of tribal people. They are, by and large, honest, having limited wants and are very sensitive. A very friendly touch is required to deal with them. This way they would not be sitting in the lap of Maoists who would not get fresh recruits. The aim should be to remove their chronic poverty and create confidence among them that the security forces are for their welfare. Doctor and Medical facilities do miracles. They can be very helping in ending the Maoist menace. Once we are able to create confidence among these tribals, they would, of their own, rush to nearby security forces station to inform the Maoist's movement in their area. Schemes initiated by the Ministry of Tribal Affairs for the welfare and development of Scheduled tribes should be implemented in letter and spirit. The schemes are described herein under :

1. **Implementation of the Scheduled Tribes and Other Traditional Forest Dwellers (Recognition of Forest Rights) Act, 2006 :**
   - The occupation of forest land up to an area of 4 hectares (maximum) can be recognized.
   - Rights are heritable but not alienable or transferable.
   - Persons living in and dependent on forests for livelihood shall be eligible.
   - Responsibility of protection of wild life, forest and biodiversity has been assigned to right-holders.
   - Support to National / State Scheduled Tribe Finance Development Cooperation (NSTFDC) for providing concessional finance including education loan to the ST people.
2. **Grants under Article 275(1) of the Constitution for raising the level of administration in Scheduled Areas at par with the rest of the State.**
   - Primarily for creation and up gradation of infrastructure in critical areas such as education, health, SSIs, forests, drinking water, food processing, processing of Minor Forest Produce (MFP), human resource development in technical and vocational spheres, water harvesting, resettlement of displaced persons, tribal lanad management etc.
   - Grants for setting up of Eklavya Model Residential School (EMRS) from Class VI-XII for imparting quality education.
3. **Special Central Assistance to Tribal Sub-Plan (SCA to TSP) for filling up the critical gaps in income generation and infrastructure incidental thereto.**
   - Supporting family / SHG / Community based employment-cum-income generation activities.

- Support to tribals below poverty line.
- Sectors : agriculture, horticulture, land reforms, watershed, development, animal husbandry, ecology and environment, development of forests and forest villages, development of entrepreneurship in Small Scale Industries (SSIs) etc.
- 30 per cent for development of infrastructure incidental thereto.

4. **Funding for Education-**
   - A new scholarship scheme launched w.e.f. 1st July, 2012 for the benefit of Scheduled Tribe students studying in classes IX and X.
   - Promoting literacy among tribal women in 54 identified low literacy districts.
   - Coaching for Scheduled Tribes.
   - Strengthening Education among Scheduled Tribe Girls in Low Literacy Districts.
   - For Post-matric scholarship for ST students, annual parental income from all sources has been increased from Rs. 2.00 lakh to Rs. 2.50 lakhs w.e.f. 1/4/2013.
   - Rajiv Gandhi National Fellowship Scheme (RGNF) to ST students on the pattern of UGC Fellowship to pursue higher studies -M.Phil. and Ph.D.
   - Top Class Education for STs for pursuing studies at degree and post degree level in 213 identified Institutes, covering the field of management, medicine, engineering, law and commercial courses. The annual parental income from all sources has been increased from Rs. 2.00 lakh to Rs. 4.50 lakhs w.e.f. the academic session 2013-14.
   - National Overseas Scholarship for ST students for pursuing higher studies abroad in specified fields of Master level courses, Ph.D. and Post-Doctoral research programmes.

5. **Development of Particularly Vulnerable Tribal Groups (PTGs) through both State Government and NGOs.**
6. **Vocational Training in Tribal Areas to upgrade the skills of tribal youth and to enable them to gain employment/ self-employment.**
7. **Grant-in-aid to the State Tribal Development Cooperative Corporations (STDCCs) etc. through their respective State Government for :**
   - Increasing the quantum of MFP; setting up of scientific warehousing facilities wherever necessary; establishing processing industries for value addition; and supplementing Research and Development (R & D) efforts.
8. **Support for Market Development of Tribal products / produce through TRIFED.**
9. **Grants-in-aid to Tribal Research Institutes (TRIs) set up by State Government/UT Administration for conducting research/evaluation studies; organizing seminars/workshops on various issues relevant to tribals, training and orientation programmes to State Government officials for preparation of Tribal Sub-Plan, tribal festivals; construction of tribal museum etc.**
10. **Scheduled Castes and Scheduled Tribes (Prevention of atrocities) Act, 1989.**
    - Implementation of the Act excluding administration of criminal justice in regard to offences in so far as they relate to Scheduled Tribes.[8]

Government had decided to launch a scheme known as Central India Tribal Plan to be implemented soon. Its execution should be by hand-picked officers with an impeccable career profile. When District Collector Vineel Krishna was kidnapped in Orissa state, Maoists confessed that he was being released since the District Collector was a good man, engaged in welfare of the district. Officers dealing with Naxalism may like to derive a lesson from this incident.

A few former Naxals who have changed and transformed themselves by way of deep study of the causes of the rise in Naxalism, have come to the conclusion that killing individual landlords etc. i.e. annihilation of class enemy etc., is no solution. The aim and ideology of Naxals is to capture State Power by way of adopting revolutionary means. Killing a few landlords here and there is not going to give Maoists the state power. For example, K. Thiagrajan @ Tiagu a Naxual who was arrested on September 27, 1970 for killing Thagappa that day had come to this conclusion. This incident or this sort of thinking should be given sufficient publicity.

There is a tendency among students of a few university / colleges to show leanings towards Communism / Marxism. They feel elated in growing their beard and keep a cotton bag hanging from the shoulder. JNU Delhi was established to produce brilliant research scholars on various subjects. Instead it started producing Marxists. Of course, a few students do qualify for Civil Services but some of them do have Marxists orientations and hold radical views. Prominent among the students of JNU was Gorakh Pandey who was also a poet and committed suicide. One of the student who was President of JNU belonged to CPI-ML and was killed. Kavita Krishnan a politburo member of CPI-ML was a former Joint Secretary of JNU Student's Union. Hem Pandey who hails from Almora (Uttarakhand) was working as a courier while studying in JNU and arrested on August 22, 2013 at a Bus station in Aheri division of Gadchiroli alongwith his two accomplices, Pandu Pora Narote and Mahesh Tirki while trying to enter the forest to deliver coded information to the Central Committee of CPI (Maoists) in Maad area of Chattisgarh.[8A] Recently in the month of September 2013 when All India Student's Association (AISA) swept the JNUSU polls, CPI-ML general secretary Dipankar Bhattacharya was very happy and issued a statement "AISA is growing as a third force in the University which marked a great moment in the history of Revolutionary Students Movement in the country."[8B]

A devoted police force is very essential to curb Maoism. The local Supdto of Police or the Commander of Security Force engaged in Naxal operation should be given full powers to deal with the situation on ground. He should be allowed to exercise these powers independently but of course judiciously and in a humanitarian way.

A Naxal is terribly afraid of police and intelligence if he is alone. He also fears police informers. All the three are deadliest enemies of Naxals. All police informers are invariably beheaded by the Maoists when caught. As such, the police as well as police informer has to be very cautious and alert all the time.

The IPS or State Cadre Police Officers who command the local police or SF unit should set an example before his subordinates as to how to tackle the problem when they come across the Maoist Columns. This writer remembers one police officer of UP Cadre Shri B.N. Sharma then Dy. S.P. who was working as CO City Meerut way back in 1965-66 who always used to be on his toes and kept a sharp eye on all the police stations functioning under his command. He would visit a police station all of a sudden at one o'clock in the night, check the police station lock up, all registers, ask about deployment of all SI, constables on patrolling duty etc. In the early morning around 6 or 6.30 am he would ride his horse in full uniform and go for a 'gust' in the city duly accompanied by a police constable following him on another horse. A dedicated, devoted, honest, strict and sincere hard task master, then CO city Shri B.N. Sharma rose high up and probably became chief of the UP police. He was an example before his subordinates. Incidently his *'Seher Kotwal'* Inspector L.N. Sharma posted in Kotwali Meerut (UP) was also *'Nehle Pe Dehla'*, equally hard working, honest and helpful to public. He would thunder *"Mere Ilake mein goonda gardi?"* and all bad characters used to fear him. Once a government servants who was travelling with a steel trunk in which some jewellery was there, was on his way to his home by a UP State Roadways Bus. The box, kept on the roof of the bus, was stolen midway and he reported the theft to Kotwali (Meerut).

The investigation was assigned to a sub-inspector who used to call the victim off and on to Kotwali Police Station. Once when the victim was sitting at PS, inspector L.N. Sharma *'Seher Kotwal'* asked him as to what has brought him to the police station? The victim narrated his plight and the frequent calling by the SI to the PS and yet doing nothing to trace his steel trunk Jewellery etc., It is a talk of 1965 and this writer happened to be present at the PS at that time when 'Kotwal' enquired about the purpose of visit by the victim. On hearing the version of the version, the Kotwal really lost his temper, abused the SI and told him to trace the jewellery etc., within three days. What sort of abuses these police walas hurl is anybody's guess. Kotwal told the SI that the victim is a government servant, how many times he can come to PS, remaining absent from his office or neglecting his office job. Lo and behold, the theft was worked out within two days. Needless to say that the Kotwal used to be much respected Police Officer in Meerut in those days simply because of his sincerity, honesty and urge to help public. This sort of behaviour goes a long way in winning over tribals or even *'aam adami'* since it creates confidence in him by the public. The tribal villagers would be on our side which would serve the real purpose of reducing Naxal's influence in the villages. Now the main strategy of Maoists is to get security forces booby-trapped to order to inflict maximum damage.[9] Injustice and exploitation ignites the minds of tribal unemployed youths.

The January 2013 attack by Maoists in which eleven (11) CRPF Jawans were killed and later IEDs were planted in the bodies of slain Jawans to increase the casualties showed that they were becoming more lethal and unpredictable.[10]

Recently around March 2013, superintendent of police Suvez Haque of Gadchiroli district had been doing real excellent work in his area by way of personally reaching out to Naxal's families and helping them through various ways. His initiative of leading from the front is worth approaching and should be rewarded. Other Superintendents of Police who are dealing with Naxals may also like to adopt his methods.

The Central and State governments must provide life insurance of considerable amount to each Jawan engaged in duties in Naxal areas. Jawans' families should not be worried on this score. They must get enough compensation in case god forbid, the Jawan sacrifices his life in the encounter with Maoists. Medical, educational, housing facilities must be extended to them. All this will boost the morale of our security forces and they would fearlessly take on Maoists.

On August 13, 2011 Union Rural Development Minister Jai Ram Ramesh stated that he had suggested to the Planning Commission to move away from District-based approach to tackle the problem of Maoists. Instead, he said, it should be based Block-wise since each district has different number of Blocks. But whatever the government gives to Districts or Blocks, it may not yield desired and effective results unless the ground staff or the administration is sincere and honest towards the given task and discharges it fully faithfully. As it is today, people who have access to the government funds by virtue of looking after the responsibility assigned to them after holding a particular post pocket most of the funds and hardly any money percolates down for the tribal welfare or development of their villages/areas. Upliftment of villages and villagers had been neglected from the very beginning resulting in the state of affairs today. No potable water, no medical facilities or schools, no roads, no employment and above all, all sorts of exploitation, are a few problems tribals or Naxal-effected villages had been facing forcing them to sit on the laps of Maoists. You stop exploitation and see that slowly the Maoists influence obliterates. Every now and then there are reports from Madhya Pradesh particularly that so and so caught with assets/cash more than his known source of income. Dishonest employees swindle away the government funds ment for someone else and for particular purpose and there is hardly any check on them.

The Indian Express newspaper has done a wonderful reporting which is reproduced below in toto. The report is by Shri Ashutosh Bharadwaj under the headline "Where does this money go" ?

Integrated Action Plan for LWE districts : Rs. 30 crore

Backward Region Grant Fund Rs. 25 crore

MINREGA: around Rs. 100 crore

Tribal Development Project: Rs. 3 crore

National Rural Livelihood Mission, Indira Awas Yojana, pensions like for old age, widows, Jal Grahan Mission, grant from the Eleventh Finance Commission, minor minerals royalty., miscellaneous programmes in Zila Panchayat : Rs 200 crore

NRHM : Rs 15 crore

Tribal Welfare funds : Rs 50 crore.

Sarva Shiksha Abhiyan : Rs 100 crore

Total Sanitation Campaign and other PHE programmes Rs. 10 crore

Ayurveda : Rs. 10 crore

ICDS, Women and Child Development Programmes : Rs 10 crore)

Rashtriya Krishi Vikas Yojana and other agriculture programmes : Rs. 20 crore

Rouds in LWE areas : Rs 100 crore

PMGSY : Rs 10 crore

Rajiv Gandhi Vidyuthikaran Yojana : Rs 5 crore

Labour Department : Rs. 5 crore

Money for 75 new Police Stations in Maoist Areas : Rs. 150 crore.

Plus, other Funds including state PWD money and funds for special schemes like national parks or sanctuaries at least: Rs 735 crore per year for each district.

Who would answer these questions ?[11]

Government may consider granting amnesty to Naxals– particularly who have become aged and are ill, languishing in Jails. A guarantee may be taken from them that they would no more involve themselves in Naxal activities. But an eye has to be kept on surrendered or captured-and-released Naxals. They may maintain their links with Maoists secretly.

It would show humanitarian angle and humanitarian approach of the Govt. Normally people do not forget the kindness shown by persons or the Govt or courts.

Generally Naxals instigate the villagers to demand a facility. If the administration, of its own, thinks in advance, provides such facilities ensurity the Naxal ranks do not swell. At times, neglecting the demand of such facility by the administration in the wake of Naxal's instigation leads to the arrival of police / security forces to apprehend them which leads Naxals to fire at police as it happened on January 21, 2012 in Garhwa district, Jehanabad.

Youths from tribal / villages should be attracted to join security forces. If need be state administration can finance their studies taking an undertaking that as soon as they complete their X or XII Standard, they would join security forces. A sense of belonging has to be cultivated among the youth. A lavish way of living by the administrative officers in front of there innocent poor villagers or looking down upon them would only aggravate the problem. One has to remember that these tribals or villagers are very touchy and sensitive. Once they feel hurt, they feel hurt forever. Injustice done by corrupt and inept administration is responsible for breeding Naxals to a great extent.

Govt may open more and more industrial technological institutes or IT professional may be asked to start their work in the Naxal effected areas of the State (s).

In order to break the neck of Naxals, caste war also can be encouraged among the Naxalites as it happened in Bihar or in Orissa where separate group was formed after breaking ties from the Yadav-majority group.

A tendency is noticed that Naxals are now concentrating in the capital and prefer to live in Delhi itself. Naxal leadership is, by and large, from urban areas hence they want their bases in urban areas. Most of the leadership of Naxals have been caught in the cities only. Otherwise also, Naxal's tactics is to move towards urban areas from villages now. Almost eleven Maoists leaders were arrested from Delhi itself during the past 3 years, i.e., till Oct 2011. Soni Sori was arrested from Katwaria Sarai in Delhi. They hide at such places only. A regular check on these areas by local police intelligence people may be helpful to tracking Naxals.

Police/Security forces should attack Maoists at their bases/ camps rather than waiting for them to attack the security forces camps, relief camps or police stations. They have to work according to the diktats of PM Manmohan Singh "Walk on two legs" (April 15, 2005) and "choke their support infrastructure" (Dec. 20, 2007).

Naxals may be tracked through mobile phone monitoring mobile tower project in Naxal-hit states, as suggested by Department of Telecommunication. This would help trace the movements of Maoists since most of them keep mobiles though their latest techniques is to avoid talking on mobile phone. This project should start in all the Naxal effected areas simultaneously without giving it much publicity.

Government has already approved 2199 Towers in nine states. The distribution for installation is Jharkhand (782 towers), Chattisgarh (497), Odisha (253), Andhra Pradesh (227), Bihar (184), West Bangal (96), Uttar Pradesh (78), Maharashtra (60) and Madhya Pradesh (22).[12]

The Gadchiroli police has taken initiative "Nav Jeevan" in Gadchiroli district to reach out to the villagers by way of presenting gifts and assuring them to fulfill their demands and aspirations in order to persuade the families of Naxals to give up their fight and join the mainstream by surrendering. In Gadchiroli there are about, 30 Naxals which includes about 50 Deputy 'Dalam' commanders. Human and humane approach would definitely go a long way to deter tribals/villagers from joining Naxal rankes. For example Supdt. of Police Gadchiroli Suvez Haque is already reaching out next of kins of hardcore Naxals like Pahad Singh and Gopi alias Nirigasay,

Darbarsing Madavi who had been active in Naxalism since 1997 and is now commander of the Korchi-Khobramenh Kurkheda Dalam. Haq met Gopi's family in Gadchiroli and helped the family by way of meeting their requirements.

The SP also met Pahad Singh's wife Shakunbai Kachlami, their two daughters. Pahad Singh had joined Naxals because of some differences with the villagers over his wife's position as 'Sarpanch'. She was ousted in a no-confidence motion and this drove Pahad Singh to join Naxals. SP Suvez Haq met the family and appealed to them to forget the past and surrender. State police should assure the Naxals of safe surrender and extend all help in rehabilitating them.

Another fine decision of the Government of Chattisgarh was to ask its IAS/IPS cadre to learn the local languages of Chattisgarh. Tribal languages of Chhattisgarh (erstwhile Madhya Pradesh) would help IAS/IPS officers to understand villagers/tribals problem better and make effective communication with them on person to person basis. Even CPI (Maoist) had made local tribal language learning mandatory for its cadres in Chattisgarh. Two main languages of Gond tribals in Dandakarnya-Haibi and Godi has to be picked up by Naxals coming from Andhra Pradesh. The bonds of language affinity are unbreakable and deep.

The govt should in the 'forgive and forget' spirit, make efforts to recruit young and energetic surrendered Naxals to join the police force. That way they will abide by law, have regular income, keep their minds busy and would give them a chance of exposure to the outside world. This scheme has probably been implemented by Chattisgarh government. Financial help and other desired facilities may be given to those who have surrendered and all out efforts should be made to rehabilitate them. For example one surrendered Maoist may like to start his own business or may enter into the world of taking up contracts of construction work. Additional Superintendent of Police Y.P. Singh of Rajnandgaon is learnt to be doing good work in the field of containing Naxals. Encouraging to surrender and extending a helpful hand definitely plays miracles. But it should be sincere with an eye of bringing Naxals to the mainstream and no stigma should be accompanied with the surrendered Naxals. If it comes to grant of general pardon, well, it may definitely be considered and their grievances should be removed satisfactorily and answered to immediately. Officers like Y.P. Singh should be encouraged for setting an example before the police force, the state government should accord him recognition. All SPs etc., who lead the forces from the front should be awarded police Medals.

But the lurking danger is that the tribal youth would join Naxals and then offer to surrender so that he gets compensation and other facility from the administration. So all the pros and cons should be examined before formulating a policy and it should also be ensured if the surrender is worked out by Maoists themselves to infiltrate the security forces. Surrender by a Naxal may entail a risk also for SF or local police or even for the surrendered Naxal himself Maoist may kill him branding him a 'police informer'. Naxals normally do not forgive those who surrender or quit their bands/outfits.

One Jija, a teenaged girl of 15 years from village Gadchiroli in Dhanora Taluka of, Maharashtra was taken away by 'Junglewalas' (Naxals) where she stayed just for one month. As she did not like staying in jungles with Maoists, she wanted to return to her parents and was permitted. Then on May 31, 2009, after a lapse of three (3) years, one night the 'junglewala' visited her when she was asleep, asked her to follow them. Her parents found her dead body next morning. But the 'Dalam' does give a fair chance to a deserter Naxal to return to their fold.

Criticising the 'anti-Naxal Strategy' of the government, Shri K.P.S. Gill former Punjab police chief said "this policy is a Flop Someone picked up the strategy from some book and forced it down the throats of para-military forcs".[13] Absolutely true. Most of the policy makers are 'armchair officers/ministers etc. They behave like J.L. Nehru who ordered the Indian Army "to throw the Chinese out" while leaving for Cylone in the wake of Chinese aggression in 1962- never bothering for army's equipment, ammunition, training, etc., 4th corps was busy in construction of houses instead of getting trained on Mountain Warfare, Coffee plants were being made instead of military hardware under the ministership of Krishna Menon..... And Nehru never scolded them which he should have done as a Prime Minister realising the threat of Chinese aggression/ intrusions.

Most of the policy makers who have no ground field/experience and never dealt with situations or a particular subject to gain knowledge, decide and direct what way a particular situation should be dealt with or handled. An example of Gen. B.M. Kaul of 1962 Chinese war could be given who was an ASC officer but was given command of a Corps which led to disaster of international ramifications for India and Indian Army. A lot many of them who have never even seen a man from ISI of Pakistan, does not know his mental status, the way he behaves, starts writing about ISI. A policy maker who has never talked to a Naxal comes to TV Channel and starts discussing about Naxalism. In fact, their position and name sells. They vomit the bookish knowledge acquired by them. One can't be expert of everything. They are called to TV channels to tell the viewers as to how the Naxal problem can be solved. Mr. K.P.S. Gill is right when he says bookish knowledge is acquired and forced down the throat of paramilitary forces. Even Shri Vikram Sood, former Chief of RAW once wrote in an article that it is no longer possible to assume that a civil service examination passed years ago qualifies a person to be an intelligence officer."[14] How difficult it is to trace or know a Naxal is perhaps not known to higher echelons of officers-particularly concerned police officers. This writer know a top class Naxal who was incidently his classmate for 3 years. Then he never knew he was a Naxalite. It is somewhere in early seventies when with some admission problem, this author visited Delhi University, accidently he met him. Of course he did help but after a few years only the author came to know that the classfellow was actually a Marxist. These Naxals are never afraid of anything except police and police informers. For years together we will not know, in urban areas particularly, that Mr. X is a Maoist. One Naxal, probably during or after the Emergency, told the Judge of Supreme Court while the hearing of his case or that of his friend's was going on and the judge spoke on Naxalism, the Marxist retorted saying please do not teach us about Marxism (Naxalism) you may teach us about law, but learn about Naxalism from us. (This story appeared in newspaper also).

Why did we let the naxal problem increase, spread in almost half of India is because nobody was interested in containing them. Officers were sure of their empanelment to higher ranks when due and lower staff was afraid of their life thinking if he dies in action what would happen to his family. Officers hardly bothered for their welfare. Most of them were whimsical and "Kan Key Kachhe" (weak of ears). If a subordinate officer approached a senior for cancelling of his transfer for the present, he would be lectured on the benefits of such a transfer. But when they themselves get a transfer order, they move the heaven and earth to get it stopped. This writer personally knows about the behaviour of so many officers who, of course, reached to top position by virtue of passing a civil service exam once as stated by Shri Vikram Sood. It is not that all the hierarchy is like that. Most of the officers are really nice, understanding and helpful and want result-oriented work from their staff. They are not the one who will crack once they are put under a little strain.

'Kan ke Kachhe' (weak of ears) reminds me of a real-life story of an employee and an officer. One of the sub inspector (SI) who got promoted to the rank of Dy SP in mid-seventies was very jealous of another SI. So jealous was he that if the SI was more qualified in academic field, this Dy SP would try to harm him one way or the other. So much so if the SI was smartly dressed, the Dy SP would try to bring him down. The jealousy arose because till the SI joined that unit, the one who later on got promoted to Dy SP was considered a very good worker but after the SI joined that unit in

1970, he excelled in the work assigned to him and the Dy SP was sort of relegated. Once when the SI wanted permission to join LL.B. course from Delhi University after office hours, the Dy SP took his application to the then DIG (who later on rose to become chief of the organisation) and told him that the SI was more interested in his academic carrier than the office work and the DIG believed. The DIG believed since he was "Kaan ka Kachha' never bothering to cross check even though both S.P. and SI were working under him. Whatever report the SI would give, the Dy SP would write a noting "file", "I have already submitted a report to this effect", "belated", etc., and it would not go to the desk of DIG with the result that he would not know what was the production of the SI. When this writer enquired from SI as to why he doubts about obtaining permission to do LLB. ? His answer was since the Dy SP had no LLB degree he can't tolerate an LLB working with him. The SI had stopped talking to the Dy SP although the Dy SP was his incharge. Ultimately the SI was transferred out of that group. After so many years the Dy SP, who ultimately retired as DIG, tried to talk to the SI who had by that time become Dy SP but he never reconciled. Not only that, this Dy SP informed another Dy SP under whom thin SI was posted after being transferred to another group asking him not to keep him (SI) with his unit. Since both of them belonged to the same community, the latter agreed. As one sows, so he will get or reap. I have mentioned this story to make those who are incharge of a unit behave in a gentlemanly manner with their subordinates if he wants good work from them. Otherwise now is the time when a subordinate would aim his rifle at the chest or head of the incharge. Justice is the prime requirement of a good leadership.

It reminds me of a unique story told to me by say Mr. X with whom the incident actually happened. X was earlier working in say Group '4' and ultimately landed in Group 'N' after a gap of 4-5 years. Unit 4 was commanded by a DIG whom we will call 'T'. When T asked the 1/C of '4' as to why the expected production of the assigned task to unit 4 is not achieved the I/c who was actually a "Reservation class promotee" blamed Mr. X stating that X was interfering in their work. DIG T got in touch with DIG "B" telephonically complaining about the interference by X who was then working under him in unit 'N'. Without bothering to ask X about the complaint lodged by another DIG, i.e., DIG 'T'–DIG B said "No he (X) can never do such things. He does not have time for all this." DIG (T) insisted on checking up with X which was refused by DIG B point blank saying "I know him through and through. Why should I disturb him. You look for the fault at your end." And the matter was stopped then. DIG B never bothered to ask X as to why DIG T was complaining ? One evening after office hours when X was walking out of the gate to catch a DTC bus for going home in Moti Bagh, DIG B also happened to pass by in his car. He invited X to go with him. Near Ashok Hotel, Delhi, DIG B told Mr. X that he wants to walk to his residence (in Chanakypuri D-1 flats). Both of them got down from the car and started walking and it was then the DIG B told him about the incident. X said "never Sir, I can never even think of such behaviour." He thankfully praised DIG B's vision and assessment. Why 1 narrate this incident is because such an accurate assessment of a subordinate officer generates utmost respect for the commands. X often, when he meets me, remembers that DIG and silently thanks him.

The Commander and Jawans have to be brave and self-confident. Remember once at passing out parade of IMA cadets, Field Marshal Manakshaw said "bravery brings you respect, you will be welcome, if you have exhibited bravery, by your parents, friends, family etc." This Bravery will generate respect from Jawans towards the company commander or Battalion commander which would be helpful in fighting Maoists.

Amicable and respectful behaviour between the chief and the staff is also a must to execute complicated and necessary task frought with life-risks. Behaviour of the captain/commander of police or security forces with his subordinates counts. The Senior

Suprintendent of Police (SSP) of Moradabad (UP) Mr. Modak Rajesh Rao who was suspended on September 23, 2013 by UP Government for allegedly beating three subordinates of his staff with a rod, broom, car wiper on Sept. 22 at his residence"[14A] left a bad taste and no respect for SP in the minds of the readers. Employees were beaten up for not informing him about Samajwadi Party (SP) leader's visit to his residence.

Proper credit should be given to a staff member/subordinate who has really produced good work. Otherwise ignoring him works as a dampener. I would narrate one example which actually took place though full details would be avoided. Way back in the year 1995 when Pakistan Army, accidently, could know about the proposed military coup against the Chief of Army Staff, theirs Corps Commanders and civilian authorities that was planned by middle level army officer for November 1995, one of the field staff officer could get to know in March 95 itself about the impending coup and had apprised the proper desks much in advance. But since the 'Desk operators' were not trained intelligence operators they could not smell the news and the report was consigned to files and records. Even the subsequent report met the same fate. But when the news in Pak press appeared that accidently during a routine check up, arms were caught while in transport for the purpose, this field staff officer told his boss who was actually from Air Force and on a secondment to a security agency that he had already given a report in the month of March 95 of the impending coup which was to be staged by middle level officers of Pakistan Army. Instead of praising the good piece of intelligence work and trying to find out as to what happened to the fate of that report, the Air Force officer said "yes, yes whenever the coup is done it is done by middle level only" and rest of the matter was ignored. The fact was he never wanted to give credit of such intelligence output to that field staff officer. Not only that, that AF officer would reject the entertainment claim of one or two Black level whiskies in which the informant was interested and always demanding. The staff knew that an Air Force man! what does he know about the coup ? Had he been from military, yes, possibly he was supposed to comprehend the gravity about it. Good work thus was consigned to records. The dealing desk was also manned by probably an officer from income tax or Revenue Service, thus not knowing the importance of such a piece of information. He also lacked the nose for news. Shri Vikram Sood, former chief of R & AW while writing an article in *The Hindustan Times* of June 21, 2006 wrote that "it is no longer possible to assume that a civil service examination passed years ago qualifies a person to be an intelligence officer". Proper credit to the staff goes a long way to produce better and best works besides it generates respect for the commanding officer. Why Mr. M.K. Narayanan, the present governor of West Bengal is praised, remembered and respected from hearts by employees in his old empire is the reason that he would always give proper credit to the staff who would do good work and praise him/them before other senior officers while in conference. The commander should command respect from those working under him by showing sincerity, honesty intelligence and his personal output, leading from the front and maintaining very amicable relations.

Pleasant behaviour with employees of the other departments of the government is also equally important particularly for those police officers who join other departments on secondment. Permit me to narrate one of the incident generated by terse behaviour of a police officer who joined MEA for a posting abroad as security incharge. This is a true incident since one of his colleague say DIG G who was known to me sought my involvement in solving the problem. The officer came from Madras and used to boss over MEA people, used words below dignity. Once while this writer went to DIG G's office to meet him, he told me if I can solve the problem of such and such officer whose Service Book, Pay slip, etc., is not being sent to the location of his posting inspite of so many reminders etc. When I approached the desk that was dealing with the case of Madras police officer, the dealing hands dealt with me in a terse manner asking me as to how I am interested in the case. He kept me standing and ignoring. I truely explained him that I neither know the officer nor there is any interest of mine except that the DIG 'G' who is very kind and nice officer and personally known to me desired me to be of some help. The Bengali SO (Section Officer) who was dealing with his case retorted 'but his colleague (i.e. the one from Madras Police) was, very rude and used cheap language for all of us here in MEA as if we are his father's servants or this is also a Madras Police office. He also said that the impression he gave was that he came to MEA as a pauper and drew every possible advance as if he was very greedy. And now he wants us to stop all work and work out his pay and perks and send his service book to his location on war footing." I could guess the grim situation and the determination of the Bengali SO to give him a befitting reply. He said he would sprinkle water all over his service book where his pay, etc., is described and send it back to Madras Police saying that since it is not readable, it should be recast for further action at their end. I became stunned hearing him. Meanwhile a pantry boy entered the room with a drum of fresh tea and served it to everybody. The Bengali gentlemen also offered me tea which 1 politely said 'No thanks'. But his mannerly behaviour gave me an inkling that basically this man must be good and that the fault must lie on the Madras Police officer. Thereafter he offered me a seat. Talks ensued and he said before one year he would not allow him to draw his salary. Of course, 'provisional' he can take. They wanted him to realise his ugly behaviour with MEA people. I politely told him that every off and on he would keep on sending cables to DIG 'G' and I shall have to trouble you. He was more furious. He said show me the cables as and when he sends it and I will get the cost of cables deducted from his salary.

However as I said the Bengali Section Officer (SO) seemed to be cultured and dignified I requested him to forget his bad behaviour for which I tender apology on his behalf.' After my three visits the Bengali SO relented and did the needful. I profusely thanked him. Later on, Madras Police officer sent a signal to DIG 'G' saying to convey his thanks to the gentlemen who got the really difficult work done for him. Otherwise he was not hopeful to get the matter settled so soon. At times, police officers behave in reckless manner when they go outside their departments which is really harmful and injurious. This writer knows a number of incidents when valuable assets were lost because of their suspicious and unintelligent behaviour. Assets cultivated carefully over a period were finished within no time because they are not bothered for 'work' since their eye is on 'empanelment' only for their further promotion.

Most of the politicians of today have become a stumbling block for bureaucracy. Even if they (bureaucrats) want to do a welfare activity for the public or frame a rule making life easy for *"aam adami'* the politicians put a spoke. Mr. Joginder Singh, former CBI Chief writes in the *Pioneer* newspaper of August 26, 2013 "The bureaucracy has become a bottleneck for the common man but the rules it implements have the approval of Ministers, most of whom are either (not well-read) or are busy politicking for making money". In Pakistan, Gen Pervez Musharraf during his rule had made graduation degree compulsory for one who intended to contest Parliamentary election. They in fact call it National Assembly (NA). Similarly, some sort of graduate degree in India also should be made compulsory for contesting legislative or Parliamentary elections. Corruption at that level or at any level causes hindrances in the governance. The whimsical and dictatorial attitude of *"Delhi to Daulatabad"* stalls the progress of the nation and generates anger among the public. The former CBI chief further writes in his article that "out of 543 Lok Sabha MPs 162 (30 percent) have declared criminal cases against themselves and 14 per cent of the current Lok Sabha MPs have declared serious criminal cases against themselves. The case of Madam Durga Shakti Nagpal IAS, SDM is well known. She had to face the politics of corruption for being strict and going strictly be rules.

Most of them are indeed very helpful and work in the larger interest of the nation. Once a doctor completed his MBBS from S.N. Medical College, Agra (UP) availing a scholarship for studying medicine after having given the undertaking of serving UP government for five (5) years as a doctor in lieu of the scholarship, He desired to join Indo-Tibetan Border Police (ITBP) in early seventies. The rules did not permit him or else he was required to refund the money of scholarship funds to UP Government. He wanted to enjoy best of both the worlds–not wanting to refund the money and at the same time joining ITBP. Incidently, he talked to me about it. Of course, with the hope that I would find some way try to rescue him. I told him that I can request the then Chief Secretary of UP Shri B.D. Sanwal, ICS though I never knew him personally. One day early in the morning I telephoned him at his residence. He himself picked up the phone. Asking for his forgiveness to distrurb him, I requested rather implored him for help in this case which I explained after introducing myself and the purpose of disturbing him emphasising that in the larger interest of the nation if the Doctor could be helped; The ICS officer replied "Let me see what I can do". Soon he got the orders amended and permission was given to all the aspirant doctors who desired to join Central Security Forces could do so without refunding the scholarship money and not rendering five years of service to U.P. government. Otherwise a very strict and honest officer, Shri B.D. Sanwal ICS was kind and very prompt in helping people for the sake of the nation. I still remember his kindness though he was not known to me personally. The doctor joined ITBP and has since retired. It is a different matter that he never bothered to thank the chief secretary nor he ever talked to me thereafter about the timely help Shri Sanwal rendered to him. Many people are thankless. Once they are helped, they simply and conveniently forget ones kindness. This particular doctor also belonged to that category.

The present Governor of West Bengal Shri M.K. Narayanan, I found, was very helpful. This writer personally knows so many occasions when he (Shri Narayanan) went out of his way to help the employees of his organization. Though very strict and a hard task master, wanting results from his staff, I was also helped by Shri M.K. Narayanan in various ways on many occasions. He always praised good work of the staff in the weekly meetings of senior officers. Highly educated staff members who were stagnating for 14-16 years in one rank were promoted during Shri Narayan's regime of intelligence bureaucracy. This trait can certainly be emulated by local SF commander or District superintendent of police whose Jawans stagnating and suffering and stand deployed on operations against Maoists.

From June 3, 2013, the Rural Development Ministry planned a 'Governance And Accelerated Livelihoods Security Project" (GOALS) in 12 districts of Chhattisgarh, Jharkhand and Orissa which are most effected by the Left Wing Extremism (LWE). It was to be run in collaboration with the United Nations Development Programme. Schemes/Projects in themselves are good if their implementation part is sincere and honest. The problem is that the money meant for these developmental schemes does not percolate down to the target. The funds simply evaporate and god knows where they go ? Yes, one fine morning one finds a lavish bungalow of the man who was responsible for tribal welfare. though his monthly salary happens to be less than thirty thousand a month. Land on his name and that of his relatives is also found when Lokayukta raids him or CBI swings into action against him. Another question mark is whether these schemes would really stop tribals moving towards Naxalism. In all possibilities, other poor population from states like Bihar, UP, etc., may also like to sit in the lap of Maoists with the hope of getting monetary benefits or benefits of these schemes. Benefits to a class sometimes works as a dampener also. But this type of lure cannot stop intelligentia or leaders of Naxal movement who are mostly from urban areas. Poverty is not the lone factor for becoming/joining a Maoist outfit. Report of the Advocates Committee on Naxalite Terrorism in Andhra Pradesh says about 90 per cent of people killed by Maoists are poor and from the labouring classes. These facilities can help upliftment of poor villagers, toiling masses and provide socio-economic justice to the poor after participating in parliamentary elections and winnig them. But it must also be remembered that the main objective of Maoists is to capture the state power by revolutionary means. Jawahar Lal Nehru had asked CPI members like P.C. Joshi to join Congress and soon to take over the government. But CPI did not agree since they believed in international communist brotherhood. It was only P.C. Joshi who was nationalist among them and was soon thrown out from the post of general secretary of the Communist party.

Centre has also planned Daily Allowance, house for surrendered Naxals to rehabilitate them. This is applicable for a period of three years. The surrendered Maoist should be provided employment like giving them contract of constructing of roads, building, supply of requirements of police or security forces, development of agricultural land, planting trees, growing (vegetables for export) or flowers and opening up of cottage industries in the cluster of villagers etc. so that they are pre-occupied with the assigned task. The maxim 'empty mind is devil's workship' should not be allowed to be applicable to them. The Orissa government encouraged surrender of more than 400 members of Chasi Muliya Adivasi Sangh. Andhra Pradesh government has decided to give the amount of declared reward on the head of a Maoist to the Maoist himself if he surrenders. West Bengal is also following this policy by way of promoting surrender promising a fixed deposit of Rs. 1.5 Lakh for three years to the surrendered Maoist. We have to watch how this policy works. But caution should be taken to see if one surrendered Naxal is playing double game i.e. continues to be a member of Naxal outfit and also takes money and avails other facilities from the state/central government as well.

Yet if the local SP or security forces commander thinks that 'action' must be taken, then the movement of the jawans should be kept secret, more than sufficient in numbers, surrounding of Naxal column or camp or base should be planned before hand.

Normally this is taken care of by the forces. Sufficient number of Jawans is a must. UAVs could be pressed into service to watch the movement of Maoists. Andhra government has pressed helicopters to monitor the Maoist's movements so that aerial surveillance could be done. The camps or columns of Maoist should be surrounded in such a way and longer period so as to starve them of food, water, etc. All their escape routes be plugged so that they become unable to go to the villages or markets to buy food or medicines. SF has to take care of the fire from Maoists when they would resort to on being surrounded and starved. This is being done by Andhra government particularly in Dandakaranya region spread over Karimnagar and Adilabad, Gadchiroli, Sironcha and Bijapur (Chhattisgarh). This practice may be adopted by other Naxal-effected states to check Maoists. The 'action' if decided, must be done sternly and ruthlessly. But SF must keep their travel routes totally secret.

In the month of January 2013 CRPF desired Bihar and Jharkhand to rehabilitate 500 Naxals (supporters/sympathisers). CRPF also claimed that it has cleared 5000 sq. km in Sarnda, Gaaru and Burra Pahar areas of Maoist influence in Bihar and Jharkhand followed by developmental project. One has to take note that the hardened Maoists would not be swayed by any amount of attractions. He would not budge from his objective of bringing in revolutionary change to get state power.

Human factors must be observed while dealing with the tribals and their girls and womenfolk respected. It was heartening to note that when Rahul Gandhi visited Niyamgiri Hills in Orissa in August 2010 he announced that he is a 'Sipahi' of 'Adivasis' in Delhi. He also proclaimed that development means that every voice, including that of poor and 'Adivasi' should be heard. These statements should be translated into action.

Harish Khare, a senior journalist and former media advisor to the Prime Minister Man Mohan Singh has summed up the crux of the problem in an article–"the UPA leadership has neither the appetite for a brutal repression of the angry tribal, nor it is likely to be able to lure the Naxalites into a democratic engagement without a demonstrable capacity to stand up to corporate greed.[15]

On June 2, 2013 Hindi daily *"Patrika"* announced on its front page captioned *"topless hokar force ko uksati hain Maowadi Yuvtian"* (Maoist women go topless to distract security forces). It wrote during encounters in the forest of Dakshin Bastar, women Maoists go topless, hurl abuses..., make vulgar gestures to distract Jawans and hence continue to hold their position." It was disclosed by Jawans themselves and 'Patrika' published it under sub headline *"Jawans ne kiya sansanikhej Khulasa"* (Jawans made a sensational revelation)"[16]

Maoists are now using social media more and more to reach the urban areas to reach out to common people after giving up the practice of issuing hand written posters and letters. Modern technology of using facebook pages promoting propaganda to widen their bases is being adopted. Recently they highlighted the Bastar carnage of May 25, 2013 in details. Maoists have started using satellite phones, coded messages etc. The government has to prepare itself to counter methods used by Maoists. The best is to intercept their couriers and win them over after finding out and identifying them with the help of intelligence men or loyal villagers.

There may be a period of lull when there may not be any activity on the part of Maoists and it should be assumed that the Maoist violence has been contained because of the security operation undertaken by the security forces against Naxals. But They make full and fool proof preparations for launching any forthcoming attack during this period examining all pros and cons and rehersing it. They are master of tactical and strategical moves. At times they make tactical retreat just to protect their cadres from attacks of SF. Meanwhile they prepare or strengthen the old base, innovate escape routes etc. The newly raised Jawans of CRPF which normally is deployed for ops against Naxals might consider this period of lull as having contained them. And when security forces relax under this notion all of a sudden Naxals appear from all sides and launch a deadliest attack. This requires round the clock alertness and vigil on the part of SF. Mostly old hands of CRPF Jawans are experienced which after having gained in operations against Naga insurgents in Manipur, Nagaland etc. can be put to use. CRPF is very much worked up because of insurgency in North Eastern states.

Security operation should be in close co-operation with Army or Air Force as the circumstance warrant. An incident occurred in January 2013 in South Chintangufa area when the 9th Battalion of Chattisgarh Armed Forces (CAF) came under heavy fire from Maoists resulting in the death of a Head Constable Besuram Mandawi and injury to Platoon commander Nand Kishore Bhadoriya. When a helicopter was called from Jagdalpur Air base to pick up the Head Constable Mandawis' body and was about to land at Temelwara helipad, rebels of People's Liberation Army fired at it from all sides. Incidently. sanitisation exercise was not done while the helicopter was to land. M. Sahu who was inside the helicopter got shot and the pilot made an emergency landing. Six IAF members who were with the chopper left it and went to Chintangufa Police Station leaving injured Sahu alone for five hours. The chopper was also left behind unattended and unsecured. Police also did not rush to Tamelwara camp to rescue wireless operator Sahu. The Helicopter and Mr. Sahu were abandoned and police did not play their part of duty in the operation. There was utter lack of coordination. It should be made sure that particularly in a difficult situation, positive and brave response is expected from all members of defence brotherhood. Though our officers who fly the Aircraft or Helicopter are brave and risk-taking but a few of them are slack in responding to the situation and not dashing. A little pressure on them makes them shiver and crack. No arm is superior than the other and each one of them has to work, according to the situation, in tendom in the spirit of nationalism, security and brotherhood. Naxals are highly trained in guerrilla methods and CRPF or state police has to match them. Ministry of Home Affairs/intelligence inputs suggest that some senior cadres of

Communist Party of Phillipines had imparted training to CPI (Maoists) in 2005 and 2011. Can a few members of our SF undergo the same sort of Training in Phillipines under the guise of Naxals. It could also be arranged at the level of government of both the countries. Phillipine Army normally must be knowing the type of Training, guerillas impart. By way of launching an operation through External Intelligence setup, perhaps, this can be tried.

On January 7, 2013 an issue arose between IAF and BSF on the question of flying choppers during combat operations when in an encounter with the Maoists in Jharkhand ten (10) security personnel were killed. Five (5) died waiting for medical help to reach hospital. IAF chopper refused to fly because of bad weather. Next day BSF chopper was summoned and it flew to the location and picked up the injured jawans for transporting them to hospital in Ranchi. This was a difficult time where a little more courage and guts were needed from the IAF pilot, of course, keeping a balance between bad whether and call of an emergent situation to accomplish the difficult task.

It reminds me of an unfortunate incident when Major K.E. Padmanabhan, son of Shri E.N. Ram Mohan IPS (Rtd.) exhibited exemplary courage and guts way back on August 15, 2008 in Leh. He piloted an Army helicopter to Tamang la pass at a height of 19600 ft to pick up an army jawan – a patient of appendicitis who needed immediate evacuation lest the appendix bursts. Major K.E. Padmanabhan was accompanied by his colleague and brother officer Major Ganpathy. The landing area usually became cloudy in the afternoon reducing the visibility considerably. Clouds would cover the valley. Without bothering much for the uncertainty of weather, Major Padmanabhan's human and humane instinct made him fly to the location to pick up the patient. But to the hard luck of all the three occupants of the chopper, while returning to the base it crashed mid-way and all of them perished. But he did exhibit his eagerness to help someone in distress even risking his own life and safety.

Since the tribals have lived in forests for ages, they should be allowed to continue to do. The Forest Act should recognise their rights to the forest, there mode of life or way of living should not be disturbed. A dialogue with Maoists must be done with an open mind recognizing tribals right to land and forest. The accommodating spirit, while carrying the dialogue, is a must. It has to be recognised that the country does not belong to the ruling government and the administration only but belongs to every citizen of the country. In fact, tribals should be preferred in granting them facilities of various types as demanded or expected by them since ours is a welfare state.

In order to develop the Naxal effected tribal areas in 9 (nine) states when cabinet committee on Economic Affairs approved a plan named "Unified Action Plan" in November 2010, the Central Commitee of the CPI (Maoist) vehemently opposed it. But it should be remembered that development of the areas is not the only solution to curb Maoism. Maoists think that development can take place after they snatch the State power. Granting forest Right through an Act would help soothing the situation to a limited extent, Strengthening and granting powers and finances to Gram Panchayats may also ease the problem. Industrialist should not be allowed to invest for mining purposes in the tribal inhabitated areas. Mining in tribal areas should strictly be prohibited. To a large extend it would reduce killing, etc., of security forces.

Surrendered Naxals should quietly be rehabiliated at other parts of the country. Of course, keeping an eye on them lest they play doubles. Some sort of suitable creative and engaging job be given to them with financial help.

The Unicon Tribal Affairs Minister Kishore Chandra Deo said to *The Hindu* "nothing can justity the attack in Bastar and it could be described as an act akin to a terrorist attack but you can not call it terrorism–that has different connotations. If the Maoist issue was to be addressed squarely, the government must first tackle the issue of mining norms in Schedule V areas (in Central India populated largely by tribals and designated as such in the Constitution). The biggest threat to the tribals is the threat of the mining. The way it is being done in these areas is both unconstitutional and illegal". He further said there are reports of a nexus between Maoists and corporators. These need to be probed as executives of big mining companies have been accused of sending large sums of money through Couriers.

To get intelligence inputs the security agencies have to involve themselves very intimately, deeply and effectively. It is a very lengthy process and takes time to select suitable staff in the units that deal with Naxals. A good study of the Maoism, their ideology, tacties and strategy, case studies, good knowledge of topography of the Naxal habitats, getting access to top class Naxals and acceptability of the information gathering apparatus etc., are a few things that are immediately required. We have to remember that "Naxalism is here and it is here to stay. Any amount of surrenders by Maoists or encounters would not deplete Naxals strength. Yes, their brutality can definitely be reduced if the administration answers their resent ments and intelligence outfits get proper inputs which can be put to use in reducing or nullifying encounters.

At the Chief Minister's Conference in New Delhi called by the Prime Minister Man Mohan Singh, the state leaders of Chhattisgarh, Andhra Pradesh, Maharashtra, Bihar and Orissa, Governor of Jharkhand and representatives of Madhya Pradesh, West Bengal and Uttar Pradesh on their part desired that the central forces should eliminate the top leadership of Naxals instead of getting involved in too many skirmishes with lower level functionaries.[17] I am afraid, if it is done it may not lead to paucity of second rung of leadership in Maoist hierarchy. If the top is eliminated, the next in rank surges forward and takes over the command. It is oil drop policy. You drop just one drop of oil in the water tank, it automatically spreads into hundred of drops. PLA guerillas must have envisaged the eventuality while chalking out the strategy and tactics. The only thing is that they are secretive and we don't know what their plans are! We have already seen that the Maoist violence did not lessen inspite of eliminating a number of top level Naxals.

R.K. Vij Additional Director General of Police in Chhattisgarh says Maoist military formations can be effectively fought only by deployment of special forces and that the incident of Jeeram Ghati in Chhattisgarh on May 25, 2013 was an act of frustration on the part of Maoist aimed at reasserting their ideology against the democratic values of the country. He may be right to a certain extent or even to a large extent but this is not the answer to the problem raised by Maoists. Maoism is not about writing good English or delivery of a good speech. It is a fight to finish by a dedicated band of devoted and determined persons. The incident of Jeeram Ghati was well planned and rehearsed to kill Mahendra Karma as main target and V.C. Shukla as second. While with the Salwa Judum, Karma had unleashed a number of atrocities 'Julms' on poor and innocent tribals. Both of them were branded as 'Public enemy'. Maoists had attempted several times to kill him. Naxals desire (in Chhattisgarh particularly) that Schedule V of the Indian Constitution should be applicable to them denying the mining areas of tribal land to big capitalists/Industrial houses. This would, to a great extent, reduce Maoist's anger against the authorities–State or Central. Enough forcs stand deployed in Chhattisgarh, still Maoists attack SF using high explosives. Forces cannot be concentrated at one area to surround Maoists. They have envisaged tactics that in case of being surrounded by SF, some of the Maoists insurgents, in fact PLA guerilla, quietly escape and take positions behind SF formations, start firing giving surprise to Jawans and taking their toll. Thus, it does not seem to be a final solution though at times, this tactic may work. Almost 13 to 15 major incidents have taken place since mid September 2005 till date despite deployment of enough police/security force.[18] Maoists press its tactical counter offensive band in such precarious situations.

There should be no detaining of a person by the police or

security forces merely on suspicion. Better avoid implicating tribals under the Unlawful Activities Prevention Act (UAPA) as person (A) associated with banned Naxalite party. In March 2013 Justice Abhay Thipsay of Bombay High Court pointed at that until the accused is proven a Naxal, mere assumption or mere belonging to a banned body did not constitute a crime. He also stated that distinction had to be made between active and non-active members.

There is a tendency on the part of security forces or their intelligence apparatus to quietly utilise a surrendered Naxalite. Not reporting his surrender, not mentioning it in the police daily diary and not producing him before the media for propaganda purposes, he is quietly sent back to the Naxal bands to report their activities to SF or Police to contain Naxalism. He should never be taken on patrol party. These days human rights organisation keep a vigilant eye on tribal areas for any atrocity on them. So the best course would be to show the Naxal's surrender and arrest. In rarest of rare cases when higher authorities of police/ SF give clearance then only he could be used or deployed for Naxal operations. The surrendered Naxal might be an infiltratee and quietly may keep on reporting the happenings in SF or their movements to the Maoists. Intelligence penetration of Maoists in the security forces is increasing. In contrast if security forces/police penetrate the Naxal outfit, it may help them in encounter with Maoists as in the case of an encounter with Naxals on September 14, 2013 at Silakota village in Malkangiri district of Orissa. This encounter was led by the Supdt of police Malkangiri, Akhileshwar Singh which killed 13 Maoists and caused a setback to the Andhra Orissa Border Special Zonal Committee of CPI (Maoist).

In drought-hit Karnataka and Maharashtra, the peasants, tribals should be given proper compensation and the Banks should be instructed to wave off the loans taken by them. This is, of course, to be done after proper verification. Since ours is a welfare state, the Central and State government should show courage to forego their debt owed to Bank so that they do not commit suicide.

Maharashtra alone, according to Crime Records Bureau, gave the data as 3337 suicides is 2011. Since 1995 a total of 57,604 farmers committed suicide. In 2012, suicide record in Maharashtra was 3786. In Andhra Pradesh in 2012 farm suicides were 2572. Governments must take up steps to stop this trend and tregedy.

The local administration in Maoist areas should hold regular meeting with the villagers/ tribals and a good and workable liaison should be maintained. District level authorities should visit these villages once a month for exchange of the point of difficulties, impediments faced by them and must try to remove them by finding solutions whole heartedly. There should be no lip service. They should be seen on ground as helping them in mitigating the problem faced by tribals. Security forces should strictly adhere to this norm.

Respect tribal customs, their symbols and above all their women folk. Our conception that the tribal women folk, are easy prey and the attitude of looking down upon them has to be stopped. This is one of the main reasons that Maoism has been taking roots in various tribal inhabited places. This writer personally knows how security forces used to behave with tribal women in North East about four decades ago. Shri Shubhranshu Choudhary in his book Lets call him Vasu with the Maoists in Chhattisgarh' narrates how forest and revenue officials behaved with women folk and what was the reply of Maoists to these idiotic acts. (Page 116 to 125). The tribal women folk must be respected if we want to contain the influence of Maoists. Their dignity must be maintained.

Lack of sufficient strength of police force could be one of reasons of not being able to eliminate the Maoists. Media (*The Hindu* of July 8, 2013 article by Sandeep Joshi) wrote that the shortage in police force in UP is 1.8 lakhs, Andhra Pradesh (30,000), West Bengal (20,000), Bihar (16,000), Chhattisgarh (13,000), Jharkhand (10000), M.P. (6000) and Odisha (2000). Ministry of Home Affairs of Government of India has instructed to relax the recruitment norms, incentives to be given to the officials posted in difficult areas of Left Wing Extremism, police to play more pro-active role in understanding intelligence-based anti-Naxal operations by special forces, state governments to prepare plans of action to completely clear Naxals from less/ moderately affected districts by 2013, best officers to be posted as SP's in the worst-affected districts who would be nodal points of operation etc. To counter Maoists a guerrilla trained police force is more essential than the number of the force. Well trained in laying ambushes and smelling the presence of Naxals is more important. Naxals usually lay mines and blow off the vehicles passing through the mined road. Under such circumstances the number of police force may be immaterial. It should be made compulsory for police officers posted in Left Wing extremist effected areas to study guerilla warfare and methods they adopt. Injustice to the villages/tribals by the government officials, forest guards and police should not be done and a strict eye should be kept on landlords so that they do not exploit the poor tribals/villagers and their women folk must be respected. And then see the results. Please read the book. *"Lets Call Him Vasu"* where he narrates the atrocities perpetrated by forest people, police, landlords, etc. Give them schools, hospitals, Doctors, teachers, roads, developmental schemes, respect their customs and see the miraculous results. At the same time efforts should be afoot to procure advance, upto the minute intelligence of the movement of Maoists, e.g., which village they visited, what transpired, when they met? etc. When police columns go out on patrolling, they should be over cautious, particularly for any obstruction laid on road, roads that are freshly dug, land mines and ambushes. Aerial survey of the area before going out for reccee by the police force should be adhered to. But "Prevention is always better than cure". We should find the answer as to why one becomes a Naxal and how to bring him back to mainstream by answering his grievances ?

But deploying large number of police force to quell the Maoist insurgency, though it is "a greatest threat" may not be the best approach to find a viable solution. According to a survey conducted by *The Hindu-CNN-IBN Election Tracker Survey 2013* by the centre for the study of Developing Societies (CSDS), 45 Percent of voters surveyed agreed with Prime Minister Manmohan Singh's assertion that Naxalism constitutes the "greatest threat to India's internal security." 43 Percent in Chhattisgarh, 51Percent in Jharkhand, 65 percent in Maharashtra's Vidharbha region shared the view of Dr. Manmohan Singh. 21 percent support an approach of deploying security forces while 50 Percent respondents believe in either addressing tribal grievances or initiating talks.[19]

The DGPs of Central Security Forces like CRPF, BSF, State police etc should ensure that there are no casualties or minimum casualties of its personnel. Let the local commander exercise his discretion so that the casualty could be zero and the assigned task is achieved. The former DGP of CRPF had done a good job by not permitting to deploy UAV's when the troops were on 'action' or on patrol duty against Naxals. Let us hope that his successor Mr Dilip Trivedi further improves upon the operational tactics since he is more dashing, vibrant and result-oriented officer with a knack of getting things done. This writer had occassions to see him in action way back in 1996. When he was a Deputy Director with a Security Agency of the Government. Hopefully he would minimize CRPF casualties and contain/eliminate Naxals.

If security forces casualties are there, Maoists feel happy and their morale boosts but if their leaders are bumped off, it certainly loosens their morale. The aim should be to target the leader and capture him alive so as to take his help in formulating our policy after interrogating him and extracting information.

Sustained operations do yield results howsoever big or small they might be. Massive operation in Palamau, Latehar and Gumla in Jharkhand led to recovery of two mortar making factories near Charadara in Chhota Nagra area in 2012. Likewise in Chhattisgarh, security forces busted training infrastructure from the interiors of Bijapur and Narayanpur districts and neutralized some top Maoists including Ratna Sambe Reddy, a member of the central Technical Committee of CPI (Maoist) who carried a reward of Rs. 6 Lakhs. Huge haul of arms from West Bengal and apprehension of top Maoists leader Ekianta Rabha, a Central Committee member from Assam further boosted the morale of the security forces.[20]

When 76 CRPF Jawans were killed in an ambush by Maoists at Dantewada on April 6, 2010, the *India Today* magazine (April 19, 2010) brought a very comprehensive article which requires due attention and compliance thereof. Pointing out the key failures of Dantewada debacle it Lists were due to failures in :

(1) *Strategy*–Reclaim and hold operations were too sparse and not backed by development programmes. Few CRPF personnel to tackle Maoists.

(2) *Intelligence*–Little ground intelligence. The company was unaware of being surrounded. It camped in a village and entered and left from the same route.

(3) *Leadership*–No recce, taking too large a group and exposing troops. A good commander would have rallied men and returned fire.

(4) *Tactics*–Cardinal rule of counter-insurgency, to stay away from the roads and adopt different entry and exits, not followed.

(5) *Communication*–Counter-ambush drills were not followed. The second company which was nearly unable to come to the rescue of besieged 'A' company. (The CRPF Jawans belonged to 'A' company of 82nd Battalion of CRPF).

(6) *Equipment*–Did not have adequate indirect fire weapons like mortars which can lay heavy fire on ambushing forces.[21]

Unless we respect our Jawans of Defence Forces or Security Forces like CRPF or BSF, who are the real defenders, we will not be able to achieve desired results. What impression our soldiers/ Jawans would derive on hearing that on August 8, 2013 Bihar's

Rural Works and Panchayati Raj Minister Bhim Singh publicly stated *"Sena aur police meyn log marne hi jate hain"* (People join the police and the Army to only die) while referring to the LOC incident of August 6, 2013 when Pakistan Army personnel fired and killed our five Jawans of 21 Bihar Regiment in Poonch distict. This sort of attitude of disrespect towards Army /Police Jawans works as a dampener for the morale of the defenders of our motherland. Later on Bhim Singh did tender an apology but the damage had been done. Perhaps Bhim Singh has no inkling as to how much our soldiers are worked up defending our borders and fighting insurgency inside the country. At Kohima (Nagaland) Cemetary an epitaph is inscribed which reads. "When you go home, tell them of us and that for their tomorrow, we gave outoday".

Our brave jawans of Army or security forces–BSF or CRPF or ITBP or SSB-give their 'Today' so that we live 'tomorrow'. The Bhim Singhs should think like 'Singh'.

Able leadership in any sphere of life is very important. Leader who can really lead from the front is the prime requirement. Most of the leaders of today are very fragile. You put them under little strain they crack. Most of them survive on other traits than the ones required by the job assigned. It is just because of fluke of luck that they pass the exam somehow and then occupy positions from where they command and then the command fails. They aim at getting good ACR, by way of 'Extra cuarricular' activities and are least bothered about acquiring qualities of character, professional excellence and giving something to the nation.

A Board of experts on Security and Terror of India today gave its opinion on what went wrong in the Dantewada ambush. Their opinion as published in the magazine is reproduced here which may certainly prove helpful to launch an all-out offensive to contain Maoism :

(1) Brahma Chellaney, Professor, Strategic Studies, Centre for Policy Studies holds corrupt politics, poor governance, class and caste inequity responsible. Decentralisation of

power has created variations in social and economic conditions across India. He suggests that the arms inflow taking place from China via Myanmar must be tackled and desires deployment of all possible force including air power to flush out the Maoists from the jungles.

(2) Ajit Kumar Doval, former Director Intelligence Bureau attributes the problem to massive field intelligence failure and desires significant tactical upgradation in coordination, synchronisation and deployment of the attack. He opines that Naxal source of weapons, explosives and finance should be targeted. Also more battalions should be raised soas to employ local youth and counter Maoist ideology through outreach efforts.

(3) Maj. Gen. (Rtd) V.K. Datta, former DDG MO (Special Operations) feels that little effort by CRPF to develop intelligence. While the rebels have graduated from guerrilla warfare and there is little knowledge of Maoist tactics He suggests a good regional intelligence network to be developed, win hearts and minds of the local population and start development in the area and locate Maoist logistic bases.

(4) Kiran Bedi, former Director General, Bureau of Police Research and Development feels that all aspeets of operational assault and preventive measures were overlooked as also the Naxals use policemen as cannon fodder to embarrass the government. She suggests that an apolitical national strategy is needed and special security zones in all six affected Naxal states. West Bengal, Orissa, Andhra Pradesh, Bihar, Jharkhand and Chhattisgarh should be declared.

(5) G. Parthasarthy, Former High Commissioner to Pakistan says poor planning, intelligence and inadequacy of the power and equipment were responsible for what went wrong. What needs to be done, is that para military forces

should be equipped with adequate training in jungle warfare and countor insurgency. Adequate and superior fire power involving army officers and ex-servicemen proactively in training and higher commands are the points, he suggests which need attention.

(6) Amitabh Matto, Professor International Polities, JNU feels colossal failure of intellingence as forces could not detect large numbers of Maoists and secondly forces did not have bare minimum of road opening parties that detect IEDs. These were responsible for what went wrong. He suggests that government should revisit each part to disarm-develop dialogue strategy and minimise collateral damage and not use air force. He also suggests to establish dialogue with Maoists by the government.

(7) Air Vice-Marshal (Retd) Kapil Kak, Additional Director Centre for Air Power Studies, holds disconnect between the 'general' and 'Specifics' of a counter insurgency operation responsible for the debacle. In his opinion it was badly planned operation in which force deployment was disregarded. He suggested constant review of counter-Maoist strategies and policies, greater co-ordination between the centre and Maoist affected states and recommends building up of technical, human intelligence.

(8) Ajai Sahni, Executive Director, Centre for Conflict Studies attributes the failure to mismatch between the magnitude of the challenge and capacities deployed. The presence of a vast region with dense forest cover, little governance and a population in extreme poverty also added to the prolem. He recommends to target Maoist capacities by reorienting police forces through training and equipment and secondly to focus on intelligence-led operations targeting Maoist leadership.[22]

A highly trained specialised force is the urgent requirement to fight the Maoists. They thrive on poverty syndrome, sympathaise with poor tribals and propagate the shortcoming or neglect by the administration of development in the areas or underdevelopment of the areas inhabited by tribals.

Maoist live in dense jungles. They set up their base in the heart of jungle–a place from where they can see all around clearly particularly if any security forces are approaching their base to dislodge them from their 'Liberated zone". They maiutain deep and round the clock surveillance of approach roads to their base which remains guarded by sentries and well laid anti–personnel mines.

Maoists are well-trained guerrillas. They adopt diversionar tactices if security approach their location. They first slow down the security forces advance and quietly forward a platoon or some cadre to engage them and try to scare them. Meanwhile other cadres start sniping from all sides.[23] By the time security forces decide which side the Maoist fire is coming from, Maoists on the other side start sniping at the forces men. Maoists fire to kill security forces personnel.

Their Training in Jungles in learning guerrilla tactics include walking through the jungles very silently without making any noise. Avoiding the obstructions laid by them on the approach road and laying of booby traps for the security forces. They, all of a sudden, charge on them changing while positions and taking the security forces column aback. Their attack on police stations or security forces camps is all of a sudden and specially at a time when the personnel relax.

To counter these tactics, the government should give a convincing action plan to the villagers that they are going to ameliorate their lot by giving them schools, hospitals, roads, employment, etc. Security forces should be instructed not to stay in the village schools not to demand or snatch chickens from the villagers/tribals etc and instead share their difficulties/grievances and give some gifts of their need. Respecting tribals is urgent requirement alongwith other developmental projects. They don't like politices, dishonesty cunningnes, etc. But when it becomes a must to conduct operations against Maoists, it must be ensured that the element of surprise is there. The moment Security Forces come across a roadblock, they should start giving a cover fire on all the four sides.

Naxals do not forgive the people who betray them. Come what may they take revenge by beheading the police informer or even the one who leaves the Naxal bands. So whenever an informer is raised from among the Naxals all precautions should be taken so that he is not exposed. Direct contact with the informer should be avoided. The intelligence unit of the security forces should find out the best way to avoid exposure of the assets and how to protect them so that the casualties of the assets as well as of the security forces is not or at least minimised. Ensure that the innocent villagers are not hurt and troubled. Elders and senior citizens of tribal villages should be accorded the respect they deserve according to our Indian culture. In Gadchiroli District of Maharashtra, the Naxal menace is at its zenith. Villagers are much troubled because of this menace. Adve Kandu, a subsistence farmer in a village at Etappally taluka says "We are like a sheet of paper between the blades of a pair of scissors. Whenever the blades clash, we get cut". He further says "The Naxals come at night and under threat of the bullet, make us help them in breaking roads. Do we oppose them? No, they have weapons. Then, in the morning the police come and punish us for being Naxal supporters. The police with their weapons, cannot do any thing, can we, with, only one axe and seythe, oppose the Naxals ?"[24]

A Community leader of Kondawahi village, a Naxal dominated village, in Dhanora Taluka says "We are governed by two "Sarkars". The official one by day, the Jungle 'Sarkars' by night. We have learnt the fine art of balancing life thus."[25]

Mumbai Police Commissioner Satyapal Singh has suggested in his article in *Indian Police Journal* (Jan.-March 2013 issue) in which he calls Maoists as 'snakes' and also to impose/slapping a collective fine and curfew on all of its residents in case a villager is found to be supporting Naxals. Alternatively the village sarpanch, police Patel and other village elders should be punished. This may be a hard approach, quite undesirable. If one villagers joins the Naxal band, punishing the entire village would tantamount to injustice to the whole lot of the villagers. Maoists already make these villagers miserable and then if security forces also do the same the poor villagers would definitely be sandwitched. It would further alienate the tribals from the mainstream. It is indeed painful to use harsh words like "Snake". Instead if a friendly word sharing warmeth towards them is used, probably it would play miracles. In the case suggested by the police commissioner, the tribal would give a clarion call *"Naxal aao, hamein Bachao"* words like 'snake' or Maoist infested areas' are very harsh and hurting. The other suggestion of Mr. Satyapal Singh is indeed very good where he desires an offer to be given to the cadres who surrender to be recruited in district police. This writer remembers a story where in 1960-61 Prof J.K. Mehta of Department of Economies, University of Allahabad fined Rs. 2 to all the students of M.A. class for making noise in the absence of the lecturer. Since I was absent on that particular day from the class I raised an objection before professor J.K. Mehta. But he was adamant and I had to pay a fine of Rs. 2 in those days. I did not argue with him since he carried much respect from all of us. But I always remember the injustice done towards those who were not present in the class that day including me.

Recently CPM general secretary Prakash Karat had stated "Maoist doctrine of revolution through guns has led to serious degeneration of revolutionary politics. Our fundamental criticism is that it has abandoned politics." He further stated "A party as they call themselves CPI (Maoists) talks about revolution minus politics. All that they think is that revolution is accomplished by the gun and it has led to serious degeneration of revolutionary politics. It has led to anarchist violence, indiscriminate killing and terror which discredits Marxism or the left movement. So we are totally opposed to it". In Naxal affected areas the SF Commander or police should be in the look out for Communist Party (Marxist) CPM activists for obtaining information on the local Naxals or movements of their bands. Most of CPM workers know a lot about Maoists plans and he can provide good intelligence.

SF/local police in Naxal areas should also be on the lookout for Nepali nationals who try to intrude into forests to meet Maoists or even an ontsider who has no business to visit those areas. Indian Mujahideen leader Yasin Bhatkal in his interrogation has revealed that "the ISI has established links with the Nepalese Maoists to further their ties with Naxals in India and intensify attacks here and bring newer areas under the ambit of ultra left extremism. Bhatkal has also revealed that the ISI is exploring ways to supply weapons and explosives to Naxal groups through the Nepalese Maoists.[27] Nepalese of yester years were a different lot but now we have to take them cautiously.

The problem of Maoism in India should not be internationalised so that it is not exploited by enemy groups sand help them with arms and money. Purulia arm drop case must be an eye opener for all those engaged in defeating Naxalism.

If the central or state governments want to tackle try in all its sincerity then the funds or equipment earmarked for Naxals must be spent or used on them only. Choppers meant for anti-operations in Orissa were used to ferry VIPs much as National Commission for SC/ST's Chairman, for State Election Commissioner. CAG has reported this lapse in his report. He had also stated that the ammunition for Maoist-affected districts was sent to non-affected districts. The Orissa DGP, in August 2010 placed an order with a Bulgarian firm for sophisticated ammunition costing Rs. 2.24 crore as these were not available with Central Paramilitary forces and ordnance factories. Of this, ammunition worth Rs. 19.35 lakh was distributed to non-affected districts of Angul, Bargarh, Muapara, Kalahandi and Jharsuguda.[28]

Inspite of all the sincere and honest efforts put up and exhibited by the security fores and local police, Naxals do not end their insurgent activities. The Security forces must come hard and strong to contain them utilising all means.

DANDAKARANYA REGION IN INDIA

Map-not to scale.

(Maoists want state power to stop Operation GREENHUNT in this region)

Security forces/local police/Central Intelligence Agencies must watch the possible infiltration of ISI of Pakistan through the sea route to the Dandakaranya region to help Maoists as they did in Mumbai on 26/11 attack. The Bay of Bengal in this region needs to be put under aerial and other methods of surveillance to check possible infiltration by Pakistan particularly. The Dandakaranya region where the government has lanched Operation GREENHUNT to contain Maoists consists of Adilabad, Khamman, Karimnagar and East Godavari districts of Andhra Pradesh, Godchiroli and Chandrapur in Maharashtra, Malkangiri and Koraput in Odisha and Bastar, Dantewara and Kanker in Chhattisgarh. All these districts/areas are by and large tribal areas and undeveloped, thickly forested by jungles etc. Maoists have made this region as their abode. We must watch for any outside infiltration through sea, i.e., Bay of Bengal.

References

1. *The Hindu,* August 30, 2011. He was commenting on the book "The Naxal Threat-Causes, State, Responses and consequences" edited by V.R. Raghavan.
2. The Naxalites and their ideology-(Prologue XII) by Rabindra Ray.
3. *The Hindu*, Aug 11, 2011 Report by Praveen Swami.
4. *The Indian Express*, December 17, 2012.
5. Taken from *The India Express*, of May 30, 2013 Report by Rahul Tripathi.
6. *The Indian Express,* July 29, 2013 "Trend reversed, more Naxal being killed, says CRPF 6" report by Vijaita Singh.
7. *Ibid.*
8. www.Tribal,nic.in

8A. *The Hindu* and the *Indian Express* dtd. August 25, 2013

8B. *The Hindu* September 17, 2013

9. *The Hindu*, May 8, 2013.

10. *Ibid.*
11. These questions are raised by Shri Ashutosh Bharadwaj in the *Indian Express* (Sunday Express) of June 2, 2013 under the heading "Bastar Betrayed".
12. *The Hindu* May 13, 2013.
13. *India Today,* April 19, 2010 issue.
14. *The Hindustan Times,* dated June 21, 2006 "Intelligence Quotient" by Vikram Sood.

14-A. *The Hindu,* Sept. 23, 2013

15. *The Hindu,* June 6, 2013 article by Harish Khare.
16. *The Indian Express,* June 6, 2013 Report by Ashutosh Bharadwaj.
17. *The Indian Express,* June 6. 2013.
18. *Ibid.*
19. *The Hindu,* dated july 25, 2013 article by prashant Jha.
20. *The Pioneer,* Angust 10, 2013 article by R.K. Singh "Naxal Desertions Burgeoning"
21. *India Today,* April 19, 2010 issue. Article "Declare war" by Sandeep Unnithan and Bhavna Vij-Arora.
22. *India Today,* April 19, 2010 issue Article "Declare war" by Sandeep Unnithan and Bhavna Vij-Arora.
23. *India Today,* October 26, 2009 issue- "Tackling the Red Terror" by Amarnath K. Menon.
24. *The Week,* August 22, 2010 issue-article "Double Mind" by Rekha Dixit.
25. *Ibid.*
26. *The Indian Express,* dtd August,19, 2013.
27. *The Indian Express,* August 30, 2013.

27A. *The Pioneer,* September 17, 2013 Report by Rakesh K. Singh.

28. *The Indian Express,* September 9, 2013 article by Debabrata Mohanty.

4
Making Bases in North East

Eastern Region Bureau of CPI (Maoist) under the supervision of Koteshwar Rao alias Kishenji was assigned the responsibility of setting foot in NE. To achieve this goal, the Naxals are establishing and strengthening their bases in Assam and Manipur to facilitate weapon smuggling and develop closer contacts with PLA. Shri Ajit Kumar Singh, a research scholar with the Institute of Conflict Management, Delhi writes in an article in *The Pioneer* of November 5, 2011 that Tingrai Orang, general secretary of Assam Chah Janajati Suraksha Samiti, President of the Assam Students' Youth Organisation Aditya Bora, after his arrest in early 2011 disclosed that a Maoist Upper Assam Leading Committee–(UALC) was already active in Assam. The UALC floated by the Maoists had received Rs. 3,00,000 in 2011 and Rs. 5,00,000 in 2010 from Maoists towards organisational expenses."

Maoists are known to have forged links with ULFA, APA, Krishak Mukti Sangram Samiti (KMSS), National Democratic Front of Bodoland, All-Adivasi National Liberation Army (AANLA) in Assam.[1]

PLA has established a base in Ruili of Yanan province in China.

Gen. (Retired) V.K. Singh, former Chief of Army Staff on September 20, 2012 attributed Naxalism to 'economic disparity' stating "Naxalism is on the rise in the country as in the year 1990, 50 districts were affected by it but today it has hit 270 districts, if situation continues to be the same then Naxalism will grow faster."

(*The Indian Express,* October 1, 2012)

In west Bengal, 'dadara' (Maoists are called as such in West Bengal state) are returning to regroup in Jangalmahal area and re-establish their organisation in West Bengal - the place of origin of

Naxalism or better said the place of revolutionaries. India should be grateful that West Bengal gave us so many great personalities who contributed in all walks of life. Simple living and high thinking people, learned, honest and graceful people of Bengal of yester years, have left their mark on all Indians. Very recently (June/July 2013) the writer had an opportunity to visit a place called Kanchrapara – probably in Nadia district or may be in 24 Pargana – to buy a book *"Let us call him Vasu"* from a book shop close to the Kanchrapara railway station. The owner of the book shop a Bengali "Bhadralok" with imposing personality, serious looking apprised me with the fact that they mostly sell text books. Incidently I do not know his name or the name of his book shop. On my asking if he can arrange the book for me?, he promised and gave me a slip to write down the name of the book and my mobile cell number. I did so and mistakenly gave him my pen also alongwith the slip. After almost a fortnight when I again visited his book shop, he smilingly gave my pen back first usking his both the hands. Till then I never realised that I had left my pen in his shop. When said that I didn't want the pen but want the book the book for which I had placed an order, the elderly and highly cultured 'Bhadralok' said yes, yes the book has been made available but the pen is also mine since I had forgotten it with him. His politeness, smiling face, honesty and good memory had really impressed me. With folded hands I thanked him and thought that I must mention about his qualities. Any amount of revolutionary zeal has not made most of Bengalis to give up their age old habits of honesty, simplicity, pleasant manners, art, music and culture. Anyway, returning to the subject proper, Maoists are reactivating their network in villages like Baliaghati, Bordanga, Deolghati, Baghgheria, Nadia and Ramchandrapur etc. Maoists hold meetings with the villagers of Kendubari area, Pondacheecha, Chunisole, Kadwasole, Chandrarekha. Earlier the 'Bon Party' (forest party i.e., Maoists concentrated in Jhargram but after the death of Kishanji in 2011 things changed and now they don't stay in villages and instead prefer forests.

West Bengal Chief Minister Ms. Mamta Bannerjee has started cracking down on Naxals and their sympathisers. On August 2, 2013 Joyeeta Dass, a graduate of Jadavpur University who was founder member of Mahila Matangini Samiti was arrested by police in Kolkata. Her husband Abhigyan Sarkar is the editor of *New Dawn*-a pro-Naxal magazine. In the beginning, Mahila Matangini Samiti played significant role during the Lalgarh movement but after Trinmool Congress came to power, Mamta started distancing herself from this Samiti.

Naxals movement in Lalgarh (2008-09) was successful and encouraged Maoists to establish Bhagirathi Teesta Regional Committee (BTRC) and Nandigram Zonal Committee (NZC) under the overall commandership of Kishanda, Incharge of the North-east. They had plans to put Nadia and Murshidabad in North Bengal and Birbhum under BTRC and coastal areas in East Midnapore and South 24-Parganas in NZC. But the arrest of Maoist secretary Kanchan alongwith BTR Organiser Barun Sur threw a spanner in the works. Meanwhile the arrest of Madhusudan Mandal and Kishanji's death on November 24, 2011, forced the Central Committee to introduce organisational changes and the North Bengal chapter was put under Party's Lower Assam Leading Committee. The interrogation of Maoist Central Committee member Anukul Naskar, the key organiser in Assam revealed that he had attended several organizational meetings in North Bengal and 'Bodoland'.[2]

S. Ramakrishnan of the 'Technical Committee' opines that Maoists are going to exist for a long time to come. The red corridor is definitely expanding. Even Home Ministry had admitted 'that despite a decline in levels of violence, the core armed capabilities of CPI (Maoists) have not suffered any significant damage'. 'Reds are expanding their area of influence besides upgrading military tactics. Large budgets, deployment of paramilitary and police modernisation schemes have not blunted their capability albeit the Director General of CRPF Shri Pranay Sahay said on July 27, 2013 before his retirement on July 31. "In 2011 we had an adverse ratio of 0.43

Naxals killed per CRPF personnel who lost his life. Three years later we have managed to bring it to 3.14 Naxals killed against each CRPF who lost his life." He also opined that there was a huge decline in the number of CRPF personnel killed since they stopped using mine protective vehicles (MPV). "There was no written order but the general instruction for the force was not to use the MPVs during operations. The design of the vehicle is such that it blew up whenever it came in contact with an IED, thereby killing the men inside it. Last year (70 Percent) of casualties were due to MPV's.

References

1. *The Pioneers,* November 5, 2011 aricle, Ajit Kumar Singh.
2. *Times of India,* Kolkata edition, July 6, 2013 article - "Maoists planning to capture new ground" by Ceaser Mandal.

5
Main Groups out of a Total of 79 insurgent Groups in India

INSURGENT GROUPS

Union Home Ministry lists 79 insurgent groups including splinter groups active in the North-East. The major groups are :

1. ULFA (United Liberation Front of Assom)
2. NDFB (Anti-talk faction) National Democratic Front of Bodoland.
3. Revolutionary Peoples' Front
4. Peoples' Liberation Army
5. United National Liberation Front (UNLF)
6. Kangleipak Communist Party
7. Kanglipak Yawol Kanna Lup
8. People's Revolutionary Party of Kengleipak in Manipur
9. Achik National Volunteers Council
10. Garo National Liberation Army
11. HynniewTrep National Liberation Council of Meghalaya
12. Factions of NSCN in Nagaland and Arunachal Pradesh
13. National Liberation Front of Tripura (Biswamohan group)
14. All Tripura Tiger Force

–*The Pioneer,* October 9, 2012

Three Maoist outfits banned under the Unlawful Activities Prevention Act 1967 are :

1. Communist Party of India (Marxist-Leninist)
2. Maoist Communist Centre, and

3. Communist Party of India (Maoist)

Besides a total of 34 groups banned by the Government (Islamic outfits, Maoist outfits, outfits operating in the North-east insurgency), it has also banned organisations listed in the schedule to the UN Prevention and Suppression of Terrorism (implementation of Security Council Resolutions) order 2007 made under section 2 of the United Nation (Security Council) Act 1947 and as amended from time to time.

6

Naxals Study Veerappan's Guerilla Methods

A study was carried out by Gangadhar for Karnataka State Committee of CPI (Maoists) on Verrappan's Guerrilla methods. Veerappan was killed on October 18, 2004 and Maoist wanted to base/study their tactics and the result of the study was posted in internet[1] by Naxalwatch[2]

The salient points of the study were :

(i) "Veerappan operated in expansive jungle terrains.

(ii) Those kidnapped and released by him establish that he adopted a guerrilla mode of his sustenance.

(iii) Veerappan relied on the support of a narrow section of people. CPI (Maoists) revolutionaries rely on the broad masses of the people.

(iv) CPI Maoists organise them in struggle against the landlords and the state on their social, economic and political demands. Maoists build mass organisations, party units, militia units among people. We educate and train the people by continuously learning from their rich practice to undertake the Democratic Revolution. Veerappan had no such social mission whereas Maoist guerrillas have lofty social objectives. We are guided by the revolutionary ideology of Marxism-Leninism-Maoism and we imbue the people with revolutionary politics and activise them in order that they realise and play their role as the movers and makers of history. Revolutionaries grow from small to big and from weak to strong as they engage the masses in the social struggle against oppressors more and more. Advanced elements from the masses identify and join the ranks of revolutionaries. This is very much unlike Veerappan who by himself had no potential for growth. Maoist imbibed themselves deep in the hearts of masses. In this sense they are like fish in water. Maoists mobilise the people to fight Hindu fascism....

Veerappan is just a local phenomena while the most armed struggles are part of not only an all-India movement, but an international movement getting all-India and international support.

The brightest illustration of the Veerappan phenomenon despite some immediate advantages it poses to the Karnataka police, is the fact that a guerrilla mode of existence can sustain a small and weak force against the might and the thousands of highly trained and well equipped forces of the centre and the States."

References

1. http//naxalwatch.wordpress.com/2004/12
2. Volume 5, No. 11-12 November-December 2004.

7
Naxal Jargons in Bihar

Barati – Policemen

Dulha – Leader of the police team

Bada Kutta – Supdt. of the police

Chota Kutta – Dy. S.P.

Dhulmul Kutee – Lax Bihar policemen

Buddha Sher – Special Auxiliary police Jawans

Khilona – Pistol

Dana – bullets

Badi Lathi – AK-47

Choti Lathi – SLR

Ghee – RDX

Churchuri – Landmine

Khad – Ammonium nitrate

Shadi – Operation

8

Annexure

FIFTH SCHEDULE

[Article 244(1)]

Provisions as to the Administration and Control of Scheduled Areas and Scheduled Tribes

PART A-GENERAL

1. Interpretation. In this Schedule, unless the context otherwise requires, the expression "State" * * *. 1 does not include the [States of Assam. 2[Meghalaya, Tripura and Mizoram. 3.]]

2. Executive power of a State in Scheduled Areas. Subject to the provisions of this Schedule, the executive power of a State extends to the Scheduled Areas therein.

3. Report by the Governor * * *. 4 to the President regarding the administration of Scheduled Areas. The Governor * * *.

4. Of each State having Scheduled Areas therein shall annually, or whenever so required by the President, make a report to the President regarding the administration of the Scheduled Areas in that State and the executive power of the Union shall extend to the giving of directions to the State as to the administration of the said areas.

Provisions as to the Administration and Control of Scheduled Areas and Scheduled Tribes

PART B-ADMINISTRATION AND CONTROL OF SCHEDULED AREAS AND SCHEDULED TRIBES

4. Tribes Advisory Council. (1) There shall be established in each State having Scheduled Areas therein and, if the President so directs, also in any State having Scheduled Tribes but not Scheduled Areas therein, a Tribes Advisory Council consisting of not more than

twenty members of whom, as nearly as may be, three-fourths shall be the representatives of the Scheduled Tribes in the Legislative Assembly of the State :

Provided that if the number of representatives of the Scheduled Tribes in the Legislative Assembly of the State is less than the number of seats in the Tribes Advisory Council to be filled by such representatives, the remaining seats shall be filled by other members of those tribes.

(2) It shall be the duty of the Tribes Advisory Council to advise on such matters pertaining to the welfare and advancement of the Scheduled Tribes in the State as may be referred to them by the Governor * * *.1.

(3) The Governor ***.

2 may make rules prescribing or regulating, as the case may be,—

(*a*) the number of members of the Council, the mode of their appointment and the appointment of the Chairman of the Council and of the officers and servants thereof,

(*b*) the conduct of its meetings and its procedure in general; and

(*c*) all other incidental matters.

5. Law applicable to Scheduled Areas.

(1) Notwithstanding anything in this Constitution the Governor 1 * * * may by public notification direct that any particular Act of Parliament or of the Legislature of the State shall not apply to a Scheduled Area or any part thereof in the State or shall apply to a Scheduled Area or any part thereof in the State subject to such exceptions and modifications as he may specify in the notification and any direction given under this sub-paragraph may be given so as to have retrospective effect.

(2) The Governor may make regulations for the peace and good government of any area in a State which is for the time being a Scheduled Area. In particular and without prejudice to the generality of the foregoing power, such regulations may -(*a*)

prohibit or restrict the transfer of land by or among members of the Scheduled Tribes in such area; (*b*) regulate the allotment of land to members of the Scheduled Tribes in such area; (*c*) regulate the carrying on of business as money-lender by persons who lend money to members of the Scheduled Tribes in such area.

(3) In making any such regulation as is referred to in subparagraph (2) of this paragraph, the Governor * * *. 3 may repeal or amend any Act of Parliament or of the Legislature of the State or any existing law which is for the time being applicable to the area in question.

(4) All regulations made under this paragraph shall be submitted forthwith to the President and, until assented to by him, shall have no effect.

(5) No regulation shall be made under this paragraph unless the Governor * * *. 4 making the regulation has, in the case where there is a Tribes Advisory Council for the State, consulted such Council.

PART C-SCHEDULED AREAS

6. Scheduled Areas.-(1) In this Constitution, the expression "Scheduled Areas" means such areas as the President may by order.

(1) declare to be Scheduled Areas.

(2) The President may at any time by order. 2-(*a*) direct that the whole or any specified part of Scheduled Area shall cease to be a Scheduled Area or a part of such an area; (*aa*).

(3) increase the area of any Scheduled Area in a State after consultation with the Governor of that State;

(*b*) alter, but only by way of rectification of boundaries, any Scheduled Area;

(*c*) on any alteration of the boundaries of a State or on the admission into the Union or the establishment of a new State, declare any territory not previously included in any State to be, or to form part of, a Scheduled Area;

(*d*) rescind, in relation to any State or States, any order or orders made under this paragraph, and in consultation with the Governor of the State concerned, make fresh orders redefining the areas which are to be Scheduled Areas;] and any such order may contain such incidental and consequential provisions as appear to the President to be necessary and proper, but save as aforesaid, the order made under sub-paragraph (1) of this paragraph shall not be varied by any subsequent order.

PART D-AMENDMENT OF THE SCHEDULE

7. Amendment of the Schedule.-(I) Parliament may from time to time by law amend by way of addition, variation or repeal any of the provisions of this Schedule and, when the Schedule is so amended, any reference to this Schedule in this Constitution shall be construed as a reference to such Schedule as so amended.

(2) No such law as is mentioned in sub-paragraph (1) of this paragraph shall be deemed to be an amendment of this Constitution for the purposes of Article 368.

9
Naxal Activities (April 1, 2011-July, 31, 2013)

Bibliography

1. Periodicals and Daily Newspapers.

The Hindu

The Indian Express

The Pioneer

Deccan Herald

India Today

Outlook

Frontline

(All the activities of Maoists from April 1, 2011 to July 31, 2013 have been culled from above referred newspapers and periodicals).

2. Books

1. *The Naxal Threat, Causes, State Responses and Consequences* —By V.R. Raghavan
2. *The Naxal challenge* —By P.V. Ramana
3. *Let's call him Vasu* (with the Maoists in Chattisgarh) —by Shubhransu Choudhary
4. *The Naxalites and their ideology* —By Rabindra Ray
5. *Naxalism – At a glance* —By P.C. Joshi

Naxal Activities (From April 1, 2011 to July 31, 2013) culled from National dailies like *The Indian Express, The Hindu,* The Pioneer.

April 4, 2011

Akkirayu Hargopal@Ramkrishna was arrested between Samiliguda and Narayanpatna area of Koraput from Ghanti and Pandayam.

April 5, 2011

A top Maoist CHENDU BHUSHNAM@Katru@Ghasi, belonging to Andhra-Orissa Border Special Zonal Committee (AOBSZC) who carried a reward of Rs. 10 Lakh on his head was arrested by Orissa Police.

April 6, 2011

Reliance Power General Manager Manoj Ojha was shot dead by suspected Tritiya Prastuti Committee (TPC) in Charta district of Jharkhand.

April 10, 2011

Police and CRPF raided a camp near Bali Parbat and recovered large cache of explosives under Diatari police station. 8 to 10 Maoists had congregated there in Keonjhar district.

April 11, 2011

Sanyasi Barge and Tapel Gangeya who were part of collector Krishna's release were killed by Maoists stating that both of them were police informers.

April 15, 2011

The Supreme Court of India granted bail to Binayak Sen who was found guilty on December 24, 2010 of having associations with top Naxal leader Narayan Sanyal.

April 17, 2011

Four villagers were killed by the extremists in Khunti and Palamau district. Activists of PLFI abducted Sukra Pahad and Balram Singh from their houses in Bandra village in Khunti district killing them on the spot. Bishwajit Yadav and Ajay Thakur of Lawadi village in Palamau district were also shot dead. (PLFI is People's Liberation Front of India) (HINDU April 19, 2011)

April 19, 2011

A CRPF Jawan Sanjay Bhadra who was critically injured in a shoot out with Maoists later succumbed to his injuries in Navigarh in Pananwa Tand area in Bihar's Gaya district. One Maoist ultra was arrested.

April 20, 2011

A senior Naxal couple – Sironcha Dalam Commander Surya alias Ramesh Gawde and his wife Jamuna@Dasri Atram surrendered to Gadchiroli Police. (This was the 14th couple to surrender since 2005). (*The Indian Express*, April 21, 2011)

April 21, 2011

Orissa High Court granted bail to top Maoist leader of Andhra Pradesh Sriramalu Srinivasulu (arrested in July 2007) and lodged in Malkangiri Jail for an attack on Orissa Police.

April 24, 2011

In Balimela area of Malkangiri (Orissa) a woman Maoist was killed by police in an encounter.

April 25, 2011

Supreme Court of India raps govt. of Chhattisgarh on hiring local for Rs. 3000/- and gun to fight Maoists.

April 26, 2011

Top Naxal cadre Diwakar, who served as secretary of North Gadchiroli Division of CPI (Maoist) and was chargesheeted by the party on 5 units recently reportedly died of Malaria as per information to his family in Talwagarh village in North Gadchiroli. But intelligence officials supect he was eliminated.

The Indian Express, April 27, 2012

April 26, 2011

A Maoist 'Area Commander' Gautam Rana was arrested near Lodhasuli under Jhargram police station in West Midnapore district.

May 3, 2011

Maoists ambushed security personnel at three different areas in Jharkhand and killed 11 members of forces in Lohardaga area.

The encounters took place in Silli area of Ranchi district, Senha area of Lohardaga.

May 5, 2011

A group of 40 armed Maoists intruded into Niliguda under Padia Block in Malkangiri district and triggered landmine explosion to blow up Gram Panchayat building.

May 5, 2011

Six members of a marriage party including two women and 5-year old, 4 others injured when Maoists blew up a Jeep in which they were travelling in Dhanora Taluka of Gadchiroli district (eastern Maharashtra).

May 9, 2011

Runita Badmajhi @ Pamila was arrested from a slum in the Nayapalli area. Top Maoist Azad @ Azad Duna Keshab Rao managed to give the police. Azad was chargesheeted in the brutal killing of Swami Laxmanda Saraswati. (*The Pioneer*, May 12, 2011)

May 10, 2011

Maoists blew up the ancestral house of JMM MP Kameshwar Baitha in Palamau district (Jharkhand State).

May 15, 2011

Naxals targeted a vehicle ferrying a polling party with a landmine blast that left one person dead and abducted seven in Jamui district as violence marred the ninth and penultimate phase of Panchayat elections in Bihar. (*Hindu*, May 16, 2011)

May 17, 2011

Five CRPF personnel were killed in a landmine blast on Sukhuma-Arrabore National Highway in Dantewada district.

May 17, 2011

A Zonal Commander Deenbandhi @ Dheeraj and two other Naxals were arrested from Kanti area in Bihar's Muzaffarpur district.

May 18, 2011

Maoist leader Azad alias Dunna Kesava Rao, Deputy to Sabyasachi Panda surrendered before the Andhra Pradesh police in Hyderabad.

A native of Mandasa mandal of Srikakulam district in AP, Azad was involved in Maoist activities since 1990. He joined CPI ML People's War in 1990 ifself worked in Uddanam area of Srikakulam in different capacity till 1997. Then he worked as Deputy Commander of Yellavaram Dalam of CPI ML PW and later as Dy. Commander of Basadhara Divisional Committee of Andhra-Orissa Border Special Zonal Committee (AOBSZC). (*The Pioneer*, May 19, 2011)

May 19, 2011

Four cops and 17 Maoists were killed in two prolonged pitched gun battles near Tadgon village.

May 21, 2011

Maoist party asked six of its Central Committee members to stay away from a top level meeting that was convened on the borders of Orissa-Jharkhand in February 2011. The Central Committee leaders were :

(*i*) Akkiraju Hargopal @ Ramkrishna

(*ii*) Varanasi Subramanium

(*iii*) Pulendu Sekhar Mukherjee

(*iv*) Misir Besra

(*v*) Malla Raji Reddy

(*vi*) One unidentified person

Incidently Varanasi Subramaniyam, Pulendu Shekhar Mukherjee and Vijay Kumar Arya, all Central Committee members were arrested in Bihar on April 29, 2011.

(K. Srinivas Reddy, *The Hindu*, May 22, 2011)

May 23, 2011

Nine policemen including Gariabandh Additional Superintendent of Police were shot dead by Maoists near Sunabeda village inside Sunabeda wildlife sanctuary in Orissa.

May 25, 2011

Police found/recovered 240 kg of explosives stored by the Maoists in jungles of Koraput in Orissa.

May 29, 2011

Aniruddha Behara @ Prakash of Arilo village under Nimada police limit in Puri district and his wife Raj Laxmi Biswal alias Nikku hailing from Paikakula village of Jagat Singhpur district surrendered at Puri. Aniruddha was a member of the Maoist Ghumusar Division, his wife worked as bodyguard to top Maoist Sabyasachi Panda. Aniruddha had joined the Maoist ranks in 2006 and Raj Laxmi in 2007. They came closer and wanted to marry which was opposed by Subyasachi Panda. They married and consequently were demoted which led to their surrender. Both Aniruddha and Raj Laxmi were involved in the attack on Nayagarh police station in 2008. (*The Pioneer,* May 30, 2011)

May 31, 2011

The Supreme Court granted bail to alleged Maoist sympathiser Piyush Guha, a Kolkata based trader who was convicted alongwith Binayak Sen and Narayan Sanyal.

June 2, 2011

Three people including a police constable killed and two others injured by Maoist at a weekly market at Tongpal in Dantewada district of Chhattisgarh.

June 6, 2011

Three landmine missiles and one manual launcher were recovered by police from Latehar district of Jharkhand.

June 9, 2011

5 policemen of Chhattisgarh Armed Forces were shot dead by a Maoist ambush in Narayanpur district.

June 10, 2011

Ten security personnel were killed including an anti-landmine vehicle when Naxals triggered a powerful blast near Gatan in Chattisgarh, Dantewada districts.

June 10, 2011

Prakash Rana and Anjali Hembrom surrendered to police with a pistol, a rifle and Rs. 10 Lakh collected by them for CPI (Maoist). They surrendered because CPI (Maoist) did not let them marry.

June 11, 2011

Three CRPF personnel at Bheji in Konta Block in Sukma of Chattisgarh were killed. Three CRPF jawans injured.

June 13, 2011

CPI Maoist politburo member Jagdish Yadav alias Jagdish Master was arrested by Bihar police at Guraru, Gaya. A resident of Kasma, Aurangabad, Yadav had alias like Akhileshji, Prabhatji and Rupeshji. He was incharge of entire armed operations and mass mobilisation in Bihar, Jharkhand, West Bengal, Orissa, Assam and Chhattisgarh. He was polit buro member since 2004, joined Naxal movement in 1968, published and edited "Chingari".

(*The Indian Express*, June 14, 2011)

June 16, 2011

In protest against the arrest of Jagdish Yadav Maoists called for the shutdown of Bihar, Jharkhand and Chhattisgarh. A portion of Railway Station and six cell towers were torched.

June 17, 2011

Three villagers including Sarpanch of Dabri village in Korchi Taluka of Gadchiroli district were killed by Naxals who dumped VBGL and MMG. (*The Pioneer*, July 25, 2011)

June 17, 2011

An office of Bihar State Bridge Construction Corporation at Sheohar and two trucks in Gaya were attacked/burnt.

June 20, 2011

One RPF Jawan was killed and another injured when CPI Maoists blew up tracks near Dania station on Gomoh-Barkakhana route in Jharkhand.

June 20, 2011

Two hardcore Maoists were killed in Usoor area in an encounter with police.

June 24, 2011

Four Maoists were sentenced to death by a court in Giridih

(Jharkhand) for October 26, 2007 Chilkari massacre of 20 villages including former Chief Minister Babulal Marandi's son.

June 26, 2011

Maoists rejected President Pratibha Patil's call for peace talks. They announeed to organise a protest week from July 4, 2011 in Chhattisgarh, Andhra Pradesh, Maharashtra and Andhra-Orissa border demanding immediate scrapping of the Army Training school project in the foothills of Abujmarh in Bastar region.

June 27, 2011

Maoists blew up a Jeep killing two constables of the district force and injuring six others in Dantewara district within hours after they killed two BSF men in Kanker district in Bastar region of Chhattisgarh.

–*Indian Express,* June 27, 2011

June 29, 2011

Juhi Kumari from Bangalore, a researcher studying Naxal movement in Bihar had gone missing from Jamui district in Bihar.

June 30, 2011

"The new Home Secretary R.K. Singh who took over from G.K. Pillar said Naxalism is a big challenge before us".

June 30, 2011

Naxals killed two villagers at Khobra Mendha in north Gadchiroli.

Vasant Shatru Katange and his uncle Nazim Shah Dalpat Katange were abducted by Naxals on June 22 and were shot dead near Khobra Mendha. –*The Indian Express,* July 1, 2011

July 1, 2011

Forces killed 3 Maoists in Jharkhand, recovered Rs. 6.9 Lakh from Telia village falling under the Vishnugarh police station in Kanaribag.

July 2, 2011

Naxals attacked village Karaili under Dharhara block of Naxal effected Munger district and shot six villagers and took away 11 villagers with them. They were realised on July 3. In another incident about 40 Maoists attacked Chando village under Barachhati police station. One of the abducted villager Laxman Koda said "they want us to join their party. We don't give them food, so they are targeting us."

–*The Indian Express*, July 4, 2011

July 4, 2011

The Central Government decided to bring 20 more districts in Naxal-hit area under its Integrated Action Plan.

July 4, 2011

A clique of Maoist leaders like Akash, Vikash and Suchitra Mahato recently held a number of meetings in the cover of darkness directing the villagers not to back the new development initiative of the Government on grounds that Chief Minister Mamata Banerjee had failed to keep her promises of releasing the political prisoners.

–*The Pioneer*, July 5, 2011

July 5, 2011

Justices B. Sudershan Reddy and Surinder Singh Nijjar of Supreme Court declared Salwa Judum groups in Chhattisgarh illegal. Their order was :

(i) The State of Chhattisgarh desist from using SPOs against Maoist/Naxalite activities.

(ii) The Union of India desist from using its funds in supporting recruitment of SPOs for counter insurgencies against Maoist/Naxalite groups.

(iii) The state make every effort to recall all firearms issued to SPOs.

(iv) The state make arrangements to protect those employed as SPOs previously.

(v) The state take measures to prevent the operation of any such group. –*The Indian Express*, July 8, 2011

Quoting from Joseph Conrad's *'Heart of Darkness'*, the Supreme Court declared that the use of tribal youths as the SPO in the

Salwa Judum movement was 'illegal' and 'constitutional'. The centre considered the verdict as encroaching upon the executive domain of the Government/Administration by way of stepping into Security Management and filed a review petition on the ground of over reach and the executive's right to decide key policies like security.

Ms Arundhati Roy in her article 'I'd rather not be Anna' (*The Hindu*, August 22, 2011) wrote "for completely different reasons and in completely different ways you could say that the Maoist and Jan Lokpal Bill have one thing in common – they both seek to overthrow the Indian state - one working from the bottom up by means of an armed struggle, waged by a largely adivasi, army, made up of the poorest of the poor - the other from the top down, by means of a bloodless Gandhian Coup, led by freshly minted saint and an army of largely urban, and certainly better off people". Communist Party of India (CPI) national secretary D. Raja opposed review of court order on Salwa Judum. On September 12, 2011 he criticised UPA govt. for supporting Chhattisgarh government. UPA and BJP found fault with the Supreme Court order banning the use of special police officers. Shri Arun Jaitley said "Instead of leaving matters related to internal security for the government to handle, ideology of the authors (of the order) seem to have become the ground for declaring the constitutionality of a mechanism .... Judges don't have to fight terror, security forces have to ..."

–*The Indian Express*, August 5, 2011

But Digvijaya Singh, Congress General Secretary said the centre should not appeal SC order banning use of SPO's against Naxalites.

–*The IE*, August 7, 2011

On August 11, 2011 Chhattisgarh Chief Minister Raman Singh termed Naxalism in the state a bigger menace than terrorism and insisted that an integrated action plan was needed to counter the problem. "If terrorism in Punjab could be solved why not the problem of Naxalism ?" Raman Singh asked. He said fully respecting the apex court judgement they have issued an ordinance to form the Chhattisgarh Auxiliary forces whereby 6000-odd tribals will be part of the force. –*The Pioneer*, August 12, 2011

On August 11, 2011 Government filed a review petition alleging judicial overreach seeking recall of the July 5, 2011 order of the Supreme Court stating that Salwa Judum case ruling was against spirit of constitution. Chhattisgarh government introduced the Chhattisgarh Auxiliary Armed Police Force Bill 2011 in the State Assembly on September 7, 2011 to deal with Naxals. The Auxiliary police forces was sanctioned a strength of 7000 personnel at a monthly salary of Rs. 6900 per month. The bill was supposed to be effective w.e.f. July 5, 2011. About 5000 SPOs were absorbed in the force.

July 7, 2011

A team of six interlocutors was appointed by the state govt. to explore the possibility of peace talks with Maoists.

July 7, 2011

The Army Chief and 7 of its Army Commanders met discrectly at Lucknow's Central Command HQ and voted against the deployment of troops in anti - Naxal operations.

–*The Indian Express,* July 8, 2011

But later Army said it would need atleast 65000 troops to combat Naxalism.

July 7, 2011

Maoists killed two policemen of Machhkund PS in Koraput district and two villagers in two separate incidents one in Rayagada district. Maoists axed the two villagers accusing them of spying for the police.

July 8, 2011

Posters appeared along the Jagdalpur - Konta National Highway 221 in Chhattisgarh's Dantewada district that singled out 12 special police officers (SPOs) and police constables for punishment at the hands of 'the people' and the People's Liberation Guerrilla Army of CPI (Maoist). –*The Hindu*, July 9, 2011

July 9, 2011

Maoists offerred 'amnesty' for SPO's who quit police in Chhattisgarh. A signed press release to this effect was released on July 7. In Koraput district (Orrisa) five homeguards of a police station resigned from service fearing Maoist reprisal.

July 10, 2011

An alleged woman Maoist Khalko Meena was shot in a gun battle in Karcha village of Balrampur (Chhattisgarh in police encounter last week).

July 13, 2011

Two Naxals escape from Narayanpur Jail. On July 12, 2011 police had arrested 6 Naxals from Dhaudai area in Chhattisgarh state. Ten policemen were suspended because of this incident.

July 14, 2011

CPI (Maoist) State Committee member Bickram said that there was no question of laying down arms in lieu of development offered by the Chief Minister. His views found support from Santras Durniti Samajwadi Agrasan Birodhi Manch (Platform against terrorism, corruption and imperialism) an umbrella organisation of a number of Maoist backed political outfit like PCPA. The new group has gone to the extent of comparing the Chief Minister's proposal to recruit 10000 local youth in police force as "another way of bringing the concept of Salwa Judum in Bengal."

–*The Pioneer,* July 15, 2011

July 15, 2011

One civilian was killed and a policeman suffered serious bullet injuries during a gun battle between Maoists and security forces in Jhalda region of West Bengal's Purulia district. Lakshmi Kanta Mehato who was abducted by the Maoists from near Toto Hills on July 14 was returning home. His release was sought by his nephew after paying Rs. four lakh ransom. Neuhen Ashwani Mehto was killed in crossfire.

–*The Hindu,* July 17, 2011

July 20, 2011

Five Congressmen were killed and many others injured in an attack on Congressmen convoy including state PCC Chief in Dhurbhagudi in Udanti area under Manipur police station in Chhattisgarh state.

July 20, 2011

Maoists blasted a coffee godown at Tumulabanda village in GK Veedhi mandal district in Andhra Pradesh.

July 23, 2011

Dilu Habika of Pilihadi was murdered by Maoists in Narayanpura block of Koraput district in Orissa on the suspicion that he was a police informer.

July 30, 2011

Five people were killed at Rohtas village by CPI Maoists in retaliation to the recent killing of their Zonal Commander by a splinter group of ultras. Virandra Yadav @ Rama Zonal Commander was killed last month, over 100 ultras swooped on Nohatta's Banda village (280 km away from Patna) and attacked the family of former Mukhiya Sugriva Kharbav, who heads an anti-Naxal group called Kaimuranchal Vikas Morcha. Naxals suspected his hand in killing of Zonal Commander Yadav @ Rana.

July 31, 2011

One Dakasa Majhi of Saragudi village was beheaded by Maoists. His headless body was found under Brahmanigon police limit. Maoists were observing "Martyrs' week" since July 28, 2011.

July 31, 2011

The bodies of three Kharwar tribals that were killed on July 30 were recovered.

August 5/6, 2011

Maoists set ablaze a hydraulic excavator hired by the forest department for euclayptus plantation work at Geesarelli village near Andhra Pradesh-Chhattisgarh border. 20 Maoists belonging to the Venkatapuram area committee chased away the excavator operator. –*The Hindu,* August 7, 2011

August 9, 2011

Human Rights activitist Mohan Singh, Samajwadi Party leader, Rajinder Sachar for Delhi High Court Chief Justice, K.B. Saxena retired IAS, Dr. Aparna Delhi CPI-ML (ND), Ashok Panda, Senior Advocate Supreme Court, Professor Imtiaz Ahmed and Praful Samand Ray, etc., held a seminar at Delhi and condemned what they said is the increasing tendency of the state to deploy armed forces to quell local and civil internal disturbances arising out of "mis-governance, social discrimination and economic exploitation." The seminar was held on the "Deployment of Armed forces in the Areas of People's struggle" organised by 'Janhastakshep'. –*The Hindu*, August 10, 2011.

August 12, 2011

Naxal ideologue Kobad Ghandy (arrested in Delhi in September 2009), Central Military Commission member Amit Bagchi and Central Committee member Nalla Ravi Sharma got bail from Andhra Pradesh High Court. They got bail in the case related to the killing of Congress MLA Narsa Reddy in a shoot-out case in Visakhapatnam.

August 16, 2011

Deepak (Telugu Deepak), who was a member of CPI (Maoist) military commission before his arrest from Behala in South Kolkata on March 2, 2010, claimed before the media that senior jailed leaders had asked the rank and file to expand their bases and prepare for yet another struggle in near future. He said "Maoists are not made for sale", criticising the government package for the development of Jangalmahal. –*The Pioneer*, August 17, 2011

(report by Saugar Sengupta)

August 17, 2011

Bad weather prevented MI-17 Helicopter to pick up three CRPF troops injured in anti-Naxal operation in Jehanabad.

August 17, 2011

Four Naxals and a policeman were killed in a gun-battle in Chattisgarh's Narayanpur district.

August 17, 2011

A joint police team from Arunachal Pradesh and Assam, including personnel of 26 Maratha L1 regiment of the Army arrested 4 ultras identified as Sanjib Daduminia, Lotik Maran, Debojit Borgohain (all from Tinsukia district) while the fourth arrested cadre Biswajit Barua hails from Assam's Dibrugarh district. They were arrested from Mahadevpur area under Namsi circle of Lohit district. –*The Indian Express,* August 18, 2011

August 19, 2011

Nine state police personnel and a civilian were killed when over 100 Maoists ambushed a police team near Metlacheru village in Bijapur district of Chhattisgarh state.

August 19, 2011

Indra Kumar Sao, a government school Head Master was shot dead at Chandni Chowk in Saraikela-Kharswan district in Jharkhand state.

August 19, 2011

Participating in a seminar at the Indian Law Institute, New Delhi, Maoist ideologue Binayak Sen criticised the arrest of civil society activist Anna Hazare.

August 20, 2011

In Makadchuha village in Gadchiroli Taluk, three policemen were killed in a Naxalite attack. A woman Naxalite identified as Chatgaon Dalam Commander Raneeta alias Ramko Hichami was also killed who resisted the police ambush single handed in a 12 hour encounter. She joined Maoists in 2000. Her husband Sunil was a member of the North Gadchiroli Divisional Committee till 2010 when he was demoted as Area Committee member for violation of no-mobile, no-motorcycle rule. –*The Indian Express,* August 23, 2011

August 21, 2011

Maoists disclosed a significant information in their annual report that they have gained an edge in Chhattisgarh and West Bengal while the Government machinary is still strong in Jharkhand. –*The Pioneer,* August 22, 2011

August 24, 2011

A group of 10 Maoists stormed Dhangiri in Jhargram and shot Trinamool Congress leader Rabindranath Mishra. It was done after a 'ceasefire' for 5 months. Among the demands that the ceasefire had hinged on a key one was the release of senior leader CPI (Maoist) founder member Sushil Roy, Former Secretary, Patipaban Haldar and Chandi Sarkar. –*The Indian Express,* August 26, 2011

August 28, 2011

Squads of Maoists from across the Orissa border targeted Andhra's Vishakhapatnam district, blowing up government machinary and cellphone towers, threatening villagers as they try to make a comeback to the area. In a first-of-its kind move to safeguard its weapons from the Maoists and other insurgents, the CRPF asked DRDO to install location finder and biometric secret code to disable and locate its weapon lost in major fight with ultras.

–*The Pioneer,* September 3, 2011

(Report by Rakesh K. Singh)

September 2, 2011

A sustained anti-Maoist drive by the police in Saranda jungles (Orissa states) made five Naxals surrender with arms and ammunitions. Surrendered cadre were active members of the platoon - 22 of Chotanagpur Division operating in the Saranda Jungles. Those who surrendered were Anmol Tirkey, Mano, Lakra @ Adam, Saban Karketta, Etwa Munda and Maheswar Singh @ Rajesh. –*The Pioneer,* September 3, 2011

September 2, 2011

Maoists gunned down Purna Chandra Dalai near his house at Chitrakonda in Malkangiri district on the suspicion of his being a police informer. Dalai was a BJP leader and a contractor.

September 9, 2011

In Chhattisgarh, a contractor B.K. Lala was arrested alongwith alleged Naxal Lingam Kodappi for carrying Rs. 15 Lakh on behalf of Essar Group to be handed over to Naxals. The Naxal Lingan is from Palnar, Dantewada.

September 9, 2011

Lingaram Kodopi was arrested on September 9, 2011 from a market in Palnar, Dantewada, allegedly while receiving money from a contractor for the Essar Group.

September 13, 2011

Purnendu Shekhar Mukherjee, a member of the Central Committee of CPI (Maoist) currently lodged in Bhagalpur Jail reportedly wrote a letter to the Jail Superintendent expressing his desire to donate his body only to medical research institute in West Bengal. Purnendu Mukherjee was arrested alongwith other two top leaders of Naxal outfit–Varanasi Subramanium and Vijay Kumar Arya at Katihar on May 1, 2011. Varanasi Subramanium also made similar request to Jail authorities. Shekhar hails from 24 North Parganas district of West Bengal is currently lodged in Bhagalpur jail.

–*The Pioneer,* September 17, 2011

(report by Amarnath Tiwari from Patna)

September 16, 2011

Prime Minister Manmohan Singh said that bringing development in the neglected regions is the lone solution to tackle left wing extremism. PM had recently met 60 collectors of Naxal-effected districts.

September 18, 2011

Ultras issued a 'Fatwa' in Maoist-hit Jangalmahal that people fall into the trap of the State Government at their own peril. They were commenting on Mamta Banerjee's move to induct tribal youth from Maoist-hit area into National Volunteer Force (NVF).

September 18, 2011

Police arrested a suspected woman Maoist and recovered explosives from her house at Katra village in Garhwa district of Jharkhand. Rukshana Khatun alias Soni Kumari alias Gudia had returned home.

–*The Hindustan*, Times September 19, 2011

September 20, 2011

Lalmohan Mehato, a local Trinamool Congress leader who organised resistance squads against Maoists was shot dead at Pukuria village.

September 21, 2011

Home Minister P. Chidambaram made a fresh offer to Maoists saying "you don't have to lay down arms. You don't have to surrender. You don't have to disband your outfits. You don't have to give up your ideology either. You just suspend violence and come forward for talks." Chidambaram also apprised that in the last two years, the centre gave Rs. 3300 crore to 60 districts effected by Naxalism across India. He also said "Terrorism is also a big challenge but the killings by Naxalites is 10 times more than terrorist killings."

September 24, 2011

A wheelchair-bound Orissa BJD MLA Jagbandhu Majhi and his personal security officers were gunned down by suspected Maoists at a public meeting while he was distributing land pattas in a village. On October 13, CPI (Maoist) claimed that they killed Majhi as he was extorting and getting many people killed in their name. –*The Indian Express,* October 14, 2011

September 25, 2011

Somaji Ayutu Made, a top Naxal Commander from Chattisgarh was apprehended in Maharashtra's Gadchiroli district.

September 27, 2011

Essar general manager DVCS Verma was arrested for allegedly paying off Maoists Rs. 15 lakh.

September 27, 2011

Two COBRA personnel were killed and four injured when Maoists attacked them near Aman village in Bokaro district.

September 27, 2011

Arun Thomas Fereira was re-arrested in Nagpur after being acquitted by the court of all charges against him. He was earlier arrested in May 2007.

September 27, 2011

Maoists killed a physically challenged youth Misra Turuk of Narayanpatna by slitting his throat and also torched his two Jeeps.

September 29, 2011

Three Naxals including a self styled, Area Commander were arrested from Bihar's East Champaran and Aurangabad district. They were identified by police as Balram Sahni, Area Commander and Bashath Kumar and Ramji Paswan.

September 29, 2011

Sujato Bhadra, leader of the team of interlocutors continued talks with Maoists inspite of renewed violence by them in Jangal Mahal.

October 1, 2011

Two Naxalites held in Delhi. Dalip and Arun also revealed the nexus between the banned group, People's Liberation Army (PLA). They provide training to the members of the military wing of Naxalites and give communications training to Naxals. Arun reportedly runs a travel agency in Pune. –*The Times of India,* October 6, 2011

N. Dileep Singh and Arun Kumar Singh Salam said that their organisation had rented some land in Myanmar for joint training of Maoists and militants from Kashmir. PLA was formed in 1978 with the objective of 'Liberating Manipur'. Singh is head of PLA's external affairs while Salam his Deputy. In October 2000 the PLA and Maoists signed a joint declaration against the Indian government.

–*The Indian Express,* October 8, 2011

(Report by Vijaita Singh and Manoj Prasad)

"In the first major evidence of Maoist link with China, the special cell of Delhi Police learnt that a top guerrilla is operating an arms syndicate from there. Interrogation of two PLA leaders (named above) revealed that the chief of the political wing of the People's Liberation Army - Irengham Chaoren - is hiding in China. The police also came to know that the banned outfit PLA having over 1500 cadres was planning to liaise with terrorist outfits based in POK, including Lashkar-e-Toiba (LeT) and separatist groups in Jammu and Kashmir and north-east."

"Following the arrest of N. Dilip Singh and Arun Kumar who were arrested from a hotel in Paharganj, New Delhi on October 1, 2011. Manipur police arrested three more persons."

–*The Times of India,* October 8, 2011
(Report by Dwaipayan Ghosh and Neeraj Chauhan)

Suspected PLA members in police custody.
in The Indian Express on October 8, 2011

The outfit PLA's militant wing comprises four (4) divisions. It is also reported to have contacts with Pakistan's ISI.

–*The Hindu*, October 8, 2011

October 3, 2011

Policemen from Chhattisgarh's Dantewada district raided PUCL general secretary Kavita Srivastava's home in Jaipur accusing her of harbouring a dreaded Maoist - Soni Sori who is victim of Maoist violence itself. Her father Madru Ram Sori was near fatalty wounded in June 2011. She said Naxals are hitting us from the front and the police from back. Soni Sori is a resident of Dantewada's Sameli village. She was earlier superintendant at a government school in Jabeli. Her husband Anil Putane is in Jail for Naxal links.

October 3, 2011

West Bengal state secretary of CPI (Maoist) Akash has proposed a month-long truce in Junglemahal provided the security forces also suspend operations.

October 4, 2011

CPI (Maoist) spokesperson in Chhattisgarh, Gudsa Usendi denied allegations of a financial agreements with Essar Group.

October 7, 2011

Three SSB personnel who were assigned the duty of protecting Salwa Judum camp were killed in Naxal attack near Geedam on NH 16 connecting Bijapur to Jagdalpur. Maoists attacked SSB convoy in a landmine blast. –*The Indian Express,* October 8, 2011

October 8, 2011

A constable attached to Anti-Naxal force of Karnataka state was killed in an encounter with a group of Naxals – 'Netravati' led by Vikas Gowda. ANF launched a camping operation when it learnt that 10-15 member Naxal group has been camping in the Manjulakadu forest range and the police swept into action. The dead constable was Mahadev Mane.

October 10, 2011

Alleged Maoist Soni Sori alleged police torture on her and suffered head and spinal injuries. She was earlier brought to Dantewada after her arrest in Delhi and lodged in Raipur Central Jail. She has been jailed for helping Naxals and accused of receiving 'protection money' from Essar group. Supreme Court in January 8, 2013 allowed her plea to shift her to Jagdalpur jail. Chhattisgarh principal secretary to the Chief Minister denied torture.

October 11, 2011

Rural Development Minister Jairam Ramesh suggested 'two-track approach' calling for dealing with the Maoist leadership and revamping of administration and governance in tribal areas. Over the next months, however, this two-track approach not only was expanded to a Three-Track strategy called '3Ps', it involved some tactical prioritisation as well. The new addition was "intensification of political activities" in the Maoist belt.

–*The New Indian Express,* Banglore, June 17, 2012

October 15, 2011

Mamata Banerjee indirectly termed Maoists as "Supari killers", "Jungle mafia" and "Cowardly goons hiding in forests".

October 16, 2011

Maoists demanded West Bengal's Chief Minister to immediately release all of their jailed comrades as a condition for peace talks.

October 17, 2011

Three CPI (Maoist) workers - Malluh Korva, Babita Devi and Milan Killah - were arrested from Sania village in Garhwa (Jharkhand).

October 18, 2011

West Bengal police forces and rebel squads exchanged fire at the Banksole forest in West Midnapore district.

October 20, 2011

One suspected Maoist Prakash Acharya visited West Bengal Chief Minister Mamata Banerjee's residence, stated that he is a Maoist and desires to surrender. On October 21, 2011 he was allowed to surrender and handed over to police for interrogation.

October 21, 2011

Six policemen were killed and three injured after Naxals ambushed a police team in Netanar area of Bastar.

October 21, 2011

Maoists claimed that they shot down a Dhruv helicopter which crashed on the border of Ranchi and Khunti district (Jharkhand state) killing three crewmen two days ago.

October 22, 2011

Naxalites killed a police Patil Ramdas Gawde from Yeragadda village in Aheri Tehsil of Gadchiroli district. They threw his body on the Alapolli Sironcha highway.

October 28, 2011

A powerful landmine was detected in Jhitka forest along the road leading to Lalgarh from Binpur in Paschim Medinipur district.

October 31, 2011

Maoists abducted 15 people in the Naxal-affected district of Jamui. Out of 15, eight were labourers, four employees of the construction committee - Bihar Bridge corporation) who were engaged in the Construction of a bridge over Bharnar river in Balthar Ghat village.

November 5, 2011

(*i*) Maoists released 15 people abducted on Oct. 31. They were freed in the forest near Charaiya area.

(*ii*) Maoist couple Duryodahan Rajwar and Lalita Rajwar surrendered to police in Ayodhya Hills in Purulia district of West Bengal.

November 7, 2011

Police carried out an operation against Naxals in Gadchiroli on receiving information of ultras being gathered there.

November 7, 2011

A state-wide 'Bandh was called by Maoists to protest against the proposed visit of Jairam Ramesh to their den in Saranda Forest (Jharkhand) on November 1, 2011. Maoists killed two men in Saranda area reacting to the announcement of Home Minister Chidambarams itinary.

November 8, 2011

Three policemen were injured in an attack by Maoists on their make-shift camp at Cone village in Latehar district (Jharkhand).

November 10, 2011

The Bengal Government had given the go-ahead for renewed anti-Maoist operations in Jangalmahal.

November 11, 2011

Mamata Banerjee told people of the Maoist-hit areas of Purulia district that they will get whatever they ask for provided they don't support the Maoists. "Anyone indulging in the politics of killing is my enemy" she declared.

November 12, 2011

Voicing protest against the recent sentencing to death of cultural activist Jiten Marandi in connection with the Chilkari massacre, Dr. Binayak Sen social activist termed it as a 'failure of democracy' with the state 'targeting social activists' in a bid to silence them. He told it at a seminar in Ranchi organised by the Jan Kalakar Jiten Bihayi Manch. 20 persons at Chilkari village were gunned down by Maoists on October 26, 2007. The seminar was held in protest against the sentencing.

–*The Hindu,* November 13, 2011

November 14, 2011

An armed Maoist squad raided a village in the Purulia area and gunned a retired school teacher Ajit Singh Sardar and his son Baku (22 year) both were TMC supporters.

November 14, 2011

Maoists call off peace talks with Bengal Government.

November 14, 2011

Two Maoists were killed and two security personnel of the 10th Naga Battalion seriously injured is an encounter that began shortly after two Trinamool Congress supporters were shot dead by a group of left wing extremists at Ghatbera in Balrampur area of West Bengal Purulia district. Gun battle continued on November 15.

November 16, 2011

Ultras killed two CISF men in an ambush in Bacheli area in Dantewada.

November 16, 2011

Mamata Banerjee CM of West Bengal said "Maoists were responsible for Gyaneshwari derailment and Shilda attack."

November 17, 2011

Jagori Baskey, one of the most dreaded names in Bengal's Maoists surrendered before the Chief Minister alongwith her rebel husband Rajaram Soren alias Sagen Santhal. Baskey was reportedly involved in the Silda camp killing in 2010.

November 18, 2011

Four months after Salwa Judum was banned across the country by the Supreme Court, it gave its go-ahead to engaging spcial police officers in anti-Naxal operations except in Chhattisgarh. SC modified its July 5, 2011 Judgement.

November 18, 2011

West Bengal Chief Minister Mamata Banerjee said that she found a 'Delhi-Kolkata-Maoist partnership' angle on in the conspiracy to eliminate the top Trinamool leadership including herself.

November 18, 2011

West Bengal State Food and Supplies Minister Jyoti Priya Mallick said that the Maoist posters threatening his life had been found outside his office. Security forces recovered a huge cache of weapons during anti-Maoist operations in Paschim Medinipur (West Bengal) during the past week.

–*The Hindu*, November 19, 2011

November 20, 2011

A member Rabi Mandi of a Maoist squad operating in West Bengal's Purulia district surrendered before the police. Rabi Mandi had been a part of Ayodhya squad for the past one-and-half to two years.

November 20, 2011

Maoists killed Sunil Dewangan, the Chairman Nuapada Panchayat Samiti was killed near Lodhra village accusing him of being a police informer and corrupt. This killing was third in the past two months in Orissa.

[On November 15, Maoists shot dead BJD ward member Krushna Panji in Orissa state. On September 24 Maoists had killed Jogabandhu Majhi, a BJD MLA from Umerkote Assembly in Nawarangpur district alongwith his personal security officer.]

November 20, 2011

Police arrested seven people for the killing of activist nun Valsa John at Pachuara village under Amrapara Police station jurisdiction in Jharkhand on November 8, 2011. Police claimed that the CPI (Maoists) were the main culprit behind Sister Valsa's murder since was pursuing of the case of a rape victim. The arrested persons were: Advin Murmu, Ranjan Marandi, Pradhan Hebram, Raksh Turi – all from Aloobera village and Paisal Hembram, Prem Turi, Tala Hembram, all from Pachura village. Police claimed Maoist involvement in nun murder.

November 21, 2011

Yogendra Oraon, a former 'Sub-Zonal Commander' of CPI (Maoist) was killed by the police at Raidih in Gumla district of Jharkhand.

November 24, 2011

Kishanji, politburo member of the CPI (Maoist) and the ideological operational face of Maoist violence in West Bengal for more than a decade was killed in an encounter at Burishol forest in Binpur (West Midnapur). Kishenji's brother Venugopal, a member of CPI (Maoist) Central Committee would not replace him.

Kishenji was born in Naachpalli, in Karimnagar district of Andhra. First arrested for burning a government bus and government property outside his school in 1969.

A graduate from the Government Degree College, Peddapalli, he was drawn into the Telangana movement when he was 20. He then joined the former CPI-ML (People's War).

By The time he joined the Maoists, he had gained quite a reputation in Peddapalli, organising mass protests for Telangana state.

According to his profile by the Andhra Special Intelligence Branch, he was a shy youth with a violent streak and was fiercely devoted to the party and the cause of poor.

Quickly Rising, he was made the State Committee Secretary and was later given charge of West Bengal, Jharkhand and Orissa where he has spent the last 20 years.

A Maoist strike in West Midnapore district in 2010.

Bengal Strategy, Strikes

• After moving to Bengal in 1994, he propounded the theory of turning mass protests into violent anti-govt. agitations. Frequently organised meetings of Maoists at Lalgarh, Palubani and Salboni.

• An Andhra Intelligence officer said the strategy of holding an area under Maoist control for long periods, unlike the usual guerrilla style, is typical of Kishenji. Was chief architect of the Lalgarh movement.

• He is also suspected to have master-minded the November 2008 landmine attack on the convoy in which former chief minister Buddhadeb Bhattacharjee and then Union minister Ram Vilas Paswan were travelling, in Salboni.

Underground for 20 years

• Kishenji had been underground for 20 years and out of home state Andhra Pradesh for nearly 30 years.

• Married M Mainakka, who also joined the Maoists. She is currently the secretary of the Dandakaranya Special Zonal Committee. –*The Indian Express,* November 25, 2011

Kishanji was also known as Mohan and Prahlad. He was one of the main architect of PWG-MCC merger. He carried Rs. 19 Lakh reward on his head.

Number 3 in Leadership Jinxed ?

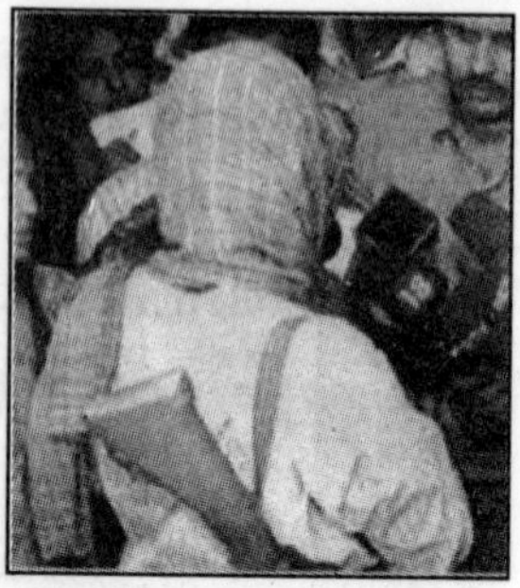

New Delhi : Is the number three rank in the CPI (Maoist) hierarchy jinxed ? Two top Naxal leaders, Kishenji and Azad, have been killed by the security forces while holding the same position. Kishenji was the third-in-command in the Naxal top body—Politburo. Azad, whose real name is Cherukuri Rajkumar, was killed in a controversial encounter by Andhra Pradesh Police last year and had been officiating in the same position, number 3, when he was killed.

CPI (Maoists) Hierarchy

General SecretaryGanapati (Reward ₹24 lakh)

Second-in-command N Keshav Rao	(Reward ₹ 19 lakh)
Kishenji	(Reward ₹ 19 lakh)
Kattam Sudarshan	(Reward ₹ 19 lakh)
Mallojula Venugopal	(Reward ₹ 19 lakh)
Prashant Bose	(Reward ₹ 7 lakh)
Mallarajji Reddy	(Reward ₹ 7 lakh)

Behind Bars

Eight Politburo members in different jails are : Kobad Gandhi, Narayan Sanyal, Sushil Roy, Mishir Besra, Pramod Mishra, Akhilesh Yadav, Amitabh Bagchi and Baccha Prasad Singh.

Setback to Extremists in 2011 (Till October)

Killed	70 (four in West Bengal)
Apprehended	1601, including 410 in West Bengal
Surrendered	44

LWE Violence-Hit

CRPF personnel killed	26
Injured	100

–*The Pioneer,* November 25, 2011

Madhuramma, in her 80, on hearing of the death of her son Kishenji said on November 25, 2011 that she had seen him for the last 33 years. Kishenji's niece Deepa, who visited West Bengal to claim his body alleged that he had been killed in fake encounter. Maoist ideologue Varavara Rao termed the killing as a fake encounter. His body was handed over to Deepa and Varavara Rao on November 26, 2011 at Midnapore hospital.

November 24, 2011

A woman CPI (Maoist) functionary Subhasini alias Anita was nabbed by police when he came to meet one of her associates at Tenught Jail. Peterwar police raided the hideout and arrested the duo on the spot. Subhasini had joined the outfit when she was 15 years of age and had been with ultras for more than 20 years.

November 26, 2011

Varavara Rao urged the interlocutors to reconsider their role in view of killing Koteshwara Rao alias Kishenji. The CPI (Maoist) state secretary Akash and two other interlocutors signed a joint statement for a month-long ceasefire on September 30, 2011.

November 26, 2011

Late Charu Mazumdar's son Abhijit Mazumdar, a member of the Communist Party of India (Marxist-Leninist) Liberation faction demand judicial probe by a sitting judge into the killing of CPI (Maoist) politburo member Koteshwar Rao.

November 27, 2011

A bandh was observed by people of Peddapalli, the native village of Kishenji in Karimnagar district in Andhra Pradesh to condemn his killing by the security forces on November 24, 2011 in Burisole forest near Jhargram in West Bengal's Paschim Medinipur.

November 27, 2011

Sitaram Yechury, CPI (Marxist) leader said killing of individuals will not provide a solution to the Marxist problem. He was commenting on killing of Kishenji of CPI (Maoist).

November 27, 2011

A 'protest week' was observed by the Maoists of Peddapalli, home town of Kishenji, from November 29 to December 2, 2011 in protest against what the Central Committee of CPI (Maoist) described as the 'brutal murder'. It called a two-day nation wide bandh from December 4, 2011.

November 27, 2011

Maoists destroyed a mobile tower of a private operator at Kanuali in Gaya district.

November 28, 2011

West Bengal Government's initiative to broker peace with Maoist suffered a set back. A statement signed by Sujato Bhadra on behalf of the 5 of the 6 interlocutors who differed on the issue said "under the changed circumstances if we carry on as interlocutors, it will only create confusion and could be ascribed as a design of the government. We do not want to be accused by being a part of such a design."

–*The Hindu*, November 29, 2011
(Report by Marcus Dan)

In the cross fire of security forces

CPI (Maoist) Central Committee

1. Mupala Laxman Rao @ Ganapthi (Secretary)
2. Prashanth Bose @ Kishanda
3. Namballa Keshava Rao @ Baswaraj
4. Misir Besra @ Sunirmal
5. Mallojula Venugopal @ Abhay
6. Katakam Sudershan @ Anand
7. Malla Raji Reddy @ Sathenna
8. Tippiri Tirupati @ Deoji
9. Dev Kumar Singh @ Nishanth
10. Jiniugu Narsimha Reddy @ Jampanna
11. Akkiraju Haragopal @ Ramakrishna

12. Kuppuswamy Devaraj @ Ramesh
13. Kadari Satyanarayana Reddy @ Kosa
14. Gajanand @ Parush
15. Chenderi Yadav @ Payag
16. Mohan @ Mahesh
17. Ranjith Bose @ Kanchan
18. Manoj @ Rajesh
19. Pulluri Prasada Rao @ Chandranna
20. Ramchandrareddy Pratap Reddy @ Chalapathi and
21. Modem Balakrishna @ Bhaskar

The list of CPI (Maoist) Central Committee appeared.

–*The Hindu,* November 26, 2011

November 28, 2011

Jharkhand regional committee of CPI (Maoist) gave a call to protest the killing of Naxal leader Kishenji in fake encounter.

November 28, 2011

A hunt was launched for the arrest of Maoist Zonal Commander Kundan Pahan in the forest of Hero, Rahe and Angarha in Ranchi district.

November 29, 2011

Mixed response to Maoist Bandh call was there in Jharkhand against the killing of Kishenji.

December 1, 2011

Maoist hijacked a bus in Khunti district. The body of the Bus Driver Partha Mishra which was lying unattended at Kenbaki village 17 km away from Sonde in Khunti was recovered on December 2, 2011.

December 3, 2011

Naxals killed 1 escort cops of Jharkhand MP Inder Singh Namdhari as he passed through Ladu More in Latehar district of Jharkhand Maoist attacked his convoy through an IED blast and then opened fire on security vehicle which was following Namdhari's car.

December 3, 2011

CPI (Maoist) cadres blew two mobile towers of private companies and kidnapped two guards posted in Jamui. Two towers were at Chai village under Jhajha police station and later they kidnapped guards Mahendra and Ramchandra Turi. Ultras had been demanding Rs. 4 lakh levy from private companies. When they did not receive the said amount, they blew up the towers.

December 4, 2011

Maoists blew up tracks in two districts in Jharkhand in their bid to enforce two day Bandh which began on December 3. In Bokaro, tracks between Gomia and Dhumri Railway Station of East Central Railway and another stretch of tracks between Hehegarha and Chipadohar Railway Station in Latehar district was blown with the help of IED blasts.

December 4/5, 2011

Maoists triggered a landmine blast inside the Block Development office at Harhargnj in Palamau district in Jharkhand.

December 5, 2011

A railway track was blown by insurgents between Mihirpur and Matari stations in Dhanbad in observance of 2 day bandh call to protest Mallojula Koteshwar Rao's killing.

December 6, 2011

To mark the 19th anniversary of Babri Masjid demolition, the Communist Party of India (Marxist-Leninist) - Liberation staged a march from Mandi House to Jantar Mantar in New Delhi to promote brotherhood and reject communal forces. Central Committee member of CPI-ML Liberation Kavita Krishnan addressed the meeting at Jantar Mantar.

December 6, 2011

Naxals blasted a culvert on National Highway 30 the only road linking capital Raipur to Jagdalpur. The blast took place at Baniagaon 10 km off Kondagon, a new district that came into effect from January 1, 2011. State Home Minister Nanki Ram

Kanwar admitted that "Naxals have become very powerful and it seems they can do anything."

–*The Indian Express*, December 7, 2011

December 9, 2011

50 heavily armed guerrillas raided construction site at Pakari village under Khaira police station and abducted seven labourers. They were kidnapped from two bridge construction sites.

December 13, 2011

Orissa police stumbled upon a huge cache of arms and explosives from a covered pit in Sitagudi forest under Chandrapur police limits in Rayagada district bordering Kandhamal.

–*The Pioneer*, December 14, 2011

December 13, 2011

In Orissa's Sambalpur district, Maoists from Jharkhand involved in arms training to Maoist in Saranda forest and his three associates. Ranbir Jharna @ Mangala and his three associates Mangalu Munda, Basant Haranz and Durga Topno were arrested.

December 13, 2011

Mails addressed to Essar Chairman Ruia in January 2011 reveals that Essar top brass intervened to release Rs. 1 crore to Naxal Conduit. Details of the letters written and calls made by Jai Johar Seva Sansthan Chairman Pawan Dube to Essar officials indicate towards this fact. On January 21, 2011 Dube had written another letter to Ruia.

December 17, 2011

Maoists razed a government school in Bihar's Jamui districts in the second such attack this week.

December 19, 2011

Naxals fired at an MI-17 Chopper deep inside Dantewada forest in Bheji police station area. Three suspected Naxals were apprehended 'Red-handed' with minor arms while they were trying to escape.

December 20, 2011

Assam Governor Janaki Ballabh Patnaik urged senior officers

of Army and police in North-Eastern states to take note of 'silent intrusion' of Maoist into Assam. Five Naxals including a couple were sentenced to life imprisonment by a local court in Bhopal for running an illegal manufacturing unit, apparently to supply arms to their cadres. Court held Krishna alias Shekhar, Ramesh Siddhi alias Dange, Tantaiah Yadav alias Satish Patil and Sunitha Patil and her husband Leela alias Diwakar Patil guilty.

December 22, 2011

Sonebhadra police arrested a hardcore Maoist couple - Jaikaran aka Ashok aka Yogesh aka Ajay aka Antu Singh and his wife Pushpa aka Lalita aka Kusumi. They were arrested while on a visit Ujiyari Tola Suwarshrut locality of Manchi Jaikaran, former sub-zonal commander of Semant Zone was earlier involved in loot at PAC camp in Khoradih locality of Ahraura in 1991 in which 13 SLR, one carbine, etc., were looted. Before fleeing Maoist had torched the camp. –*The Pioneer*, December 23, 2011

December 23, 2011

A constable engaged in anti-Naxal operation was killed in rebel fire.

December 26, 2011

After 30 years of Naxal violence in Andhra State in 2011 only seven civilian deaths were reported. Even Naxal violence cases were down. Andhra dealt with a heavy hand and as a result Naxal movement shifted to other neighbouring states.

December 31, 2011

Police recovered the bullet-riddled bodies of 4 persons kidnapped in Jamui district. They belonged to Ansari community and were shot dead by the rebels from a village in Jhajha block.

January 2, 2012

An encounter between the police and ultras took place in Kilhar Tola of Matiyon village under Chutia police station in Rohtas district. Three Naxals were killed and one was arrested. The bodies were identified as that of self-styled area commander of the neighbouring district Kashi, Prasadji also from UP and Santosh Yadav from Jharkhand. The arrested Naxal was Sushil Chowdhury.

January 4, 2012

Maoists had called a 2-day Bandh and set ablaze at least three mobile towers at Baragada area in Ganjam district of Orissa. One person was killed in a landmine blast in Kandhamal district.

January 5, 2012

On the second day of their 2-day Bandh, Maoist triggered a landmine blast in Kandhmal district blowing up a police vehicle killing three policemen on the Kotagad-Srirampur road.

January 9, 2012

The BJP legislator of Manoharpur (Jharkhand) Gurucharan Nayak was attacked twice by suspected Naxals while on a visit of Harta village for laying foundation stone in Chaibasa. First the Maoists attacked the legislator while he was attending the function at Aarta village and again he was attacked on his way back to Manoharpur.

January 10, 2012

Comrade Sahyadri, Secretary of Maharashtra unit of CPI (Maoist) said Home Minister Chidambaram is the 'biggest terrorist' of India. His anger against the people is indicative of the defeat of his terrorist policies. Chidambaram has expressed regret at lesser police attacks on the people of Gadchiroli, Gondia, Chandrapur..."

–*The Indian Express,* January 11, 2012

January 13, 2012

West Bengal have about 350 active Maoists men and 40 women in their ranks. Their two surviving 'military experts' Jayanta Mahato of West Midnapore and Ranjit Pal of Purulia were asked to retire to Jharkhand. Akash, Maoist Bengal Secretary, who used to look after Kishenji's security was the man who ditched him. Akash who was untraceable for the past couple of months was unhappy with the alleged 'closeness' between Kishenji and his wife.

–*The Pioneer,* January 14, 2012

January 16, 2012

Naxalites began their secret conclave at a place in the mineral-rich district of Saraikela in Jharkhand which began from January 12, 2012 in connection with holding Tenth Congress of CPI (Maoists). The 9th CPI (Maoist) Congress was also held in Jharkhand.

–*The Indian Express,* January 17, 2012

January 21, 2012

Naxals set off a landmine to blow up a police vehicle, opened fire on them killing atleast 13 and leaving two seriously injured. Looted weapons of dead policemen. The incident took place on the road to Bargar 60 km from Garhwa near Bhandaria police station in Jharkhand by 50 Naxalites. Naxalites abducted Garhwa Zila Parishad Chairperson Sushma Mehta and her bodyguard.

January 21, 2012

Subhash alias Satish from Chattisgarh, was killed in an encounter in the forest of Rayagada district. He was ZIC of CPI (Maoist) Bansdhara division founded by Orissa top Maoist Sabyasachi Panda.

–*The Indian Express,* January 22, 2012

January 22, 2012

Naxals seem to have drawn an elaborate plan under which they instigated a village protest and then targeted the police team. Initial enquires by police showed that CPI (Maoist) Zonal Commander Mritunjay held the serious meeting with the villages of Bargar immediately before in incident and encouraged them to demand relocation of a primary health centre.

–*The Indian Express,* January 23, 2012

January 22, 2012

A Maoist camp was destroyed and several weapons and explosives were seized in Tehguda forests in Orissa's Malkangiri district.

January 24, 2012

Bargar Panchayat Mukhia Ram Dass Minz who was suspected

to have played a role in the ambush by Naxals that left 13 policemen dead on January 21, 2012 was arrested.

January 26, 2012

Police killed Chitrakam Reddy alias Sitru, area commander for Bandhugaon in Koraput district. His wife was also killed alongwith him in an encounter with District Voluntary Force (DVF).

January 28, 2012

Naxalites killed Bhamragarh Panchayat Samiti Chairman and Bhamragarh Tehsil Congress unit Chief Bahadur Shah Alam close to Bhamgarh police station in Gadchiroli. Alam had been on the hit list of Naxals after he shared the dias with K. Madhukar Rao, leader of Salwa Judum movement in Chhattisgarh who had brought his campaign to Gadchiroli in March 2011.

–*The Sunday Express,* January 29, 2012

January 28, 2012

Maruti Kurwatkar, a member of the State Committee and Secretary of Chandrapur Committee of CPI (Maoist) was arrested at Talodhi in Chandrapur district.

January 28, 2012

The CPI (Maoist) wanted former secretary of PUCL Shashi Bhushan Pathak to negotiate with the State Government on behalf of the organisation for the release of abducted cop Sunesh Ram who was abducted 9 days back when red rebels had killed 13 police cops in a landmine blast in Garhwa.

–*The Pioneer,* January 30, 2012

January 29, 2012

CPI (Maoist) Commander, Arvind Ram alias Kaushalji was arrested by police from Chutia village in Rohtas district. Arvind Ram, a native of Navadih village was said to be CPI (Maoist) area commander of Tilouthu-Nauhata region of Bihar's Sheohar and Munger districts. Another self styled area commander Sunit Raut was nabbed from Bashi Jagdishpur village in Sheohar district. Yet another Maoist Anil Manjhi was arrested from Bhangalwa village in Munger district. –*The Hindu,* January 30, 2012

January 30, 2012

Four Naxals who surrendered to Kanker Chhattisgarh police said they were forced to undergo vasectomy operation by their leaders based mostly in Andhra Pradesh. Surrendered were East Bastar Division Committee member Sunil Kumar Matlan alias Rajesh Kumar and his wife Jaini alias Jayanti Kutari, Partapur Area Committee member Ramdas, Panidobir local organisational squad deputy commander Susheela, Sitapur LOS commander Jaylal and his wife Asmani alias Sanay and member of Platoon number 25 of Raoghat area, Samo Mandvi.

–*The Indian Express,* January 31, 2012

February 3, 2012

Sabyasachi Panda's bodyguard, Rajendra Kumar Raita alias Suraj alias Sangram surrendered before police in Orissa's Ganjan district.

February 3, 2012

Social Activist Swami Agnivesh urged CBI director AP Singh to hold impartial probe in Azad's killing on July 1, 2010.

February 5, 2012

A Maoist squad leader Yudhistir Mahato was killed in Jamtal Jungles in West Midnapore district. Mehto, hailing from Barikul area of Bankura district was a member of Madan Mahato squad.

February 7, 2012

Kishenji aide surrenders with wife—Chiranjit and Anima Mahato, a Maoist couple surrendered to the police in Paschim Medinipur district of Jangal Mahal region. Chiranjit was Kantpahari area commander and close aide of politburo member Kishenji who was third-in-command and gunned down on November 24, 2011 in a forest in Midnapore. Chiranjit Mahto's wife Anima Mahato was a member of Badal Mahta squad. –*The Pioneer,* February 8, 2012

February 9, 2012

One of Chattisgarh's most effective and successful anti-Naxal fighter who was described by the police as mentor and first commander of SPOs was killed in an ambush in Sukma district. Kartam Surya was a former special police officer (SPO) or Koya Commando was killed Maoists near Morgunda village - about 60 km away from Raipur.

February 9, 2012

Odisha Organising Committee Secretary of the Communist Party of India (Maoist) Sabyasachi Panda admitted before the select group of journalists at a undisclosed location in Kandhmal district (Orissa) that "ideology should control the gun and not vice-versa. Many of our cadres who are armed do not know about principles. As a result they resort to killing without doing much homework." "Those joining the movement do not know its objective. They are coming under different circumstances. They neither know about society nor about communism."–*The Hindu,* February 11, 2012

(Report by Satya Sundar Barik)

February 10, 2012

Four personnel of BSF - commandant of J.R. Khaswan, Dy. Commandant Rajesh Saran, Subedar Ashok Yadav and Asstt. Sub Inspector Jitendra Sahu were killed in an ambush by Maoists while they were on their way to Chitrakanda from the BSF camp at Balimela. They were travelling in a SUF when their vehicle overturned in a landmine blast about 9 km from Balimela.

–*The Hindu,* February 11, 2012

February 15, 2012

In a 10 page press release, written in Oriya and signed by secretary of divisional committee Poonam Chandar, Maoists admitted February 10, 2012 landmine blast on Balimela-Chitrakonda road in Malkangiri. "It accused the government of pushing operation Greenhunt for protecting corporate interests. Hydro electric projects like Balimela and Machhkund that benefit corporates have displaced thousands of people. Bauxite mines of

Nalco in Damanjodi and Hindustan Aeronautics in Sunaboda have caused immense loss to tribals. In Narayanpatna block of Koraput, tribals are fighting for their land rights." "In the last two-three years, our leaders Azad, Kishenji, Sooryam, Sakhamuri Apparao and others have been killed by security forces in false encounters. In Malkangiri three BSF Battalions have declared war on poor tribals in the name of Operation Greenhunt. There are 14 such camps in Malkangiri. What is the purpose of deploying BSF inside the country instead of border areas ?" They alleged that BSF personnel attacked tribals in Origel village in which 8 people were hurt and in Andral, Bonda tribals were assaulted by Jawans." *–The Indian Express,*

February 16, 2012 report by Debabrata Mohanty

February 15, 2012

Maoists took control of Panchayats in about 30 blocks of Malkangiri and Koraput districts in Orissa Panchayat Polls. All of their nominees were elected unopposed.

February 19, 2012

Two Naxal cadres surrendered to Gadchiroli police. Somi alias Nirmala Kulmethe and Sukhran Sonu Madavi were active in Naxal movement since 2000 and 2008 respectively. Both have taught at the Naxal school at Metapara in Abujmad.

February 29, 2012

Sadanala Ramakrishna @ RK stated to be the head of the Central Technical Committee of CPI Maoist was arrested. A mechanical engineer from Karimnagar district of Andhra Pradesh, he was believed to have been entrusted with carrying out Maoist activities in West Bengal after the death of outfits politburo member Kishenji in November 2011. Four other CPI Maoists, Dipak Kumar, a resident of Chattisgarh was arrested from the College Street in Kolkata. Sukumar Mondal, Bapi Mudi and Shambhu Charan Pal were arrested from the Beniapukur area.

–The Hindu, March 2, 2012

(Report by Shiv Sahay Singh)

February 29, 2012

Five suspected CPI (Maoist) cadres were arrested in Jharkhand. Four of the five cadres were Mohan Yadav, Arjun Yadav, Manish Prasad and Surendra Prasad. The fifth Devsagar Yadav is also Naxal.

March 1, 2012

Police busted well-organised units of weapons in Kolkata and Mumbai. They fabricate rocket launchers, pressure-activated mines and hand grenades. Sadnala Ramakrishna was the Incharge of Central Technical Committee (CTC) which was given the responsibility of fabricating weapons and explosives. CTC consisted of 5 or 6 members and worker under the direct supervision of the Central Military Commission (CMC) of the Maoist Party. Ramakrishna hailing from Antakkapet village in Karimnagar district of Andhra Pradesh. He is B. Tech in mechanical engineering and joined the movement around 1978. He was found using aliases Santosh, Vinod, Bhanu and Kasturi. A weapon-making unit in Bhopal on January 10, 2007 and another workshop in Rourkela on January 12, 2007 was raided by police.

–*The Hindu,* March 2, 2012
(Report by K. Srinivas Reddy)

March 3, 2012

Students, Union election in Jawahar Lal Nehru University in Delhi brought Communist Party of India (Marxist-Leninist) Liberation affiliated All India Students Association (AISA) sweeping 4 seats.

March 3, 2012

Vittal Malekudia alongwith his father Lingappa Malekudia was arrested by Karnataka state government for his Maoist links. He was granted conditional bail by Beithangdy Judicial Magistrate on June 3, 2012.

March 4, 2012

Five Maoists who were arrested by Kolkata police on February 29 revealed that an appartment in Birati located in eastern fringe of the city was purchased by Maoist Ramakrishna who posed as a businessman. Rs. 35 lakhs in cash, instruments used for manufacturing rocket launcher and some Maoist documents were seized. Maoists used to hold meetings in this flat. A chain of supply of arms and ammunition manufactured in Kamarhati in North 24 Parganas used to be sent to Chhattisgarh. 7 transport operators who used to carry arms to Chhattisgarh from Kolkata were also identified.

March 4, 2012

Armed Maoists attacked a stone crusher unit of a private builder and set fire 15 of its vehicles in Nuapada district.

March 4, 2012

Twenty three Maoists surrendered before the police with arms and ammunition in Bihar's Muzaffarpur district.

March 5, 2012

Four cadres - Tapeshwar Gahyhu from Latehar and Anil Ram from Palamau district–only two bodies could be identified - were killed and a CISF personnel injured during an encounter in Chatra district of Jharkhand.

March 7, 2012

Fourteen vehicles engaged in road construction in Chhattisgarh's Kanker district were set on fire by Naxals.

March 7, 2012

Police chargesheeted Essar GM DVCS Verma, suspected Naxals Lingaram Kodapi, Soni Sori, Company's Chief Contractor B.K. Lala and top Naxal commanders Raghu and Vinod.

March 9, 2012

Suchitra Mahato, wife of slain Maoist leader Sashadhar Mahato, surrendered before the Chief Minister alongwith her latest husband Prabir Garai - a Bankura based contractor. She was later admitted to a private nursing home for surgery for bullet wounds.

March 14, 2012

Two Italians identified as Paulo Boscusco a tour operator who has been living in Puri intermittently for 14-15 years, who had gone to Daringibad hill station (Orissa) on March 12 accompanied by driver and two others were abducted on March 14 by Maoists from somewhere in Daranbadi Block near the Sorada police station area of Ganjam district. The locals were released two days later and they informed about the abduction of Italians. Maoists claimed responsibility for the abduction. Sabyasachi Panda alias Sunil, State Secretary of CPI (Maoist) Orissa State Organising Committee listed 13 demands for the release of foreigners. His key demands were:

(i) Stop combing operations and exploitation of tribals.

(ii) Release Mili Panda, Ganapath Patra, Azad and Kameshwar Rao.

(iii) Release 672 innocent tribals.

(iv) Enlist Konda Reddy and Muka Dora communities as STs.

(v) Stop Polavaram protect.

(vi) Issue Pattas to tribals of KBK district whose lands have been forcibly grabbed by non-tribals.

(vii) Drop cases against Maoists.

(viii) Order CBI enquiry into the rape of Arati Majhi of Gajpati. Panda's wife Subhashree has been in Jail for the last two years on charges of being a Maoist operative.

–*The Pioneer,* March 19, 2012

–*The Indian Express,* March 19, 2012

(ix) Tourists should not be allowed in Tribal area, withdraw ban on CPI (Maoist) and other people's organisations.

(x) Arrest and trial of the SP and police official for murdering Lalit Dehuri and Junesh Pradesh, etc., were the other demands of ultras.

(xi) Release of Maoist Commander Chenda Bhushanam alias Ghasi (arrested on April 3, 2011).

March 16, 2012

CBI in a report submitted to the Supreme Court said that the killing of Cherukuri Raj Kumar alias Azad and journalist Hem Chandra Pandey by AP Police on the night of July 1, 2010 were not fake encounters as alleged in the petition.

The Seven on Maoist List of Demands

The Orissa abduction crisis seems no closer to a resolution with one of the negotiators questioning the state government's sincerity towards meeting the 13 demands made by the Maoists to release two Italians. Among other demands, the Maoists want these seven to be set free.

People outside the closed office of abducted Italian, Paolo Bosusco

Ashutosh alias Motilal Soren (41) : Jharkhand-born Ashutosh is one of the 21 members of the CPI (Maoist) central committee as well as part of its seven-member 'Central Military Commission'. He is said to have been involved in the conspiracy to murder VHP leader Laxmanananda Saraswati in Kandhamal during August 2008 and in the killing of former Jharkhand chief minister Babulal Marandi's son Anup in October 2007. Soren was arrested in March 2009 from Rourkela and has been in a Bhubaneswar jail since then.

Subhashree Panda alias Mili : The wife of Sabyasachi Panda, secretary of the Orissa state organising committee of the CPI (Maoist), Mili was arrested from her Bhubaneswar house in January 2010 on charges of being a professional revolutionary. The 40-something was the first Maoist in Orissa to be charged under the Unlawful Activities (Prevention) Act, 1967. Though the Orissa High Court quashed the proceedings against her in October 2011 on technical grounds, the police filed more cases against her, which has kept her in prison. The police say that while Sabyasachi planned and executed daring attacks on the police establishment, Mili was incharge of transferring Maoist leader from one base to the other. She allegedly also looked after the publicity part of the organisation as well as printing of Maoist literature. The Panda couple have a 12-year-old daughter, who now lives with her grandfather.

Kamalakanta Sethi and Sujata Kutruke Alias Chandramma : In their thirties, the husband-wife duo were allegedly involved in several murder and landmine blasts and were arrested from Gudari area of Rayagada district in May 2008 by the Spcical Operations Group of the Orissa Police during a combing operation. Though Maoist sympathisers describe Kamalakanta as a *lungi*-seller, some gelatin sticks, detonators, banners and Maoist literature were reportedly seized from the duo.

Manjulata Muduli : Manjulata, who hails from Lachhmakana village under the Erasama police station in Jagatsinghpur district, was allegedly involved in Maoist activity in western Orissa for six years. She is said to be a member of the Sambalpur area committee. Suspected to have been involved in the Nayagarh armoury attack of February 2008, Manjulata was arrested a few days later.

Pratap Kimbaka : Hailing from Chandrapur village of Muniguda police station area in Rayagads district, Kimbaka was allegedly involved in Maoist violence in Koraput, Kandhamal and Kalahandi districts. He was arrested along with Manjulata.

Gananath Patra : Advisor to the Chasi Mulia Adivasi Sangh, an alleged Maoist frontal organisation in Narayanpatna block of Koraput, 71-year-old Patra has been fighting for tribal land rights in poverty-ridden south Orissa for over two decades. His persistent demand has been that Scheduled Area (Scheduled Tribe) Land Transfer Regulation of 1956 that prohibits transfer of land from a tribal to a non-tribal be strictly implemented. Patra became a target of police after the November 2009 firing in the Narayanpatna police station in which two tribals were killed. He has been in Koraput jail since January 2010 after his arrest from Bhubaneswar on charges of murder and abduction.

March 18, 2012

Jailed architect of the Lalgarh revolt, Chhatradhar Mahto wrote a letter to intellectuals asking them to explain why they were not raising voice against "the pathetic condition of political prisoners in so called correctional homes in West Bengal and torture in police lock up." –Report by Rajib Chatterjee in

–*The Indian Express*, March 19, 2012

March 19, 2012

Responding to State Government (Orissa) offer for talks to end the Italian hostage crisis, the Maoists named Narayan Sanyal, politburo member of CPI (Maoist) - then lodged in Jharkhand Jail, social activist and Jan Adhikar Manch convenor Dandapani Mohanty and lawyer Biswapriya Kanungo.

March 20, 2012

Police recovered the missing laptop of slain Maoist politburo member Kishenji from Kushaboni forest in the Jangalmahal area of West Midnapore district.

March 20, 2012

Spiritual guru Sri Sri Ravi Shankar said that government schools are breeding grounds for Naxalism and that they should be privatised.

March 21, 2012

Police said that abduction of foreigners is Sabyasachi Panda's desperate attempt to gloss over his past failures. Short-tempered and whimsical the most wanted Maoist stands sideline in his outfit.

March 22, 2012

Orissa Assembly adopted a unanimous resolution appealing to the Maoists for the safe release of two foreign nationals-Italians who have been under their captivity since March 14.

March 22, 2012

Cadres of Andhra-Orissa Border special Zonal Committee of Maoists killed Krushna Chandra Rath, a Sub-Inspector of Police in Mudulipada police station in Malkangiri.

March 23, 2012

Delhi police filed a supplementary chargesheet against top Maoist Leader Kobad Gandhy, accused of trying to set up a network of the banned outfit in Delhi.

March 24, 2012

Maoist kidnapped a ruling BJD MLA Jhina Hikaka near Tayaput in Koraput district of Orissa.

March 25, 2012

Sabyasachi Panda stated before newpaper men that there is disunity in Orissa cadres. At least 5 CPI (Maoist) divisions are working in different regions of Orissa.

March 25, 2012

The abducted BJD MLA Jhina Hikaka was in the custody of Koraput-Srikakulam Zonal Committee Deputy Commandant Sarita who is No. 2 hardcore Maoist in the committee. Daya is the commandant, in charge of the division.

March 25, 2012

One of the kidnapped Italians Cpandio Solangelo was released by Maoists.

March 26, 2012

Two days after Laxmipur MLA Jhina Hikaka was abducted, Maoists of Koraput sent a wish list that included immediate halting of combing operations and release of Chasi Mulia Adivasi Sangh (CMAS) activists lodged in Jails. The letter in Telugu was signed and sent by secretary of Koraput-Srikakulam divisional committee Daya alias Chemala Krishnamurthi and one Jagabandhu a representative of Andhra-Orissa Border Special Zonal Committee on their CPI (Maoist) letterhead.

March 26, 2012

Bihar police busted a hideout of Maoist leader Dev Kumar Singh alias Arvind in Aurangabad district arrested his five men and seized arms and ammunition.

March 27, 2012

IED blast at Pushtola (Gadchirli in Maharashtra. 13 CRPF personnel killed and 30 injured.

March 28, 2012

Kobad Ghandy was freed by the court-by Additional Sessions Judge Pawan Kumar Jain - of charges under anti-terror law-Unlawful Activities (Prevention) Act. He was arrested on September 1, 2009 from Bhikaji Cama Place in South Delhi.

April 1, 2012

Divya alias Wallasi (26), a woman Maoist involved in the abduction of former Malkangiri district collector R Vineel Krishna in February 2011 was arrested near Janbar in Malkangiri. She was an Area Commander of the Maoist group for the past 11 years under the Galikonda Naxal division.

April 1, 2012

Delhi police filed chargesheet against two Manipur militants of PLA who were arrested last year. N. Dilip Singh alias Wangba and Alok Kumar Singh alias Willow were arrested from a Paharganj hotel in Delhi on October 1, 2011. They stated that PLA and CPI (Maoist) had signed a memorandum of understanding on October 22, 2008 for extending help to each other in fighting war against the government.

April 2, 2012

Talks for release of hostages were resumed as Maoist released new audio-tape. Dandapani Mohanty and B.D. Sharma represented Maoist.

April 3, 2012

The wife of Maoist leader Sabyasachi Panda, whose outfit claimed to have abducted Italian national Paolo Basusco on March 14, 2012 appealed to the ultras not to harm the hostage - Italians as well as MLA. They asked Orissa government to fulfill its demands including release of jailed rebels latest by April 5, 2012.

April 3, 2012

A Maoist ultra was killed in an encounter with security forces in a forest in Keonjhar district.

April 4, 2012

A hardcore Maoist identified as Pondu Panki Ray and his three accomplices were arrested and a landmine seized from Sundergarh district. Pondu is a native of Nuagaon Purantoly under Saraikela police limits in West Singhbhum district of Jharkhand.

April 4, 2012

Dunna Kesava Rao alias Azad, the Maoist leader who allegedly killed Vishwa Hindu Parishad leader Laxmananand Saraswati in Kandhamal in August 2008 and then surrendered before AP police in May 2011 was given a reward of Rs. 10 lakh by Andhra Pradesh police. The money was handed over to Rao's mother by a team of Andhra police officials at Jharpara jail in Bhubaneswar where the former rebel in currently lodged.

April 5, 2012

Six Maoist, COBRA Jawan killed in an encounter in the deep forest of Karamdih under Barwadih police station in Latehar district.

April 5, 2012

Maoist's fire damaged BSF helicopter that was flying from Latehar to Ranchi with two injured personnel.

April 5, 2012

Orissa Chief Minister Naveen Patnaik announced names of 27 Maoists to be freed. The 4 persons who would be released for securing Paolo's freedom included Subshree Das alias Milli Panda, wife of Sabyasachi Panda, Secretary of the Orissa State Organising Committee of CPI (Maoist). 15 members of Chasi Mulia Adivasi Sangh whose chief is Nachika Linga and eight Maoist from different Jails for the release of Hikaka and four others for release of Paolo. Eight Maoists whose release was to be facilitated by the government were - Narsi Kendruka, Joruka Kendruka, Deba Madhi, Ganga Sodi, Bhima Padiami, Mangaraj Darua and a married couple from Andhra Pradesh Murla Neelam Reddy and Setu Pangi.

April 6, 2012

Rosalin, wife of sub-inspector Ajit Bardhan, who was abducted and killed by Maoists while on patrol duty in Sundargarh in July 2009 said the governments move to release 27 Maoists would set a wrong precedent.

April 8, 2012

Maoists of AOBSZC demanded release of 5 more Maoists in lieu of BJD MLA Jhina Hikaka's release. The five are Chenda Bhushanam alias Ghasi (his wife Kavithakka, Secretary of Andhra-Orissa Border Committee had surrendered before Andhra police in 2007), Gananth Patra advisor of Chasi Mulia Adivasi Sangh, Suno Pangi a woman Maoist from Potangi Block of Koraput, Wadeka Walsi, a Chasi Mulia activist and Singa Nachika.

April 8, 2012

Maoists have been reading the coaching material to crack the IAS exam (prepared by Delhi-based Rau's IAS study circle, literature on making rocket launchers and on hunting down choppers. The Maoist literature was seized by security forces from Hikonar (Orchha block of Narainpur). The literature recovered also included (on March 15) included the 1954 edition Communist Guerrilla warfare written by Brigadier C. Aubrey Dixon and Otto Heilbrunn apart from a book in English of critical essays on the Marxist cultural movement in India. (*The Indian Express,* April 9, 2012 report by Ashutosh Bharadwaj).

April 9, 2012

Orissa Police Association threatened to go on strike if any hardcore Maoist was released in a swap deal.

April 9, 2012

7 CRPF COBRA and Jharkhand policemen were injured in an encounter with Maoists in the forest of Saniya village in Latehar district in Jharkhand.

April 10, 2012

Subhashree Das alias Milli Panda, wife of Maoist Sabyasachi Panda was acquitted by a Rayagada Court due to lack of evidence.

April 12, 2012

The 29-day hostage drama of Italian national Paolo Basusco ended when Maoist leader Sabyasachi Panda freed him. The Italian was from Condove in Turin, Italy and was abducted alongwith Claudio Colangelo on March 14, 2012 while tracking in the forests. Colangelo was released on March 24 as a goodwill gesture. For release of Hikaka, Maoist spokesman Jagbandhi in a statement said "The BJD MLA's fate will be decided by a 'praja' people's court unless the government releases all 30 prisoners all BJD lawmakers in Koraput will face dire consequences."

April 13, 2012

A teacher's 'Training Camp' was conducted in Pune district and Naxal training was imparted.

April 13, 2012

A group of 21 jailed Maoists, led by former Sub-Zonal Commander of Sone-Ganga-Vindhyachal Zone Sudama Oraon accused senior comrades of 'living in town' and exploiting the lower cadre, most illiterate and poor tribals. Oraon, accused of killing Rohtas District Forest Officer Sanjay Singh in 2002 has been in Rohtas Jail since 2006. Oraon hinted at a caste war within CPI (Maoist) with OBC Yadavs as the dominant group.

April 13, 2012

A Naxal action team gunned a prominent local NCP leader Kewalrao Atkamwar alias Raju near the police station of Etapalli town in Gadchiroli district.

April 13, 2012

Naxals fired at an ambulance in Sukma district in Chhattisgarh.

April 15, 2012

Maoists extended the deadline for MLA Hikaka's release. But the police threatened to boycott anti-Maoist operations in the state if Ghasi @ Chenda Bhushanam and Maoist leaders like Sunno Pangi, etc., are swapped or released.

April 15, 2012

Four persons were arrested on charges of supplying arms and

ammunition to Naxals. Contractors Irfan and Ahmed Qureshi have mostly beer working in Gadchiri and Gondia districts of Maharashtra.

April 16, 2012

Home Minister P. Chidambaram stated that Assam has emerged as the new theatre of Maoist activity.

April 17, 2012

Former Naxalite leader belonging to People's War, Khambhan Gnana Satyamurthy (K.G. Satyamurthy) died at Kandulapadu in G. Kondur Mandal of Krishna District of Andhra Pradesh. Born on July 15, 1931 at Sankarampadu, a helmet of Polukonda near Gudivada in Nandiva Mandal, he was a close associate of Charu Mazumdar, a contemporary of Kondapalli Seetharmaiah, he entered People's war in 1968.

April 19, 2012

Maoists produced BJD MLA Jhina Hikaka before a People's Court to decide his fate. On April 18, 2012 the state government had announced that it would withdraw cases against 13 Maoists and their sympathisers in exchange for MLA's freedom.

April 19, 2012

Naxals gunned down a SRPF Jawan Ramkobal Ramadhar Pandey in Gadchirli's Dhanora Taluk in Maharashtra district.

April 20, 2012

A deadly attack on the convoy of a Bijapur legislature of Chattisgarh ruling BJP, Mahesh Gagda was made triggering a powerful landmine blast in a forested area Pegrapalli in Bijapur district. Bijapur district collector Rajat Kumar was also travelling with the legislator in the convoy of eight vehicles. Two district unit leaders of the BJP and the driver of their vehicle were killed on the spot.

April 21, 2012

Maoists kidnapped Sukma (Chattisgarh state) collector Alex Paul Menon IAS, killed his two security guards accompanying him. Two Guards were shot for resisting abduction at a function in Bastar. They were abducted from Manjipara village.

April 22, 2012

After abducting Sukma Collector Alex Paul Menon, the CPI (Maoist) sent a list of demands, including immediate halt to all police activities in the area and release of eight fellow comrades whose names were : Madkam Gopanna, Nirmal Akka, Devpal Chandra Shekhar Reddy, Shantipriya Reddy, Meena Chaudhary, Korsa Sanni, Madkam Sanni. Deadline of 72 hours was also set and warned that if by April 25, action is not taken, they (Maoists) will have to decided the collector's fate in Jan Andalat (People's court). Villagers, students held a silent rally in support of the collector seeking his release. Besides Maoist also demanded release of two elders—Ashit Kumar Sen and Prafulla Kumar Jhan. Thus, making it a total of 10.

Capturing hostages is believed to be the only way for Naxalites to get the government to lend them their ears. So by agreeing to talk only when kidnapped, are we not asking to be held at gunpoint ? At left, Maoists during a training session in the Dantewada forest. (Right) Sukma Collector Alex Paul Menon, accompanied by an interlocutor, following his release by the Maoists in the forests of Chintalnar in Chhattisgarh, in May last year.–Photos : Akhilesh Kumar

The Hindu of January 8, 2013

–Author

April 23, 2012

Human rights leader Binayak Sen appealed to the CPI (Maoist) to release the abducted District Collector of Sukma in Chhattisgarh Alex Paul Menon. He also expressed grief over killing of two guards of the collector. Maoists named Prashant Bhushan lawyer, B.D. Sharma former Bastar collector who now has an NGO and Sukma-based Chief of Adivasi Mahasabha, Manish Kunjam as mediators. R. Vinod Krishna, another IAS officer had words of hope and reassurance. Earlier in 1994 a committee for concerned citizens (CCC) comprising of former Bureaucrats, Journalist, intellectuals etc. was convened for Andhra Peace talks.

April 23, 2012

Chhattisgarh government suspended all Naxal operations in Bastar region as a first step towards securing release of Sukma collector Alex Paul Menon.

April 24, 2012

State Govt. forwarded two names as mediators–former Chief Secretary Chhattisgarh Suyogya Kumar Mishra and former Madhya Pradesh Chief Secretary, Nirmal Buch. Kunjan and Prashant Bhushan rejected Maoists offer to mediate, the CPI (Maoist) propose the name of Professor Hargopal.

April 25, 2012

WB Chief Minister Mamata Banerjee in Kolkata asked people to remain watchful.

April 25, 2012

Maoists killed one in April 24/25 night in Etapalli Tehsil and two were murdered - Ramsay Narote and Deorao Usendi in Markegaon in Gadchiroli as the Maoists may try to regain ground under the guise of different organisations. At Lalgarh congregation she urged people not to provide any shelter to the rebels. "Those who cover their faces and kill people are cowards" she said.

April 26, 2012

Biju Janata Dal (BJD) MLA from Koraput, Jhina Hikaka was released by Maoists after 34 days. At a press conference at Koraput, Hikaka said that the reported decision made at the 'Praja' court that he would have to resign as MLA. He was taken hostage at Tayatput village on March 23 night by Maoists belonging to Andhra-Orissa Border Special Zonal Committee.

April 26, 2012

Negotiations between abductors and government of Chhattisgarh began for release of Sukma Collector.

April 26, 2012

Maoists formed a new Westen Maharashtra Area Committee to spread its subversive agenda. A separate Golden Corridor Committee has been formed to build the outfits base in the industrial areas of Gujarat and Maharashtra. The outfit has also formed a new Vidarbha Divisional Committee for pursuing the issue of separate Vidarbha state. —Report by Rakesh K. Singh

The Pioneer, April 27, 2012

April 28, 2012

CPI (Maoist) leader-Area Commander Mahesh Yadav was arrested from Tekapatti police station jurisdiction in Katihar district.

April 30, 2012

A Delhi court accepted a fresh set of charges filed by Delhi Police against Kobad Ghandy under Unlawful Activities Prevention Act (UAPA).

May 1, 2012

Noam Chomsky, liberal philosopher and Institute Professor at the Massachusettes Institute of Technology through a letter to the Prime Minister sought justice for Soni Sori thus joining a band of 250 Indian foreign intellectuals to write an open letter protesting brutal treatment meted out to Soni Sori, a Chhattisgarh women.

May 2, 2012

A press release dtd May 2, 2012 signed by Maoist spokesperson Abhay stated that, the party claimed that the motive behind NCTC is to "crush with more centralised methods the people of our country fighting on their issues and for democratic rights."

May 3, 2012

Sukma collector Alex Paul Menon released.

May 3, 2012

In Jajpur a women maoist Sini Sai of village Gobarghati was arrested from the dense forests bordering Jajpur and Keonjhar.

May 3, 2012

Maoist gunned down a farmer Balram Nayak in Tentuligumma village under Baoipariguda police station. A letter recovered from his body alleged that Nayak was working as a police informer.

May 3, 2012

Supreme Court finally gave verdict that Naxal leader Chirukuri Raj Kumar alias Azad was killed in a genuine encounter on July 1, 2010 by Andhra Pradesh police.

May 4, 2012

Chhattisgarh Chief Minister Raman Singh said that the centre put in place a national policy to deal with hostage crisis which should not have any provision for negotiation even if Chief Minister is kidnapped.

May 4, 2012

A loyal bodyguard of top Maoist leader Sabyasachi Panda surrendered in Gajpati district. Sushant @ Prasad Majhi, Panda's bodyguard joined Maoists in 2005 when he was a high school student. He was a resident of Tudukpanka village in Gajpati district.

May 7, 2012

The Supreme Court of India granted bail and suspended the life sentence of CPI (Maoist) activist Narayan Sanyal who was held guilty of sedition alongwith Dr. Binayak Sen by a court in Chhattisgarh in the year 2010 (December 24, 2010 by Raipur court). A Bench of Justice G.S. Singhvi and S.J. Mukhopadhya left it to the trial court concerned to impose any conditions for bail on Sanyal. Narayan Sanyal was in jail since 2006.

Narayan Sanyal

Photograph appeared in The Indian Express of May 8, 2012

Narayan Sanyal was prime accused when nearly 300 Maoists attacked a police training centre in Giridih on November 11, 2005, killed five policemen and looted 193 weapons.

May 8, 2012

Maoist struck in the Western Orissa district of Naupada, killing an Asstt. Sub-Inspector of Orissa police after abducting him a few kilometers away from a CRPF camp. The police officer Kriparam Majhi was escorting a water tanker to CRPF camp.

May 9, 2012

Gadchiroli police caught Deputy Commander of Potegaon Dalam Lalsu Walko alias Subhash who was main playcase in a landmine blast that claimed 13 CRPF men on March 27 near Pushtoda in Dhanora Tehsil. Walko had joined Naxal ranks about four years ago.

May 9, 2012

Assam police gunned down four Maoist cadres in an encounter that took place at Sadiya in Tinsukhia district bordering Arunachal Pradesh. Those killed were : Siddhartha Buragohain Aditya Bora, Rajib Gogoi, Arup Chetia and Kamala Gogoi.

May 11, 2012

Pradeep Kumar Singh, active member of People's War Group in Jharkhand who was allegedly involved in an ambush in which Supdt. of Police Lohardaga Ajay Kumar Singh was killed in 2000 in Jharkhand. Pradeep Kumar Singh had joined PWG in 1990 and was arrested from Sector 24 in Rohini in Delhi. He was resident of Latehar in Jharkhand.

May 13, 2012

In a deadly attack on a patrolling team of CISF in Dantewada, six Jawans and a civilian driver were killed at Kirandul - 420 km south from Raipur. Maoist walked away with AK-47 of all the 6 CISF men.

May 13, 2012

Maoists killed CISF men, in Indian's biggest iron ore mine -

NMDC in Kirandul (Dantewada), yet the complex remained unguarded.

May 14, 2012

Maoists kidnapped two people including a local BJP leader in Sukma district of Chhattisgarh in separate incidents. Sukma district BJP secretary Mochaki Joga and Mochaki Kacche, a trader was abducted in Dornapal area.

May 14, 2012

Maoists are staging a come back into Andhra Pradesh. They crossed from Chhattisgarh and held a 'people's court' in a village in Khamman and fired and injured the Sarpanch.

May 14, 2012

Maoists beheaded a villager Ramlal Kayam at Kudaburu dubbing him a police informer. They left posters behind warning villagers against helping the police.

May 15, 2012

A Maoist Sub Zonal Commander Satendra Paswan wanted in the abduction and subsequent release of Latehar Development Commissioner and two engineers last year (2011) was arrested alongwith another person in Palamau district. Paswan had taken shelter at the residence of Sahendra Yadav at Polpol village.

May 15, 2012

The Director General of Orissa State Police Manmohan Praharaj stated that the state police and the Central forces have been able to eliminate 27 Maoists in different Naxal districts between January 2011 and May 2012. Similarly, during this period 194 red rebels were arrested and 60 others surrendered before the police.

The outlawed CPI Maoist had given a 24-hour bandh call to protest against the proposed National Counter Terrorism Centre (NCTC) and operation Green Hunt. Maoists posted posters on massive scale at Odiapentha, Balipeta, Narayanpatna, Almonda, Kaberibadi areas of the district and on the entire road connecting Bandhugaon with Rayagada district.

May 15, 2012

Maoists detained a passenger train in Jharkhand's West Singhbhun district for nearly 20 minutes with a one kg can bomb hung from the front of its engine, ahead of Bharat Bandh called by ultras on 16 May.

The Bilaspur-Passenger train which was detained at Posaits station on May 14 ran for another 15 km with the can bomb dangling from the Engine to Manoharpur station where it was defused and removed. —*Deccan Herald*, May 16, 2012

May 16, 2012

A letter released by Gangadhar of CPI (Maoist) notes that they intend to create a new front in Kodagu Chamrajnagar, the Nilgiris, Satyamanglam and Wyanad areas. The statement said "it is true that we have not been able to spread our roots in South India. But we have not given up and will take the movement forward by beginning a new front at the point of convergence of Karnataka, Tamil Nadu and Kerala. We will move forward based on our experiences in the Malnad and coastal areas. It will not be possible for the enemy to decimate us. We have people on our side and we will certainly win." —*Deccan Herald*, May 22, 2013

May 22, 2012

Deba Gageranga, a BJD activist and husband of a lady 'Sarpanch' Lahari Gageranga was shot dead by Maoists in Naxal infested tribal district of Rayagarh in southern Orissa. They alleged that the BJD activist was a police informer.

May 23, 2012

Seven members of CPI (Maoists) including the security guard of slain Naxal leader Kishenji surrendered their weapons in the presence of D.G. West Bengal police Naparajita Mukherjee. Security guard Jagannath Soren alias Hero surrendered his INSUS rifle, 56 rounds of cartridges and two magazines. He was followed by Sashadhar Mahato alias Subal, Khagpati Mahato, Buddeshwar Hansda, Niranjan Nag, Lalit Mahato and Sukhendra Baskey.

—*Deccan Herald*, May 24, 2012

Naxalites have improvised the indigenous rockets with repeated field trials in Dandakaranya. Around Rs. five crores were spent for manufacturing the rockets. In 1989 Maoist leader Sadanala Ramkrishna, who did graduation in mechanical engineering graduate from Warangal Regional Engineering College headed the Technical Research and Arms Manufacturing and was responsible for producing arms/rockets for Naxals. *The Times of India*, Bangalore of May 28, 2012 gave an estimate of 6000 rockets possessed by Maoist at present.

May 28, 2012

National Investigation Team (NIA) arrested a member of Manipur-based People Liberation Army (PLA) identified as Ebatambi Asem from Gopalpur town in Ganjam district of Odisha. An identity card bearing the name of A.V. Sharma was recoved from his possession.

May 29, 2012

Union rural development minister gave a call to Maoist to drop guns for politics, asked them to join electoral politics instead of indulging in violence which derailed development and welfare of the poor.

June 2, 2012

Maoists caused an explosion on a bridge on National Highway No. 30 in newly formed Kondagaon district of Bastar region of Chhattisgarh state. Blast ripped through the vehicle carrying 25 people, including 19 prisoners. All sustained injuries.

June 8, 2012

A Maoist couple Seema Azad and her husband Vishwa Vijay were given a life imprisonment sentence by an Allahabad Court. She is a Journalist/Editor of Dastak magazine. The couple was lodged in Naini Jail in Allahabad and were involved in anti-national activities and were peddling provocative literature.

June 10, 2012

A CRPF jawan and two ultras were killed and nine security

personnel injured in an encounter with security forces and armed Maoists in Balthar forests in Bihar's Gaya district. The CRPF Jawan Sachindra Sharma fell to the Maoist's bullets.

June 10, 2012

Andhra Pradesh police arrested Maoist leader Cherukuri Raj Kumar alias Azad's wife in Khanapuram village in Warangal district. Azad's wife Padma alias Sitakka was leader of women's wing of CPI- Maoists. Azad himself had been gunned down in Adilabad district on July 2, 2010 by police.

June 12, 2012

Naxal fear triggered mass resignation of 68 elected representative of civic bodies forcing them to put in their papers. 18 of them were heads of villages, 44 Panchayat Samiti members and one from Zilla Parishad at Bhamragah in Gadchiroli district. Most resignations were from a couple of villages in Dhanura and Korchi Tehsils which are largely Naxal-affected areas.

June 14, 2012

Two hardcore Maoists, accused in several murder cases, Bishram alias Sudhir Bhuyian and Hubil Hora belonging to the West Singhbhum district of Jharkhand were arrested from Saranda forest bordering Odisha and Jharkhand at Lungra Ghati under K. Balang police station. —*DNA,* Bangalore June 15, 2012

June 17, 2012

The Central government decided to permit Maoist-hit states to rent helicopters from private firms and use them for anti-Naxal operations till it acquired eight MI-17 V-5 choppers.

June 20, 2012

Maoists abducted 19 Railway employees, including a station Master in Bihar's Jamui district. All of them were released later. Maoists were attempting to regroup in Malnad area of Karnataka state which includes/comprises seven districts of Chikmagalur, Shimoga, part of Udupi, Dakshina Kannada, Hassan and Kodagu and had deputed Central Committee member Kuppu Swami to establish a base and recruit cadres. Kuppu Swami hails from Bangalore and has assumed identities such as Kuppu Devraj, Jogesh and Yogesh. —*Deccan Herald,* June 21, 2012

June 20, 2012

The annual report of the UN Secretary General on Children and Armed conflict says children are recruited and used by Naxalites particularly in Chhattisgarh and some districts in adjoining states.

June 22, 2012

During combing operations in Maoist-hit Koraput district, police seized some weapons gadgets and Naxal materials from Baipariguda area.

June 24, 2012

CPI-ML (Liberation) general secretary Deepankar Bhattacharya said that his party would abstain from the July 16, 2012 Presidential polls as it disapproves of policies and programmes of both the UPA and NDA.

June 26, 2012

Maoists killed a former tribal ward member Pidika Sarba at Gumaroput village after taking him away from his home. The rebels slit his throat and dumped his body on the outskirts of the village. Naxals suspected that Pidika, former Panchayat ward member had been passing information to police.

June 27/28, 2012

Maoists launched multiple attacks and ambushed a police bus, blew up railway properties and a bridge at three different places in Jharkhand.

June 28/29, 2012

Security forces killed 19 Maoists in the 'liberated zone' of Chhattisgarh. It was the second coordinated attempt by the security forces to launch an operation on the Maoists in Chhattisgarh–first being Ambujmad. 6 Cobra commandos were injured in the gun fight. CRPF police party also got engaged in another battle with Maoists at a place called Penta. Two rebels were shot down and a few taken hostage. But controversy over the Bijapur encounter heightened further with the Chhattisgarh Congress Committee's fact finding team claiming that there was no evidence to suggest the 19 killed were Maoists. The Chhattisgarh unit of the Congress came to a preliminary conclusion that more innocent tribals than Maoists were killed in the June 29, 2012 encounter in Bastar.

July 7, 2012

T. Palani (45) of Periyal Dravidar Kazhgam (PDK)–a breakaway faction of Dravidar Kazhgam (DK) was beheaded after he was shot dead.

July 8, 2012

One People's Liberation Front of India (PLFI) militant was killed and four others injured in a fierce gun battle with the police in a forest on Orissa-Jharkhand border and a large number of arms ammunition seized from these members of militant group. PLFI was responsible for the killing of ruling BJD leader Hardip Singh in Sundergarh district on July 7.

July 11, 2012

Barely three days after the killing of a former Naib Sarpanch in Malkangiri district, armed Maoists killed the son of a ruling BJD leader and Block Chairman in Bolangir district–the house of Kharprakhol block chairman, Ganeshram Bhoi in Sanaguchibhatra was raided to locate his son Sashiram Bhoi.

—*The Deccan Herald*, July 12, 2012

July 13, 2012

Mrs. Subhashree Panda wife of Maoist leader Sabyasachi Panda stated that her husband would surrender if government withdraws cases against him.

July 13, 2012

Centre hiked reward for surrendered Naxals from Rs. three to five lakhs.

July 23, 2012

Two CRPF personnel were killed and five injured in a gun

battle in Porahahatt jungle in Rania in Khunti district–around 70 km away from capital Ranchi.

July 29, 2012

In a Naxal attack in Malkangiri district, a special police officer was killed and another sustained serious injuries. The incident took place when Maoists are observing a 'Martyr Week' in different districts of Orissa. The week-long programme will come to an end on August 3. —*Deccan Herald*, July 30, 2012

August 2, 2012

In an interview with Zee News and DNA, Union Home Minister Sushil Kumar Shinde said Naxals are our brothers and we will look at their problems.

August 2, 2012

After Maruti Chairman R.C. Bhargava hinted at Maoist links in the pre-planned violence of July 18 in its Maneshar place, the centre announced to probe the allegations. In the violence one senior HR executive Awanish Kumar Dev was killed.

August 3, 2012

Maoist leader Ranjan Munda and another squad leader were arrested from West Midnapore district.

August 6, 2012

Maoists blew off a mine protected vehicle with the help of an Improved Explosive Device (IED) killing a CRPF personnel and injuring few others in a place under Aranpur police station in Dantewada district in Chhattisgarh.

August 7, 2012

Two CRPF commandos were killed in an IED blast. A Tata-407 vehicle was blown up near Rajpeta village under Basuguda PS area of Bijapur district killing two commandos.

August 8, 2012

Minister of State (MoS) for Home, Jitendra Singh said in Rajya Sabha that Maoists are collecting money through the sale of illegal poppy cultivation in Maoist dominated areas of Chhattisgarh, Jharkhand, Odisha and Bihar.

August 10, 2012

CPI (Maoist) expelled Sabyasachi Panda, the organisation's secretary of Odisha State Organising Committee for working against the party's interest. The Central Committee of CPI (Maoist) issued a statement to the press on August 3, 2012 declaring that Sabyasachi has been removed from the post of general secretary of the party's Odisha state committee for his 'anti-organisational activities.'

August 12, 2012

Subhashree Panda, wife of sacked Maoist leader Sabyasachi Panda said that there is threat for her husband's life from police and militants alike.

August 13, 2012

5477 km road length to be laid in eight Naxal-hit states to improve connectivity, was approved by the Union government.

August 13, 2012

Johnson Munda, an Area Commander, active in Western Singhbhum in Jharkhand and Keonjhar and Sundergarh in Orissa who was arrested by Jharkhand police was asked by Odisha police for interrogation. Munda belonged to Bitkilsoya village under Jareikela police station area in Odisha.

August 15, 2012

Maoist threat on the eve of Independence Day disrupted train services on the Howrah-Delhi route. About 25 Maoists arrived in Ismailpur Railway Station of Mughalsarai Division and stuck posters and banners carrying a warning that train movement should be stopped. —*The Times of India*, Bangalore August 15, 2012

August 14, 2012

CPI (Maoist) leader Sabyasachi, who was expelled from the party by its Central Committee said CPI (Maoist) is anti-tribal. He said he had severed ties with organisation for the past seven months and formed a new organisation 'Odisha Maovadi Party' to fight for the cause of the downtrodden in Kandhamal, Ganjam, Gajpati and Rayagada districts. "We cannot serve as slaves in a party that denies internal democracy and works against the interest of common people. The CPI (Maoist) is doomed unless it corrects itself" Panda said.

August 22, 2012

Naxals adopted new tactics of using women and children as human-shields during exchange of fire with security forces, Govt said.

August 23, 2012

The National Investigation Agency filed a chargesheet against five Maoist leaders in Kolkata in a special court accusing them of manufacturing local weapons illegally to "intensify the war against the country." They were arrested by anti-Naxal force Greyhounds of Andhra Pradesh in March 2012.

August 24, 2012

In an encounter near Maraskol village in Narayanpur district, 2 Jan. Militia members were killed in an encounter.

August 25, 2012

Security personnel recovered explosives including one pipe bomb from the Naxal-affected Ghatsila sub-division of East Singhbhum district in Jharkhand.

August 29, 2012

CPI (ML) general secretary Dipankar Bhattacharya was to court arrest in Jantar Mantar, New Delhi to demand resignation of Prime Minister Manmohan Singh in view of corruption, privatisation policies that promote corporate plunder of natural resources etc.

August 29, 2012

Minister of State for Home Jitendra Singh told the Rajya Sabha that 84 districts in 12 states were affected by Maoist violence, while Maoist front organisations were active over-ground in 119 districts (in 20 states). What are the parameters for classifying a district or a state as Maoist effect is not told.

August 31, 2012

Jharkhand police had seized a M-16 assault rifle, one AK-56, 4 mm pistols, bullet proof vest from senior CPI Maoist cadre Anil Yadav and arms supplier Prafulla Malakar. These were US Army issued rifles etc. Maoists acquiring modern weapons.

September 8, 2012

A CRPF Jawan was killed and five others were wounded in a gunfight with Maoists near Pandrukhia forest on the borders of Gaya and Aurangabad districts.

September 10, 2012

Orissa police found that between 70 and 80 per cent of armed Maoists in the state do not belong to the state and have come to Orissa from outside state.

—Report by Debabrata Mohanty in *IE*
September 10, 2012

The centre decided to urge Naxal-effected states to lower the norms of recruitment in government jobs to open up employment opportunities for more number of local youth and prevent them from succumbing to Maoist propaganda.

—*The Indian Express,* September 11, 2012

Police said that seven out of 17 people killed in an ambush in Basuguda area of Bijapur district had Naxal records. The operation was conducted on the night of June 28 and 29. Now police claim that not seven but one had Naxal links. Amid allegation of human rights violations, the Chhattisgarh government had ordered a judicial enquiry into the case.

—Report by Vijaita Singh in *Indian Express,* September 11, 2012

September 11, 2012

Centre cautioned Assam that extreme left wing extremists with links to Maoists from Central India have found foot-hold in the Amorpur village which falls in Sadiya sub-division of Tinsukia district. On June 1, 2012 a senior Maoist leader of 15 yrs standing in Orissa asked an ideological question – whether the path of

Protracted People's War (PPW) was still suitable to Indian conditions. What he wanted to convey was that people are not yet ready for PPW. Panda, who owed allegiance to the party unity before it merged with PW which subsequently merged with Maoist Communist Centre (MCCI) to form CPI (Maoist), in his letter indicated that the reunification of Maoist forces hailed as a milestone for the movement has not gone down well at the field level. The Maoist Central Committee responded on July 16, 2012 reaffirming its commitment to the path of PPW to build the movement to "finally seize political power all over the country by spreading from smaller as vaster areas, isolated areas to all over the country and by developing from a small force to a mighty force." The 4-page statement signed by Anand, a member of Politburo and also secretary of Central Regional Bureau saw Panda's rebellion as part of multi-pronged offensive launched by Indian security forces.

Panda also wrote a letter to Maoist Chief, Ganpathi in June 2012 complaining about lack of internal democracy. He criticised Maoist indulging in mindless killing. He asked "where is the provision of annihilation of one party member in that party constitution, even if he acts as enemy agent ?" Earlier also there was a vertical split in PW in Karnataka and the expelled members went on to form a new Maoist outfit called Karnataka Maoist Swatantra Kendra (KMSK). —Report by K. Srinivas Reddy

The Hindu, September 13, 2012

September 12, 2012

The arrest of Abhishek Mukherjee alias Aranya, a Maoist leader, believed to be dead, revealed his links with Jadavpur University where Abhishek studied. He revealed that Maoist's Kolkata City Committee now have 14 member. It was dissolved in 2011 after the new government came to power. When it was restructured Abhishek is said to have been made secretary, a post he had held in 2010 too. In Jadavpur University Campus, United Social Democratic Front is said to be a front for Maoists.

—Madhu Pruna Dass from Kolkata–*The Indian Express*

September 13, 2012

STF source revealed that Mukherjee and two other Maoist– Nil alias Sushil Mandal and Sameer were arrested while holding a secret meeting in Tala Park in North Kolkata. Abhishek's wife Debolina Chakraborty had been in jail for two months now.

September 19, 2012

A sub-Inspector was killed and two other policemen injured in Naxal attack in Jamui (Jharkhand) near Sidheshwar temple. A CRPF personnel was killed and other injured when suspected Maoists attack a helipad in Bastar region of Chhattisgarh.

September 23, 2012

Sabyasachi Panda's mother Krishna Kumari Panda asked her son to lay down arms and return to social mainstream.

September 23, 2012

Maoist Central Zone Committee member Sashi Shekhar Singh was held in Nagaryawan village in Gaya district alongwith Vinay Das.

September 24, 2012

Two village guards locally known as 'gram rakshish' – Manik Khilo and Jagbandhu Khilo from Handikal and Joda Amba respectively were killed by Maoists claiming them to be police informers. They were murdered by Maoists in the cut-off area of the Chitrakonda reservoir in Malkangiri district in South Odisha. Their bodies were found near Panapput on September 25.

September 30, 2012

Rise of Naxalism was attributed to "Economic disparity" by the former Chief of Army Staff General V.K. Singh (Retired).

September 30, 2012

CRPF's anti-Naxal operations are set to go high tech as it plans to deploy GPS-enabled satellite trackers and mobile video conferencing system.

October 1, 2012

In Metala forest of West Midnapore, two CRPF personnel

were shot dead—R.N. Mahato of Balasore (Orissa) and Vijay Bhashkar of Mehboobnagar (Andhra Pradesh).

October 2, 2012

The Supreme Court said that Naxalism was as a result of an oversight of constitutional provisions relating to administration of schedule areas and tribes of the country. "Nobody looks at Schedules V and VI of the Constitution and the result is Naxalism."– said a Bench led by Justice A.K. Pathak.

October 2, 2012

Maoists fired a 'missile' like object at Golapalli police station in Sukma district of Bastar region of Chhattisgarh.

October 13, 2012

The Union Home Secretary R.K. Singh stated before a parliamentary panel earlier this year (2012) "...this Naxalism is an issue in which we believe is a major internal security problem, a major problem for the country because the areas which are under the control of the Nxalites are actually outside the sovereign control of the State Government and therefore of the Central Government." He admitted that areas under the control of the ultras are outside the control of the government.

October 18, 2012

Six CRPF Jawans were killed and nine others seriously injured when their anti-landmine vehicle was blown up by Naxalites at Barha village in Gaya district. Naxalites triggered an IED blast blowing the CRPF anti-landmine vehicle. The martyred CRPF Jawans were identified as Sub-Inspector Ramji Ram, constables Vikramaditya Yadav, Ashok Nirala and Raj Singh and the driver Babu Lal.

October 18, 2012

Sanatan Sardar, an important local leader of CPI (Maoist) from Kolkata was areested in the Binpur Thana area of West Bengal's Paschim Medinipur district.

October 22, 2012

Two men were killed by the Maoists after accusing them of stealing goats at Banalhat village in Orissa. The Zonal Commander Nakul Yadav caught Laxman Lohra and Raj deo Khervar at the village under Bishnupur police station and convened Kangaroo court. The ultras later chopped off their hands and beat them to death on made up charges that the two had stolen goats in the village. —*The Pioneer,* October 23, 2012

Meanwhile, Maoists leader Daya claimed that he was responsible for the slaying of a tribal villager Gumpha Kadraka of Gurumeda since he was suspected to be a police informer. His body was spotted at a nearby Nilabadi village.

October 22, 2012

In a raid conducted by Ranchi police, a wanted Maoist Birendra Singh Munda alias Mahesh was arrested from Raisa near Bundu in Ranchi district. Mahesh was third in power in the Kundan Pahan squad. He was currently functioning as secretary of Gautamhara Area Committee under Zonal Commander Rammohan in the regions falling in between Ranchi-Tata Road and Ranchi-Muri Road said SSP Ranchi, Saket Kumar Singh. Mahesh's father Heera Singh Munda was one of the founding members of the Maoist movement in Jharkhand during the initial phase.

October 26, 2012

People's Liberation Front of India (PLFI) Area Commander Surya Dan alias Subar Singh and his bodyguard Churu alias Seyon Topo were arrested from the Odisha-Jharkhand border area.

October 26, 2012

MHA issued an advisory to nine-Naxal affected states to use Central Rehabilitation fund to carry out reverse vasctomise for Maoist return to the mainstream.

October 29, 2012

Two hardcore CPI (Maoist) activists Samuel Odeya and Mumtaz Ansari were arrested from Ranka Jungle – Kokakocha village in Seraikela – Kharswan district.

November 3, 2012

Two Maoist activists, Sukdeb Mahato and Chiranjeet Mahto, who had surrendered on January 12 and February 7, 2012 respectively in the Jhargram area of Paschim Medinipur district of West Bengal were held outside the residence of Chief Minister Mamta Banerjee. They were taken to local Kalighat police station for interrogation.

November 4, 2012

Two CISF personnel were killed when an attack was carried out at a checkpost on a hilltop at Akash Nagar – close to Bailadila hills in Dantewada district in Chhattisgarh by heavily armed Maoist who opened fire at an iron-ore mining area.

Kudiam Gujja, Nagesh and Shivaji, three Naxals were book for raping two minor girls in Muded area in the Bijapur district. The minors were forcibly picked up from their houses and made them to work as Bal Sangham members and then repeatedly assaulted them.

November 4, 2012

CRPF stumbled upon a 'list of children' maintained by Maoists for sexually exploiting them. The list had various heads such as 'women, girls and little girls.' The centre stepped into help the minor girls and gave them Rs. five lakh each for rehabilitation.

November 8, 2012

Mahendra Karma, senior Congress leader and former leader of Opposition in Chhattisgarh who was on his why to Barsur was attacked by Maoists when an IED blew up his bullet-proof vehicle. Karma was on 'hit list' of Maoist as he had launched Salwa Judum in Bastar several years ago.

November 9, 2012

Three policemen and a prisoner were killed when Maoists opened fire on the police escort carrying prisoners to Girdih jail in Jharkhand. Eight Maoists and 25 other prisoner who were being taken from the court to jail absconded in the incident.

November 10, 2012

Girdih police arrested seven persons in connection with Naxal attack on November 9.

November 10, 2012

A hardcore Naxal Dhakad Salam, resident of Nariya Kilepar village was arrested near Bayanar police station by Kondagaon police.

November 14, 2012

At least five Maoists gunned down by security forces in a forest on the border of Odisha, Ganjam and Gajpati districts. A red rebel was captured, arms and explosives seized and two security personnel was also injured in Bhaliagada jungle under Mohana police station. The bodies of all the five Maoists were identified and they were from Kandhmal district.

November 14, 2012

Rebel leader Sabyasachi Panda escaped being killed near Bhaliapada village on the border of Ganjam and Gajpati districts. His 5 associates were killed in encounter. Panda had been expelled from CPI (Maoist) about three months earlier. His wife Mili said the encounter reflected State Government's attitude in dealing with rebels. "They just want to be trigger-happy. First they say Sabyasachi can surrender and then they attack him." Panda formed the Orissa Maovadi Party after being expelled from CPI (Maoist) in August 2012. He had over 50 criminal cases against him apart from the murder of Laxmanand.

November 16, 2012

Various terror charges were framed against Yogender Singh Bhokta under Unlawful Activities Prevention Act (UAPA). Bhokta who was arrested by special cell of Delhi Police on May 3, 2009 from Badarpur area of Delhi was self styled Commander of CPI (Maoist).

November 18, 2012

The Central Regional Bureau of Maoists appointed former 'Military Commander' Kadri Satyanarayan Rao alias Kosa after the death of Kishenji. He is also known as 'Sadhu', 'Gopanna' and carries a reward of Rs. seven lakh on his head.

—*The Indian Express*, November 19, 2013

Kosa, considered to be in the 24-25 in the hierachy of CPI (Maoist), till a year ago was believed to have been the mastermind of 2010 Dantewada massacre in Chhattisgarh in which 76 CRPF personnel were killed by Maoist.

November 18, 2012

Odisha Maobadi Party Chief Sabyasachi Panda who had suffered bullet injury released a tape inspite of the fact that police were chasing him. During an encounter with the police at Mohana Block in Gajpati district on November 14, five of his men were killed–Chasiram Bargshingh, Ayub Padra, Samson Majhi, Sanatan Mallick and Laxmikant Nayak of Kandhamal. Panda through the tape demanded a compensation of Rs. 10 lakhs to each of those killed to be given to their families as they were innocient villagers.

November 20, 2012

Police arrested from Bhaliaguda under Mohana block in Gapati district. The arrested were identified as Kalia Mallick, Jalendra Mallick, Surendra Mallick and Bulu Mallick from Bhaliaguda where five Maoists were gunned down in police encounter on November 14.

November 22, 2012

Samson Mallick and Arun Sona Majhi of Dhusana and Gaheju village of Hatimunda GP under Barhanigaon police station in Kandhamal district surrendered before Ganjam S.P.

November 22, 2012

The police in Bijapur claimed that "they had unearthed a racket that supplied minor girls to top Maoist."

November 22, 2012

Two Maoists, who were Panda's aides – Samson Mallick and Arun Sona Majhi of Dahusana and Gaheju village surrendered before S.P. Ganjam.

November 25, 2012

A woman Naxalite was killed in a police encounter in the forest area of Abapur village near Ghot in Chamorshi Talka.

November 25, 2012

The Koraput police arrested two hardcore Maoist from the Durmbaguda area. They were identified Habitea Lingama and Habiha Tamaya.

November 25, 2012

Maoists in Bengal are planning a stunning strike in the state to tone up their dismembered organisational network as well as avenge the encounter death of one of the Supreme Commander Kishenji killed by police in November 2011. Two of their senior leaders Bikash and Madan, have been doing rounds of Binpur and Belpahari area for the purpose.—*The Pioneer,* November 26, 2012

November 25, 2012

Commandos of Gadchiroli police killed a women Naxal (25) in an encounter with a group of Naxals in the forest of Abapur village. The killed women was Rinki alias Rakhi alias Laxmi Likami.

November 26, 2012

Eight Naxals were arrested in Chhattisgarh in two separate operations. A joint team of Bijapur police and Chhattisgarh Armed Forces nabbed Kalmumi Minoo alias Manoj near Ghudsakar village. In Etebalka village, Kankar police arrested three more Maoists were arrested - Santosh Kumar Anchala, Bir Singh Anchala and Baisakhu Ram–all of them were accused of ambushing a police team near Etebalka on July 21, 2010.

November 27, 2012

Hardcore Maoist Laxman Raita alias Patul who was involved in the abduction of two other women cadres of the Odisha Maovadi Party led by Sabyasachi Panda surrendered before Ganjam SP at the district police HQ at Chhattisgarh.

—*The Pioneer*, November 28, 2010

November 28, 2012

During a raid in Chhattisgarh CRPF seized the pictures of Prashant Bose @ Kishanda No. 2 in Maoist hierarchy. (His wife Sheela Marandi, a member of the core committee of CPI (Maoist) was arrested in 2006. In 2008 Bose signed a deal with Manipur based PLA to get arms and train the Maoist in Guerilla warfare.

—*The Indian Express,* November 29, 2012

Prashant Bose alias Kishenda alias Nirbhaya is in the centre, carrying an umbrella. To the far right, waaring glasses and white beard, is Shamsher Singh Seri alias Karam Singh. The CPI (Maoist) announced Karam Singh's death of natural causes in October 2005. If that is true, this picture would be from at least 2005 or earlier.

—*The IE November 29, 2013*

November 29, 2012

At Semitiguda Press Club held its annual function at, Minister for School and Mass Education, Rabi Narayan Nanda called upon media to play an efficient role as a watch dog. The Kandhamal police + SOG + CRPF Jawans seized a powerful landmining weighing 20 kg and other explosive material during a combing operation in Badabanga forest under the Darinbadi police limit in Kandamahal district.

December 1, 2012

Union Minister for Rural Development Jairam Ramesh said while addressing a Press Conference in Guwahati that his ministry has moved the proposal for including Tinsukhia and Dibrugarh in the list of Maoist insurgency (or LWE).

December 1, 2012

Public Sector Bhilai Steel Plant (BSP) is to go to extraordinary lengths to ensure that its Rs. 5000 crore plan to extract quality iron ore from mines located in the Maoist hinterland in Rowghat Hills in South Central Chhattisgarh.

December 2, 2012

Dr. Prakash Amte son of Baba Amte conducted vasectomy surgery on Maoists at his community centre in Maharashtra Gadchiroli district. Surrendered Maoists have often said that they were forced to undergo sterilisation by their leader.

—*The Indian Express*, December 3, 2012

December 2, 2012

Maoists gunned down a tribal man after accusing him of being a police informer at a habitation of Gutti Koyas near Thatilanka village in Chintur mandal near Chhattisgarh border. The killing coincided with the peoples liberation guerrilla army week celebration which began on Sunday the December 2, 2012.

December 2, 2012

Two hardcore Maoists Jadurai Soy alias Chamara and Bijoy Honhaga alias Rakesh who were highly active in Saranda forest in Jharkhand-Odisha Border surrendered before Rourkela SP. Honhaga was secretary of Jana Militia squad and President of Krantikari Kissan Committee. —*The Pioneer,* December 5, 2012

A group of 60 Naxals set fire on at least two tipper trucks used in road construction work in Tongpal area of Sukma district in Chhattisgarh. —*The Pioneer,* December 5, 2012

December 5, 2012

Sangran, son of Dandapani Mohanti, a Maoist sympathiser

who acted as an interlocutor in the negotiation for release of two Italian tourist was arrested alongwith an associate, Kailash, Mandal by police from Gajpati district in Berhampur town of Ganjam district, stapped with sediton charge. Maoist literature and leaflets were seized from them. 100 rounds of bullets and firearms were also recovered from them.

—*The Indian Express,* December 6, 2012

December 5, 2012

A woman Naxalite was killed in an encounter near Hikker forests in the Etapalli division of Gadchiroli district. Police recovered one rifle, two back packs and some Naxal literature.

December 6, 2012

Assam police arrested a top Maoist leader Anand Singh Kharwal @ Anandji from Tezpur town in Assam. He was most wanted Maoist leader in Chhattisgarh in Jharkhand and carried a bounty Rs. 5 lakh. The purpose of Anandji's visit to Assam is being investigated.

December 7, 2012

Chinnram Gota, a leader of erstwhile movement against Naxals, Salwa Judum in Bijapur was killed by Maoists at Pusler village under Farsegarh police station. Gota's guard Mangal Kursam was also killed.

December 8, 2012

A woman Maoist Manasi Baske (27) alias Sita who hails from Salboni area was arrested from Lalgarh area of West Midnapore district in West Bengal. She belongs to Bikas squad.

December 9, 2012

Communist Party of India (Maoist) has carved out a new zone for their operations comprising Gadchiroli, Gonia and Balaghat areas in Maharashtra and Madhya Pradesh in a view to re-assert their presence in central India. Pahad Singh was to look after the unit. —*The Indian Express,* December 10, 2012

December 9, 2012

Buoyed with success of the anti-Naxal operation 'ANACONDA-1' which began on July 31, 2011 and lasted till

September, another operation ANACONDA-2 was launched involving more than 1200 troops from CRPF, India Reserve Battalion (IRB), and anti-Naxal Cobra force, Jharkhand Jaguar and Jharkhand police in the dense Saranda forest of West Singhbhum. Three banned organisations CPI (Maoist), Kissan Krantikari Samiti and Nari Mukti Sangh were active in the area.

—*The Pioneer,* December 11, 2012

December 12, 2012

On December 12, police fired on tribal children attending a Maoist camp and killed a teenager namely, Chainu Mandawi and arrested nine others in Abujh Maad a 4000 sq km forest area most in Chhattisgarh. Police raided the day-long camp that was being attended by over 20 tribal children between the villages Sitram and Bala in Paralkot Reserve Forest area, 10 km inside the Maad. Armed Maoist cadre escaped.

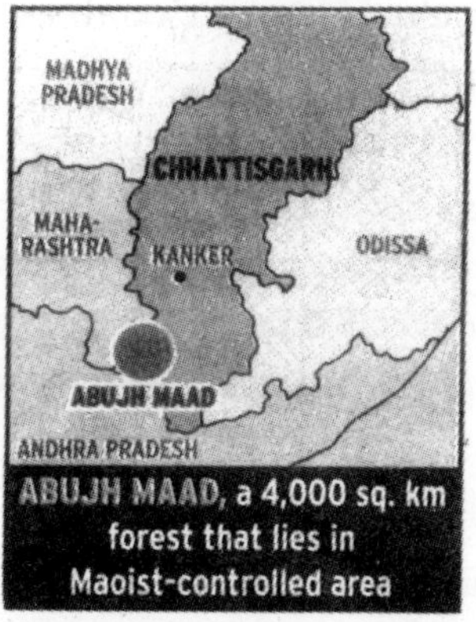

ABUJH MAAD, a 4,000 sq. km forest that lies in Maoist-controlled area

—*The Hindu*, November 20, 2012 (Report by Suvojit Bagchi)

On December 21, the villagers/residents of four villages inside Abujh Maad in South Chhattisgarh passed a unique resolution resisting both the Maoist and the police.

December 13, 2012

27 Maoists surrendered before the police in Bihar's Muzaffarpur district. Maoists included one Area Commander.

December 14, 2012

One suspected Maoist was killed and nine arrested in Abujhmaad, Chhattisgarh under an operation "12-12-12". The arrested included six men and three women. Two Maoist camps were busted under "12-12-12". Maoists tried to regain their grip at Dalma, Bodam and Patamda where they been almost wiped out from in an anti-insurgency operation.

December 14, 2012

A Rajya Sabha member and Odisha Jan Morcha (OJM) chief reportedly cited an interview with Maoist interlocutor Dandapani Mohany who claimed that Odisha govt. to have bribed Maoists for release of R. Vineel Krishna and Laxmipur BJD-MLA Jhina Hikaka.

—*The Pioneer,* December 15, 2012

Eight Naxalites were killed by Security Forces and nine captured during a raid on the ultra's training camp in Bande forest area of Kanker district.

December 15, 2012

CPI (Marxist-Leninist) (Liberation) seeks total prohibition in Bihar. Deepankar Bhattacharya, General Secretary alleged that profit to Liquor mafia are several times more the state revenue "Liquor mafia enjoying state protection" said Meena Tiwari CPI-ML leader.

—*The Hindu*, December 16, 2012

December 16, 2012

Leader of Opposition in the Odisha Assembly and Congress Chief Whip Prasad Harichandan demanded resignation of Chief Minister Naveen Patnaik for alleged nexus of State Government with the Maoists and demanded a probe into the case by National Investigation Agency (NIA). —*The Pioneer*, December 17, 2012

December 16, 2012

CRPF launched a major offensive in the forest of Laheri in Gadchiroli (Maharashtra) and recovered SBML guns, assorted ammunition and explosives, a huge cache of arms and ammunition, 23 backpacks and some literature. The Maoist unit that came under attack could belong to People's Liberation Group Army (PLGA). PLGA's head Chandna surrendered last year in Andhra Pradesh.

—*The Indian Express,* December 17, 2012

The teacher's strike in Chhattisgarh in December 2012 was supported by CPI (Maoist). On December 15, 2012 a 'bandh' called by the CPI (Maoist) was observed in Narainpur district supporting teacher's demands.

December 17, 2012

BSF and local police, in an operation against Maoists, seized a large number of steel containers filled with explosives from the Musalmunda forest in Narayanpatna of Koraput district. Three landmines each weighing 22 kg, three tiffin bombs weighing about five kg each and a country-made gun alongwith huge amount of wires, safety fuses and control system used to blast landmines was seized from or den in the forest. The explosives were dumbed by the Maoist in the forest in half-prepared condition.

—*The Indian Express,* December 19, 2012

December 17, 2012

Maoists torched 18 vehicles involved in a Railway tunnel in West Singhbhum district in Jharkhand. The tunnel is 680 meter long and Naxals wanted the use of manual labour to prolong work whereas the contractor had requested the Railways to let him use manual labour and machines.

December 21, 2012

About 300 residents from four villages met inside Abuj, Maad in South Chhattisgarh and decided that they will continue giving food to the Maoists as they raise our issue of protecting land and forest. But we will not send the children to camp to give the food. Villagers decided that children will not interact with police or Maoists.

December 22, 2012

The arrest of three persons including the Manager-cum-Supervisor for Sushee Infra Pvt. Ltd. (a firm based in Hyderabad) by Gadchiroli police from Hyderabad on December 22 has again sparked apprehensions about a possible resurgence in the Southern State. The two persons held with the Manager Venkatarama Reddy were Chinmaya Soyam, a former Sarpanch of village in neighbouring Adilabad district of Andhra and a local NCP leader and former Chairman of Sironcha Panchayat Samity, Suryanarayan Parpatwar. The infrastructure firm was working on the Pranhita-Chevella inter-state irrigation project which is expected to be a soother for the strife-affected Telangana region. Telangana sentiment are in a way helping the Maoist resurrection in AP.

—*The Indian Express,* December 26, 2012

December 25, 2012

Bijoy Singh Sardar and Moumita Paharia surrendered before the police in Purulia district. These Maoist members also handed over two double-barrel guns. Both Sardar and Ms Paharia were active since 2008 and were associated with Dalma squad and Ayodhya squad of the outfit along the West Bengal-Jharkhand border.

—*The Hindu,* December 26, 2012

December 27, 2012

Naxals killed Mudiyam Naga (45) a sarpanch of Hirapur village in Basaguda area (Awapalli village of Bijapur district, Chhattisgarh. He was stabbed by 4 Naxalites with sharp weapons.

December 28, 2012

Two policemen and a woman were wounded in the leg as Maoists opened fire at a village in the Etapalli Taluka of Maharashtra's Gadchiroli district.

December 29, 2012

Five (5) Maoists identified as Rajesh of Mavelikkara, Baluleyan of Njarayilkonam, Devarajan of Kollam, Gopal of Rajilpakkon in Tamil Nadu and Mannuar Ajayan were arrested from a lodge in Mavelikkara, Allappuzha district in Kerala for recruiting juveniles in Kerala by CPI (Maoist). Two minors had also attended the meeting in the loge. Six mobile phones and a laptop were also seized. All the five were released by the Kerala court for want of sufficient evidence. Police had identified the two minors as daughters of Maoist couple Roopesh and Shyna. Roopesh is former state secretary of CPI (Maoist). They have been accused of harbouring Malla Raji Reddy, the politbureau member of CPI (Maoist) who was nabbed by Andhra Pradesh police in 2007. Now NIA has taken up this case.

—*The Indian Express,* May 30, 2013

December 30, 2012

Security forces busted a Naxal training camp in the forest area of Kamkanar, Chokanpal and Jampemarka of the Bijapur district in Chhattisgarh. A couple of detonators, battery, wire, Maoist literature, ration, medicines in large quantities and other Naxal related materials were recovered from the camping site.

January 1, 2013

Assam Chief Minister Tarun Gogoi stated that the presence of Maoists in Assam was a big problem. The CRPF has claimed that in the last one year it has cleared over 5000 sq km in Saranda, Gaaru and Burra Pahar areas of Maoist influence in Jharkhand and Bihar which was followed by development projects. It wanted Jharkhand and Bihar governments to rehabilitate more than 500 odd Maoist sympathiser.

—*The Indian Express,* January 3, 2013

(Report by Vijaita Singh)

January 2, 2013

Naxals stabbed to death the 'Sarpanch' of Mankeli village in Bijapur. Budhram (45) who had shifted to Bijapur from Mankeli after Salwa Judum was stabbed by four Naxals with sharp weapons in Nayapara locality of Bijapur district Hqrs.

—*The Pioneer*, January 3, 2013

January 4, 2013

Rebel Trinamool Congress MP, Kabir Suman disclosed the involvement of Maoists in the agitation led by his party in Nandigram in 2007. Speaking to some TV channels, Suman pointed out that the late Koteswara Rao alias Kishenji, former polit bureau member of CPI (Maoist) has exhorted his supporters in Paschim Medinapur district to take up the Trinamool Congress Party flag and defeat CPI (M) in Assembly elections.

—*The Hindu*, January 5, 2013

On January 5, 2013

Former Chief Minister Buddhadeb Bhattacharjee state that the police action in Nandigram in the West Bengal's Purba Medinapore during the earstutile left front government was not to acquire land forcefully but to put a check on Maoists activities in the area. —*The Hindu*, January 5, 2013

January 6, 2013

Letters seized from Maoist 'Commander' Ghasi alias Chenda Bhushanam who was arrested in April 2011, indicate that Maoists were in touch with Koraput MP Jayram Pangi and Koraput MLA. Raghuram Padal apart from Congress MLA Ramchandra Kadam.

In a letter written in February 2011, on a CPI (Maoist) letterhead, Daya, Secretary of Koraput-Srikakulam Divisional Committee of the Maoist asked MP Pangi, MLA Padal, Laxmipur MLA Jhina Hikaka and a Biju Janta Dal (BJD) leader from Pattangi, Prafulla Pangi to atted their (Their) meeting in the Narayanpatna block. The letter sent by a Maoist courier was acknowledged by Koraput MP Pangi at 6.10 pm on February 6, 2011.—Report filed by Debabrata Mohanty

—*The Indian Express*, January 7, 2013

January 6, 2013

During a combing operation against Maoists in Gandhamardarn a reserve forest near Saapmund, Mahulpali and Beherapani village in Khprakha block of Balangir district. In the heavy exchange of fire between the Jawans and Maoists, one SOG Jawan was injured in the crossfire.

January 7, 2013

Bimal Gudia, wanted in over two dozen cases of Naxal violence including landmine blast was nabbed from Saranda forests under Manoharpur police station in West Singhbhum district.

Seven CRPF personnel were killed and 12 Jawans injured in a fierce encounter with the CPI Maoists at Hehegarha under Barwadih police station in Latehar district (Jharkhand). The four-hour encounter is believed to have been headed by Arvind who stood to be holed up in the area for the past 25 days. Perhaps CRPF personnel could have survived, had they been evacuated in time.

January 8, 2013

Revising the death toll, CRPF said four (4) of its personnel and not six (6) as initially reported – were killed in the encounter with Maoists on January 7. A constable of Jharkhand Jaguar Special Task Force was also killed.

January 8, 2013

A court in Dantewada acquitted all 10 (ten) tribals accused of 6th April 2010 killing of 76 security personnel (75 CRPF personnel and one state policemen) at Taadmela village (then Dantewada district now renamed Sukma). The Additional Sessions Judge Anita Deharia freed Kartam Joga, Co-petitioneer with activist Nandini Sundar and others in the Salwa Judum case. Case collapsed after nearly all the 43 prosecution witnesses turned hostile. Those who walked with Kartam Joga were : Poyam Ganga, Podiyam Hidma, Poyam Hidma, Kawasi Budra, Duro Joga, Warse Lakhma, Madkam Ganga, Rajesh Ganga and Madvi Dula. All 10 were charged with murder, criminal conspiracy, unlawful assembly and under provisions of Arms Act and Explosives Act. Police had named 93 accused but could arrest only 10. —*The Indian Express*, January 9, 2013

January 7/8, 2013

In a Maoist ambush two civilians and three security personnel were killed and a local resident injured in a landmine blast in Amwatikar village. CRPF were able to retrieve the bodies of 5 CRPF personnel on January 9, 2013 who went missing during an encounter with Maoist on Monday the 7th of January. Maoists had mutilated the bodies of two of the personnel–one had his eyes gouged out while the other had been hacked. On 9th January,

CRPF revised the death toll to 13 – 10 security personnel and three civilians. The Maoists believed to be around 200 of them and led by Central Committee member Dev Kumar Singh alias Arvindji were armed with AK-47 rifles, Insas, light machine guns and grenades. —*The Indian Express*, January 10, 2013

January 9, 2013

Gadchiroli police reported that the dreaded Naxal leader Thakapalli Vasudev Rao alias Assanna alias Satish alias Sujit had entered Gadchiroli. Assanna is a resident of Warangal district in Andhra Pradesh. He is believed to be mastermind behind an assassination bid on the then Chief Minister of Andhra Pradesh N. Chandrababu Naidu, near Tirupati in 2003.

January 10, 2013

In the first incident of its kind, Maoists placed a 2.5 kg. Improvised Explosive Device (IED) fitted with the gelatin sticks, detonator and battery, packed in a plastic container, inside the stomach of a CRPF personnel killed in an encounter in Latehar on January 6. The body of constable Babulal Patel (29) from Allahabad was recovered alongwith four other bodies of security personnel on January 10, 2013. Doctors found that the abdomen had been cut open horizontally with "surgical precision" and sutured again. Vital organs like intestines and spleen had been removed to fit the bomb.

The bomb taken out of the body of the CRPF man in Ranchi on Thursday (January 10, 2013)

The group of around 200 Maoists, led by Dev Kumar Singh (65) alias Arvindji was trying to crossover to Saranda forest when the encounter took place. Arvindji is a former member of People's War Group (PWG) and carries a reward of Rs. 7 lakh on his head.

—*The Indian Express*, January 11, 2013

Maoists had chopped off the tongue of Baijnath Kisku of CRPF's 112 Battalion and ruptured the stomach of another Jawan. 'In an eight-minute audio clip sent to 'the Hindu' on January 10, 2013 night, CPI (Maoist) special area military commission (Bihar, Jharkhand, North Chhattisgarh) spokes person Toofan claimed that People's Liberation Guerilla Army (PLGA) had killed 17 Security personnel 'PLGA killed seven on January 7 and 10 more the next day and seized sniper rifles, LMG's etc. The central forces beat local villagers and forced them to act as shields and carry corpses. This is against the norm of any war and we condemn this and express regret for the death of five innocent villagers – Jogeshwar Bhuia, Manav Singh, Vijay Turi, Promod Sau of village Navadi and one more ....." he said.

January 11, 2013

Belly bomb sewn into soldier's body article by Anumeha Yadav, *The Hindu,* January 11, 2013

Jawans shifting the bodies of security personnel who were killed in the Kakatiya forest in Latehar on Thursday.

The Maoist squad that attacked security personnel in Latehar on January 7, surgically implanted bomb inside the bellies of two–not one–slain men. The second bomb placed inside the abdomen of CRPF man Baidyanath Kisku actually went off unlike Babulal Patel which was found by Doctors at Ranchi's Rajendra Institute of Medical Sciences (RIMS) and subsequently defused. Two zonal commanders of the Maoist Army Harinath Singh and Dinesh Singh alias Panditji were arrested for the attack on January 11.

January 12, 2013

At least seven Maoists and a Greyhound constable sustained injuries in an exchange of fire on January 12 night at the border area of Andhra Pradesh and Chhattisgarh in Khamman district. Two tribals, a pregnant woman and a minor girl went missing from Nimmal gudem village in Sukma (Chhattisgarh) after a team of Khamman police and Greyhound raided the village.

January 13, 2013

Maoists set on fire 26 vehicles deployed in north Gadchiroli for road construction work. The incident occured between Lekha and Dodalwahi village in Dhanora Tehsil.

January 13, 2013

Milli Panda, wife of Odisha Maoist Party (OMP) President Sabyasachi Panda declared that she would contest as an independent candidate in the next polls. "I have decided to join mainstream politics after discussing with people", she said on January 13 at the meeting under the banner of Janamanch Odisha which she floated recently.

January 15, 2013

The villagers of Amwatikar – about 40 km from Latehar town – have alleged that security forces used their men, women and children as 'human shields' and forced them to look for and recover the bodies of CRPF men killed in the encounter of January 7. 22 Naxal-affected districts will not be able to build critical public infrastructure even in forest land – Ministry of Environment. 13 categories of public utility infrastructure include construction of school buildings, anganwadi centres, drinking water facilities, rural roads, Panchayat Bhawans/Community Halls, godowns/PDS shops and health centres.

In order to take on the Naxals, MHA cleared a proposal whereby worst affected state of Chhattisgarh, Jharkhand, Odisha and Bihar would raise specialised police forces trained in guerilla warfare and equipped with modern weaponary. These states would follow Andhra Pradesh model to hound Maoists.

January 16, 2013

Badarpu Malliyya alias Shekhar, the in-charge of South Gadchiroli divisional committee of CPI (Maoists) who surrendered before Andhra Pradesh police in November 2013 told *The Indian Express* that the government's twin strategy of security with development has begun to hurt the Maoists leaving the morale of their cadre affected. Originally from Macchupeta village in Karim, Shekhar was in Gadchiroli for questioning by police. Shekhar who is partly suffering from kidney and liver ailments and also because of "disillusionment" following the suicide last year by senior Maoist Divakar. Shekhar surrendered along with his wife Ponnan Saroja alias Vijaya. Shekhar had joined the Manthni Dalam in Karimnagar district in 1988 at the age of 24.

—*The Indian Express,* January 17, 2013

January 18, 2013

An IAF MI-17 helicopter on its way to rescue policemen injured in an encounter with Maoists crash landed after extremist fired at it in Chhattisgarh's Sukma district. The helicopter was on its way to rescue constable Besuram Mandawi and Assistant Platoon Commander Nand Kishore who were injured in a gun battle with Maoists in the Jungles of Sukma district. Yem Lal Sahu (29) a wireless operator who was aboard the MI-17 was also hit in abdomen by the Naxalites.

January 19, 2013

The Chhattisgarh police has found that Maoists are at an advanced stage of developing indigenous propellers and rocket launches which indicates that their strategic strength a rising and they pose a serious threat to aircraft in Bastar region.

January 20, 2013

A Maoist camp was busted and a huge cache of explosives and other materials was seized by the security forces from a forest in Ganjam district. The camp was traced to be located in Adipanka village, a hillock area under Gajalbadi Beat House of Saroda police station.

The Gadchiroli police alongwith Maharashtra's C-60 Anti-Naxal Force in an anti-Naxal operation gunned down at least six Maoists near Jimalgatta in Aheri Tehsil (Gadchiroli). The deceased Naxals were identified as Shankar Anna alias Muneshwar Lakda, member of South Gadchiroli divisional committee of CPI (Maoist), Vinod alias Chandrayya Kodape, Aheri local organisational squad Commander, Vinod's wife Geeta, a deputy commander of platoon 14, Zuru Mattami, Mohan Kowase and Sunita alias Pale Bandy Kodape. Shankar Anna was leading the Maoist squad that organised a meeting on the night of January 19 at Govindgaon.

January 20, 2013

A pressure bomb planted by Naxals which exploded at Jamiajara in Bokaro, bordering Ramgarh and Hazaribag district to target CRPF men when they were returning from a long-range patrolling at Jhumra Hills. 8 (eight) CRPF men were hurt.

January 23, 2013

After an encounter with Maoists on January 7, 2013 where 11 security personnel were killed, panic stricken villagers continued to flee Nawadh and Amvatikar village in Latehar district. four villagers were killed in a blast triggered the next day when they lifted the body of a CRPF trooper on police instructions. A hand written note signed by Bihar-Jharkhand North Chhattisgarh special Area Military Mission spokesperson Toofan, sent to the HINDU on January 21 stated "The PLGA had sewn a time-bomb with an ordinary circuit inside the Jawan's belly, not a circuit connected to stitches as the government claims. The bomb was set to explode at the site to maximise casualties among security forces but did not do so because fluids entered the circuit. We condemn the use of villagers to lift bodies."

(Latehar was carved out of Palamu district in 2001 identified as one of India's poorest 100 district in 1997).

January 24, 2013

Odisha Maovadi Party Chief Sabyasachi Panda issued an audio Tape indicating his interest to come to the dialogue table. "For a suitable atmosphere to initiate peace process and start dialogue with us, the government should stop violence and oppression on us" Panda added.

January 27, 2013

Naxals kidnapped eight (8) construction workers from Khaira in Jamui district of Bihar who were engaged in Bihar Rajya Pul Nirman Nigam for construction of bridge over Badalidih river.

January 29, 2013

Maoists killed a tribal 'Kabaddi' player during a village-level match to mark the Republic Day celebration. The match was organised between teams from two villages in Umarpal, Rajnandgaon district on January 26. Maoists suddenly opened fire at Parmeshwar (30) a resident of Kanker district. Another player Birbal was injured.

February 2, 2013

In an encounter between security personnel and Maoist, an active member of Kundan Pahan squad named Binda Pahan was killed in Khunti.

February 4, 2013

Maoist sympathisers Siddhartha Bhosale of Kondhwa, an economics student at Fergusson college, Deepak Dhangale, a poet-singer of Punee-based cultural group Kabir Kala Manch (KKM) and two girls-Mayuri of Nagpur and Anuradha Sonule of Chandrapur got bail from Bombay High Court which said "suspects could be sympathisers of Maoist philosophy but none can be said to be active members of banned CPI Maoists."

Maharashtra ATS had arrested the four in April 2011 alongwith three others – Angela Sontakke including from Pune and Thane.

February 3, 2013

The Andhra Pradesh-Chhattisgarh border area in Khamman district is again turning into a Maoist hotbed. Maoists flee back to Chhattisgarh after attacks in Andhra.

February 3, 2013

Seven hardcore Maoist-Sarbu Miniaka, Sona Wadeka, Lati Hikka, Jugal Mandingi, Iswar Hikka, Dcuru Miniaka and Hari Minika were arrested in the Jungles of Murlaput under the Laxmipur police limits during a combing operation in Koraput.

February 3, 2013

Gadchiroli place solemnised the marriage of Santhosh alias Nevra Kiddikola (28) and Shanta alias Nirmala Kudiyami (23) surrendered Naxal cadres at a temple at Aheri in South Gadchiroli. Santosh was Platoon No. 7 commander while Shanta was member of Perimili Dalam. Officials of Gadchiroli police played the role of family elders.

February 8, 2013

Maoist interlocutor Dandapani Mahanty was arrested from his residence in Berhampur town in Ganjam district over his alleged involvement in blowing up a mobile tower in Adipanka area of Gajpati district two years ago, i.e., in 2011. Mohanty was convenor of Jan Adhikar Manch and was trying to revive Maoist cadre.

February 9, 2013

Three persons–all residents of Howrah who have been involved in supplying arms to Maoists in Jharkhand were arrested in Kolkata.

February 11, 2013

Heavily–armed Naxals ambushed a CRPF patrol party in the jungles along the Chhattisgarh and Maharashtra border. The incident took place at Sirpur village of Pendri.

February 12, 2013

Soni Sori, the tribal accused of acting as a courier between

Essar Steel and CPI (Maoist) was acquithed by the additional sessions court of Anita Dehariya for want of evidence to substantiate the allegation.

February 13, 2013

Authorities confirmed the presence of armed Maoists in the jungles of Kerala-Karnataka border. They were first spotted by Malyalee plantation workers in the forests at Mankundi near Kanamvayal on Kerala-Karnataka border on February 1, 2013. Six Maoists armed had reached Kerala though anti-Maoist combing operation are on in Kerala forest.

Maoist were likely to attack certain police stations in Wayanad district on February 18, 'The Martyrdom day' of Naxalite Varghese and on February 19 the anniversary of the massive police action against Adivasi Yogi, who was killed. I Muthanga district.

February 18, 2013

Biju Janta Dal (BJD) member Pradeep Maharathy demanded in the State Assembly that Chief Minister Naveen Patnaik make a statement on the alleged nexus between Odisha Jan Morcha leader and Rajya Sabha member Pyarimohan Mohapatra and the Maoists.

The Supreme Court held that appointment for the post of a civil Judge cannot be rejected on only ground that a candidate's husband had appeared for some of the CPI (Maoist) leaders in bail matters. A Bench of Justices A.K. Patnaik and H.L. Gokhale criticised the Andhra Pradesh High Court for rejecting a candidate for selection for the post of Civil Judge.

February 19, 2013

More than 400 members of the Chasi Muliya Adivasi Sangh (CMAS) in the past one month surrendered in Koraput (Orissa) (since January 2013). Its a frontal organization of CPI (Maoists). CMAS was believed to be behind the 2011 abduction of BJP MLA Jina Hikaka of Laxmipur constituency.

February 19, 2013

The Odisha Jan Morcha's (OJM)'s students wing president

Prafulla Kumar Naik filed an FIR at the capital police station in Bhuwaneshwar against Chief Minister Naveen Patnaik and school of Mass Education Minister Rabi Narayan Nanda for their illegal nexus with the Maoists.

February 21, 2013

Sanik Munda (26), Great grandson of freedom fighter Birsa Munda (who lead the movement against the British rule in the 19th century) was brutally killed by extremists near Binda village under Murhu police station in Khunti (About 50 km from Ranchi). There was the war of supremacy between CPI (Maoist) and splinter groups and killed for providing shelter to one Pankaj Munda, who had formed his own group after estrangement from PLFI. Sanika Munda's body was found mutilated with the head crushed by stones and one of the hands chopped off. He was missing since February 20. Birsa Munda's, another great grandson Budhram was also threatened in 2011 by Kundan Pahan group. Shyam brother of Pahan had been asking for levy.

February 21, 2013

There was an encounter between police and Maoist in Harhanj but no casualties.

February 22, 2013

Maoists killed eight people including six policemen by triggering a landmine blast at Majhaulia village under Roshangunj police station area of Gaya district in Bihar.

February 22, 2013

Journalists of South Bastar boycotted Maoist and decided not to carry their reports until they punish their cadres responsible for the murder of Sukma based journalist Nemichand Jain (42) who was found brutally murdered in Tongpal, Sukma on February 12. 50 journalist from the region held a rally in Dantewada on February 21. Maoists immediately accepted the murder but later denied their role claiming 'Jain was a police informer'.

February 24, 2013

Panchayat Samiti member, Athnas Ba, was shot dead near his home in Simdega district by People's Liberation Front of India (PLFI) cadres.

February 26, 2013

The Delhi High Court asked the Delhi Police to reply to a bail plea filed by Kobad Ghandy (65) lodged in Tihar jail for more than three years on charges under the Unlawful Activities (Prevention) Act (UAPA) and also on charges of impersonation, cheating and forgery under various sections of the IPC.

February 27, 2013

The social activist Niyamat Ansari who had been fighting corruption in the Mahatma Gandhi National Rural Employment Scheme (MGNREGS) in Latehar. Apparently acting at the behest of culprits behind Ansari's killing, local Maoists have now threatened his sister Saida Bibi and even abducted Bhukhan Singh, the whistle-blower Ansari's close aide and companion in his struggle on the Centre's flagship programme. The ultras approached Saida bibi and threatened her with dire consequences. The party people (Naxals) told Saida to change her statement in court. They pressured her to say that she does not identify the persons languishing in jail (for murdering Ansari) and instead blame the 'party' for the crime. Seven (7) accused are behind the bars for the March 2, 2011 murder.

March 2, 2013

The Maoists were taking away foodgrains meant for mid-day meal in schools and public distribution system and even controlling projects under MGNREGA in Naxal affected areas of West Singhbhum district. This was revealed by an arrested hard-core Maoist identified as Chirwa in Jharkhand.

March 2, 2013

Suspected CPI (Maoists) beheaded a quack at Hudagada village in Seraikela-Kharswan district of Jharkhand. The torso of victim identified as Vijay Kumar Dey (37), a quack and the severed head were found lying within a distance of 15 meters.

March 2, 2013

People's Liberation Front of India (PLFI) cadres were believed to be behind the killing of a Kesalpur Panchayat member Athnas Ba in Simdega district on February 24.

March 8, 2013

A bench of Justices Aftab Alam and Ranjana Desai while considering the West Bengal state's appeal challenging the August 8, 2012 High Court verdict stayed Calcutta High Courts Judgement directing West Bengal to treat arrested members of the banned Communist Party of India (Marxist-Leninist) as "Political Prisoners" by declaring the outfit a 'political movement'. The Calcutta High Court had declared CPI (ML) spokesman Gour Narayan Chakraborty, who was facing charges under the Unlawful Activities (Prevention) Act "a political prisoner" under the West Bengal Correctional Services Act 1992. Six (6) other Maoists facing similar charges — V. Venkteswara Reddy, Sambhu Soren, Sagan Murmu, Chatradhar Mahato, Sukanti Barkey and Prasun Chatterjee – had also secured similar privileges from the High Court. The accused first sought 'political prisoner' status on July 4, 2011 but the trial court rejected the plea.

—Report by J. Venkatesan, *The Hindu*, March 9, 2013

March 9, 2013

Two woman Naxal were killed in a gun battle between ultras and a joint team of security forces. The team of security forces comprised of Bijapur police, CRPF and Greyhound force of Andhra Pradesh police. Incident was that of Chhattisgarh. One of the slain women was identified as Kunjan Deve of Kanchal. Maoists claimed the police killed two women and raped five during the raid. 10 villagers were also injured as per statement issued by Dakshin Bastar Division Committee of CPI (Maoists).

March 9, 2013

Maoists torched the house of PLFI zonal commander Laxman Yadav in Paki in Palamu.

March 11, 2013

The Orissa police claimed to have moved closer to nab Maoist leader Sabyasachi Panda (44) after they killed his right hand man Pradip alias Gobind Majhi (26) an encounter in the forests of Gajpati district. Pradip was second-in-command in Panda's set up and hold the rank of division committee member. (Panda was expelled in August 2012 by CPI (Maoists) for criticising general secretary and supreme commander Mupala Laxman Rao alias Ganpathy as 'autocratic' and 'dictatorial' in a letter.

March 12, 2013

A special task force Jawan Angad Kumar was killed and another Jawan Yashwant injured in an exchange of fire between security force and ultras in the forest of Chintagufa and Dornapal police station area in Chhattisgarh's Sukma district.

March 13, 2013

Jharkhand Maoists trapped 250 policemen on top of a hill for over 24 hours engaging them from below and preventing 1000 other cops from reaching them untill a team led by DG police finally rescued them. However, DGP Rajiv Kumar had denied that his troops were encircled. The encounter took place at Hill Number 974 between Sibil and Saksari villages of Chainpur block, Gumla. (Last time police suffered major casualties in Chainpur in 2001 when Maoists triggered a blast in Kurumgarh). —*The Indian Express,* April 11, 2013

Report by Ashutosh Bhardwaj

March 14, 2013

A special court in Ranchi sentenced two Maoist William Marandi and Shahdeo Mahato to life imprisonment and also imposed a fine of Rs. 5000 each for killing of 29 police personnel at Baliba in West Singhbhum district, Jharkhand on April 7, 2004. It was first major strike by Maoists after Jharkhand bifurcated from Bihar on

November 15, 2000. The rebels had been booked under Prevention of Terrorism Act (POTA).

The 12-hour 'Odisha Bandh' call given by Odisha Maovadi Party Chief Sabyasachi Panda in protest against the security forces killing his chief aide Gobind Majhi alias Pradip in an encounter in Karanjaguda forest under the Mohana police station on March 11, 2013. The bandh seems to have evoked little response.

March 12-14, 2013

In Karakona forest in Gumla district, a joint team of Jharkhand Jaguars, COBRA personnel and the district police conducted an operation to take on Arvindji, a central committee member of CPI (Maoist) Arvindji alias Arvind Singh has several aliases and hails from Sukul Chak village in Bihar's Jehanabad. He was leading Maoists when security forces were attacked/ambushed at Latehar's Katiya forests killing 11 personnel and they planted IED in the bodies of two slain security personnel. Arvind remained elusive. Jharkhand Director General of Police Rajiv Kumar himself joined the operation at Gumla. The forces rescued two personnel, Brajesh Licha and Bikram Roy from Maoists captivity after a prolonged gun fire. Maoists used them as human shield. The security forces deactivated 30 landmines and recovered 12 handguns. This operation also saw a casualty – Manoj Bakkla. Gopal, spokes person for Bihar-Jharkhand North Chhattisgarh special Area Committee refused the claim and said only one cadre of PLGA was killed in encounter.

March 18, 2013

Two commandos were injured in an encounter with Maoist in forest area near Maratola village of the east Maharashtra district.

March 22, 2013

Sriramalu Srinivas alias Sudarshan (55), a senior and top Maoist who was freed to ensure the release of abducted Malkangiri collector Vinod Krishna in 2011 was arrested from Wyra area of Khamman district in Andhra Pradesh. He is senior member of the Andhra-Orissa Border Special Zonal Committee (AOBSZC) of CPI (Maoist) and carried a reward of Rs. 20 lakh on his head and was operating in Kalimela area of Malkangiri in Orissa. An engineering graduate, he was a senior leader of People's War Group before it merged with Maoist Communist Center to form CPI (Maoist) in 2004. He was arrested by the Orissa police in 2007 near Chitrakonda in Malkangiri.

March 27/28, 2013

At least 10 cadres of the CPI (Maoists) including those occupying senior positions in the Bihar-Jharkhand-North Chhattisgarh Special Area Committee (SAC) were killed in Chatra district in a gunfight with a breakaway group. Tritiya Prastuti Committee (TPC). Police recovered 10 bodies at Kakramanda village. Lalesh Yadav, secretary, Madhya Zone of SAC, Jai Kumar Yadav, a platoon commander of SAC and two area commanders - Dharmender and Paul Yadav were among those killed. Tritiya Prastuti Committee (TPC) led by its founder Brajesh Ganju is active in Latehar, Chatra and Ranchi districts. TPC shot Maoists in cold blood and showed CRPF the bodies.

March 28, 2013

The National Investigation Agency (NIA) probing a 'larger conspiracy' by the Maoists declared Muppala Lakshman Rao alias Ganapathy and four other top leaders of the Central Committee as 'wanted' in connection with the procurement and manufacture of sophisticated arms and ammunition including Rocket Launchers. CPI (ML) (Liberation) leader Congraram Koul was murdered at Panitola in Tinsukhia Local CPI-ML committee filed an FIR naming local MLA Raju Sahu and some other Congress functionaries.

March 30, 2013

Maoists apologised for their act after their cadres murdered journalist Nemichand Jain in Sukma on February 12, 2013. They also requested Bastar journalists to end their boycott. Jain was branded by Maoists as a 'police informer'.

March 30, 2013

A Delhi based firm which was raided is being investigated for reported procurement of night-vision equipment by Maoists and its supply to Maoists in Chhattisgarh and Jharkhand.

(each piece of the night-vision equipment was estimated to cost nearly Rs. 20 lakh and can be used upto a distance of four kilometers).

March 30, 2013

Chatra police made efforts to trace 25 Maoists abducted on March 28, 2013 in Kunda Jungles of Lakarbandha, the Tritiya Prastuti Committee (TPC) decided to release them after having received a call from a Kangroo court. Abducted Maoist's families were also informed.

April 1, 2013

The Assam government announced a CBI investigation into the murder of Gongaram Koul, a CPI (ML-Liberation) leader in Tinsukhia. CPI (ML-Liberation) had accused Legislator Raju Shah and several local Congress leaders including Panchayat leaders Bijoy Gohain and Mridul Neog and a PDS agent Purushottam Singh for the murder. Sahu denied the allegation.

April 1, 2013

Tritiya Prastuti Committee (TPC) rebels released 16 out of 25 abducted CPI (Maoists) by April 1 from Lawalong jungles of Chatra about 100 km from Ranchi. The released Maoists also had to sign an undertaking that they will not re-join the Naxal outfit again.

It seems there is trial of strength between Maoists and TPC in the state. They clashed on March 27, 2013 at Lakarmanda village of Chatra district when the former were moving from Gumla to Bihar after being cordoned off by the security forces. In route to Bihar, Maoists were attacked by TPC. Maoists have alleged that TPC is being used by state police.

April 2, 2013

Two members of Kabir Kala Manch, (a cultural organization

having links with Maoists) surrendered before the Marine Drive police in South Mumbai. Two surrendered Manch activists were Sheetal Sathe and Sachin Mali.

April 1-2, 2013

Tritiya Prastuti Committee was founded in Chatra by Brajesh Ganju in 2004, a dalit, who had left the Maoists Communist Centre (MCC) citing the dominance of Yadavs in the party leadership and discrimination against Dalits. TPC is separated from CPI (Maoist). In a statement, Maoist (CPI-Maoist) alleged that the police and their 'vigilante group' TPC had cooperated to carry out the operation against them "We resolve to avenge the death of the People's Liberation Guerilla Army martyrs' said Bihar-Jharkhand North Chhattisgarh Special Area Committee spokesperson Gopal in a statement declaring Bihar-Jharkhand bandh on April 6 and 7. —*The Hindu*, April 3, 2013

April 3, 2013

Kurmanur Panchayat Sarpanch Bhagban Krisani was brutally killed by Maoist rebels in Malkangiri district's Chitrakonda area suspecting him to be a police informer. About 25 Maoist visited Krisani's home and asked him to accompany them to attend a meeting. But he was taken to the jungle, tried by Praja Court which awarded him death sentence. The reason for the killing seemed to be rivalry between tribals and the Kondareddy community, which aspires for tribal status. Kirsani, a tribal leader did not get alongwith the Kondareddy community in his gram panchayat. "The Maoists are supporting the Kondareddy community's demand of ST status. The killing is a tactics to scare the tribals into supporting the Maoist," according to Malkangiri SP Akhileshwar Singh. A Panchayat office was blown up by Maoist on April 2 night (i.e. 2/3) at Seeram village in Lohardaga district of Jharkhand.

April 3, 2013

Leaders and over 800 delegates of CPI (Marxist-Leninist) Liberation passed a resolution on the national and international situation, including the agrarian and rural struggles, on the movement against violence and for equal rights and the working class movement on the second day of the parties 9th Congress held in Ranchi. The convention was attended by CPI-ML delegates from Nepal, Bangladesh and Australia. The congress opposed the United Progressive Alliance's 'privatisation of natural resources and in sectors dealing with people's basic rights like education and healthcare.' The resolution also opposed the projecting Gujarat Chief Minister Narendra Modi as BJP's prime ministerial candidate in 2014 Lok Sabha elections.

CPI-ML (Liberation) General Secretary Dipankar Bhattacharya stated "Repression is the default setting of the Indian State's response to people's movements. Our party will back resistance movements and progressive adivasi struggles going on in Jharkhand. The left movement played an important role in the movement for creation for Jharkhand after independence. Now the state's politics is dominated by a nexus of corporate and politicians and we are open to allying with other left forces to challenge this. 'The Fifth Schedule norms, laws such as Santhal Pargana Act, Chhota Nagpur Tenancy Act are being openly violated in the state. Panchayat elections were conducted after over 30 years in 2010 but no power has been given to Panchayatiraj institutions. It is the same pattern in the setting up of POSCO plant in Odisha."

April 4, 2013

At Chainpur's crowded Thursday market, Maoist surrounded a police vehicle and opend fire killed five (5) policemen of Jharkhand police (JAP) in Gumla when their patrol was attacked near a Bus Shelter in the Chainpur police station area. An Asstt. Sub-Inspector, a Havaldar and three constables were killed. Maoists took away three INSAS rifles, 600 rounds of ammunition and eight hand grenades. The victims have been identified as Dilip Bedia of Ranchi, Ram Narayan Ram of Garhwa, Bhola Singh of Chapra in Bihar and Chotelal Murmu of Godda all from the state police. K. Anita alias Kaloari, head of the women's wing of the group and Bikram Mallick the head of the overground worker were arrested from Talpatnam jungle near Badagada. Gadchiroli police commandos killed five Naxalites in the south of Bhamragarh town of Gadchiroli. The encounter took place near Bhatepur village on the banks of Pranhita river.

April 5, 2013

Communist Party of India (Maoists) gave a call for 24-hour 'Bandh' on April 8 in Dandakarnya to protest the killing of cadres in Chhatra district of Jharkhand and Bhamragarh of Gadchiroli in Maharashtra, according to a press release signed by Gudsa Usendi, spokesperson of Dandakaranya Special Zonal Committee. The press release further pointed out that some important local level leaders and active party workers who died in the separate encounters were – Comrade Lalesh Yadav, a member of Bihar-Jharkhand-North Chhattisgarh Special area committee and Central Zonal Committee incharge of Bihar, Comrade Dharmendra Yadav, a Sub-Zonal Committee member, Comrade Prafful another Sub-Zonal Committee member, Comrade Jay Kumar Yadav, a platoon commander, Camrade Bha, Comrade Albert and Comrade Pramod.

—*The Hindu,* April 6, 2013

April 6, 2013

Maoists trigged an explosion that damaged the block Headquarters.

April 6, 2013

A suspected Maoist, Shyam Charan Tudu (26) was arrested by West Bengal police in Coimbatore district for his alleged involvement in the Silda camp on February 15, 2010 that killed 24 Eastern Frontier Rifles personnel.

April 7, 2013

MHA opined that TPC killing Maoists could be a sign of caste war.

April 7, 2013

A group of Maoists who attacked a police station in Gumla district were forced to flee after being counter attacked by the police. Maoists fired at Chanpur police station.

April 6, 2013

Maoists blew up a Railway track between Hajipur and Sarai stations. The blast was part of their two-day bandh in Bihar.

April 7, 2013

Communist Party of India (Maoist) blew up part of a Railway track between Chhipadohar and Hehegerha Railway stations in Latehar district in West Jharkhand. They also attacked public buildings in other districts during a 48 hour bandh declared by them protesting the killing of 10 Maoists in Chatra district on March 27-28.

In Chainpur, Gumla district, Maoists opened fire on Chainpur police station–no one was injured.

100 Maoists blew up part of power sub-station in Naxal dominated Jamui district under the Jurisdiction of Khaira police station. It was a part of 48-hour bandh protesting killing of 10 cadres in Jharkhand. Maoists also struck an Airtel mobile tower in Aurangabad district.

April 10, 2013

The National Investigation Agency (NIA) announced a cash reward of Rs. 15 lakh on top Maoist leader Mupalla Lakshman Rao alias Ganpathy and Rs. 10 lakh each on four of his associates for waging war against the government–4 associates are - Nimbala Keshav Rao alias Basavraj, Thippiri Tirupali alias Deoji, Balmuri Narayan Rao alias Prabhakar and Somji alias Shahdeve. Babu Mahopatra and Agni Polai were arrested on April 10 near Badagada. Both were Maoists of Sabyasachi group.

April 11, 2013

Seven buildings of Water Resources Department at Misirbigha village under Deo police station area of Aurangabad district were blown off by the Maoists. A live can bomb was also recovered from the spot. More than 50 Maoists were involved.

April 12, 2013

Seven people (four Naxalites, two civilians and a Jawan of

Maharashtra's special anti-Naxal force C-60 died in an encounter between Gadchiroli police and Naxals near Sindesur village in Dhanora division of Gadchiroli district of Maharashtra. The deceased police Jawan was identified as Govinda Farkade (41).

April 12, 2013

After seizure of "cylindrical shaped components" from Arjun Gunja and Mohan Vishwakarma, suspected members of the Central Technical Committee and Technical Research and Arms Manufacturing unit of CPI Maoists, the National Investigation Agency (NIA) began proble into Maoists plan to manufacture grenades. Both Arjun Gunja and Mohan Vishwakarma were arrested in West Bengal. West Bengal police also allegedly busted hideouts on the outskirts of Kolkata where Maoists were assembling grenades. Sadanula Ramakrishna, alleged Central Technical Committee head and brain behind the plan to transport grenade components to Jharkhand, Chhattisgarh and Orissa Maoists was arrested in February 2012. —*The Indian Express,* April 13, 2013

April 12, 2013

Four Naxalites and a policeman were among seven people killed in an encounter between rebels and police in the forest of Gadchiroli. The slain Naxals were identified as Pandu Gawade (38) and three women cadres – Chanpa Tursam (21), Vasanti Masru (17) and Sangita Atram (25). [Pandu is the husband of Indrakka, a divisional committee member of South Gadchiroli division. He was arrested in 2003 at Rajnandgaon in Chhattisgarh. After coming out of jail in 2008, he re-joined the rebels and married Indrakka].

April 12, 2013

Villagers of Sindhepur village in Gadchiroli district, where seven people died in an encounter between the police and Maoist on May 12, 2013 alleged that during the encounter that took place in a forest near the village, the rebels tried to use some of the villagers as human shields.

April 14, 2013

The National Human Rights Commission (NHRC) gave a

clean chit to the Chhattisgarh government on the treatment meted out to the tribal school teacher Soni Sori who was accused of acting as a courier between Essar Steel and Maoists.

April 14, 2013

Security personnel destroyed a Maoist camp and seized a huge cache of firearms and arrested a Maoist cadre in the triangular area of Badagada at forests of Orissa's Ganjam district. A Maoist by name of Ramjanam Yadav was overpowered by villagers and handed over to the police in Tandwa village under Amba police station in Bihar's Aurangabad district.

April 16, 2013

In one of the biggest operations in Dandakaranya, security forces killed nine (9) Maoists including five (5) women, in Sukma district of Chhattisgarh at Puvarti under Jagargunda police station. Among those killed were member Marri Ravi alias Sudhakar who carried a reward of Rs. 20 lakhs. Sudhakar was North Telangana Special Zonal Committee member. Sudhar's gunman Ajay was also killed. Other identified Maoists were (*i*) Pushpak, divisional committee member (Karimnagar), (*ii*) Sabitha (Warangal), (*iii*) Arelli Venkat alias Kiran (Karimnagar), (*iv*) Maddi Seetha alias Navatha (Mangpait), (*v*) Jagan Raju alias Durga Ram Raju (Warangal). All of them operated from Andhra Pradesh.

—*The Indian Express,* April 17, 2013

Sudhakar and other Maoists killed.

April 16, 2013

Ten (10) left wing extremists including a senior leader of CPI (Maoists) were killed and a dozen injured in an encounter with police forces of Andhra Pradesh and Chhattisgarh in Chintalnaar forest a of Bijapur district on the border of Andhra and Chhattisgarh. One of the killed has been identified as Kanakala Raji Reddy member of Central Committee of CPI (Maoist). A resident of Karimnagar district, he carried a reward of Rs. 12 lakh on his head. He was accused of attempt to murder two Chief Ministers N. Janardhan Reddy and N. Chandrababu Naidu.

April 17, 2013

A BSF helicopter involved in airlifting commandos conducting anti-Naxal operations in Andhra Pradesh Greyhounds was fired at in the jungles of south Bastar in Chhattisgarh – AP border to Bhadrachalam in Khamman district in Andhra.

April 17, 2013

Breakaway Naxal leader Sabyasachi Panda is becoming lonelier by the day. Panda lost about 50 cadres in a year – most of them arrested or surrendered. On April 15, camp follower Bighna Jagaranga surrendered before Raigarh SP. On April 11, Kandra Dalabehera alias Peter of Patachanchara was arrested during a joint operation by security forces.

April 18, 2013

The Bombay High Court rejected the bail application of Angela Sontakke (42), an alleged Naxal who was arrested by the Maharashtra Anti-Terrorism squad in April 2011 alongwith six others for their association with the banned outfit Communist Party of India (Maoist).

Naxalites killed a Reserve Inspector Shiv Prasad Babu of Greyhounds of AP police after capturing him while he was returning from an encounter site in Sukma district of Chhattisgarh on 16 April 2013. He was injured and sick and missed the helicopter which was to fly him back to the base camp. He managed to trek back but lost his way in the forest. Earlier six personnel were reported missing but five reached Khammam safely later. Shiv Prasad (Vishwa Prasad)'s body was reportedly kept at Korabutta village near Sukma. Local Bijapur journalists tried to negotiate with Maoists to retrieve the body of slain Greyhound.

April 18, 2013

A tribal youth, working as "under cover" policeman filed a petition in Bilaspur High Court seeking protection as the state police wanted to eliminate him. He was working in Surgujya region of north Chhattisgarh since 2002. He learnt about the links of top policemen with the Maoists during his employment as "under cover" and informed the state Home Ministry and later on he wrote to Union Home Minister P. Chidambaram on July 28, 2010. State police then approached him and asked him to keep quiet. Bilaspur High Court held the proceedings in-camera-press and outsiders were not allowed and also asked the state government to provide him security. —*The Indian Express,* April 20, 2013

April 19, 2013

Two ultras identified as Ohar Singh Jade (27) and Ramesh Nareti (25) were arrested during a search operation in Bastar region of Chhattisgarh – from the forest, of Kodogaon village in Kankar district. In another search operation in Narayanpur district two Maoists Ramder (24) and Mishir (22) were apprehended from Basing forest area.

Maoists attacked a jeep of police party when it was on its way to Basaguda from Bijapur and injured two CRPF Jawans.

April 19, 2013

Two members of the CPI (Maoist) Sabyasachi Goswami alias Kishore (the state committee member), Jakir Hussain were arrested from Kolkata's Jadavpur area.

April 24, 2013

A team of CRPF Jawans which was returning after search operation was fired at by Maoists in between Naimed and

Peddakodepal. A 10 kg improvised explosive device (IED) was recovered. Maoist were hiding in the bushes when they fired/ambushed which lasted for one hour.

April 26, 2013

1. Two Maoists – Aklanta Rabha and Siraj Rabha were arrested from near Gauhati from Jorabat on Assam-Meghalaya border. Arms etc. were recovered from them by the police. Aklanta is also known as Maheshji alias Saikia and is fluent in ten (10) languages. He is a lone member of the Maoist Central Committee from Assam in CPI-ML-Liberation. Siraj Rabha alias Bijoy Rabha was the chief training instructor of Maoists for the Jharkhand state.

2. While delivering the Rohini Ghadiok Memorial lecture at India Habitat Centre, Dr. Binayak Sen said there is a need for greater level of participation from the middle class in dealing with issues such as famine.

April 26, 2013

Two police personnel were killed in a Naxal attack in Chhattisgarh's Kanker district on a day when a bandh called by CPI (Maoist) effected life. Sub-Inspector Santosh Ekka and Head Constable Aliram Usendi were killed and two injured. The attack was led by the Madh division of the rebel's Dandakaranya Special Zonal Committee.

In a separate incident in Kanker district, around 100 Naxals torched a Bamboo depot of the forest department in Bande police station area.

April 27, 2013

Maoist insurgents put on fire the forest wood depot and the residential units located at Bodal village 18 km from the Bastar divisional Hqrs at Jagdalpur. Property worth 5-6 lakhs alongwith Government records gutted in the fire.

Rourkela police and CRPF, etc., seized 30 kg explosives from Saranda forest under the K. Balang police limits in Sundargarh district.

April 29, 2013

The Vice President of district unit of BJP Shivdayal Tomar was shot dead by Maoists in Kawad village under Katekalyan police station area in Dantewada district.

Three Maoists were killed in an encounter with the Jharkhand Jaguar Special Task Force and Commando Battalion for Resolution Action (COBRA) of CRPF in the Peerhi forest near Garu in Latehar district. The encounter took place less than 15 km from the Katiya forest, where 11 CRPF and Jharkhand Jaguar STF personnel were killed by Maoists on January 7, 2013. One INSAS Rifles and two. 315 Rifles were recovered from Maoists.

—*The Hindu,* April 30, 2013

May 2, 2013

A hardcore Maoist Mathew Bedbaka who is a close associate of Maoist Central Committee member Modem Balkrishna as well as a former associate of renegade Maoist Sabyasachi Panda was arrested in the forest of Kandhamal district (Orissa). Mathew Bedbaka hails from Rayagada district and was involved in several bomb blasts including the infamous ambulance blast of November 2010. He was picked up from his hideout in Meragudi village at Kotagarh area of Kandhamal.

Soni Suri who is branded as Maoist by Chhattisgarh police was acquitted by a Dantewada court for want of evidence. A tribal teacher she was named in the case related to Maoist attack on Congress leader Awdhesh Gautam on 7th July 2010. She is also named in Essar-Naxal pay off case in October 2011 as a conduit between the rebels and company. This case is still pending in the court. Soni Suri was acting as a courier between Essar Steel and the outlawed CPI Maoist.

Two Maoists cadres of Daula Dalam were killed in Kochora village, Narayanpur district of Chhattisgarh. Killed Maoists were identified as Phool Singh, Depty Commander of Daula Dalam and a member Jai Singh.

May 2, 2013

Maoists abducted three residents of Mahulapadara village under Mathili police limits in Malkangiri district.

May 8, 2013

The Odisha and Chhattisgarh police seized explosives weighing around eight kg in the Dharambandha forest under Sunabeda sanctuary 15-20 Maoists were residing in that make-shift camp in forest.

May 8, 2013

An encounter between Chhattisgarh Armed Force (CAF) and Naxalites took place in the jungles of Kistaram police station area (Sukma district) while carrying on combing operation. A security personnel of CAF was killed and three others injured.

A very senior leader and policy maker of CPI (Maoist) Anukul Chandra Naskar alias Goer Chandra Naskar alias Pareshji was arrested in Assam's Cachar district. Naskar hails from Balia under the Sonapur police station in 24 Parganas district of West Bengal. He joined Maoist Coordination Committee (MCC) in 1967 and rose to become a Central Committee member in 1985. When MCC and People's War Group (PWG) merged to form CPI (Maoist) in 2004 he was made a member of Central Committee and Polit Bureau. His presence in Cachar came to notice during the interrogation of Aklanta Rabha @ Maheshji and Siraj Rabha @ Bijoy Rabha who were arrested on April 26 on the outskirts of the city of Gauhati.

Manju Avlam (18) and Avlam Aaytu (21) Maoist courier were arrested from the forest village of Kaika (Bijapur).

May 12, 2013

Maoists attacked Akashwani and Doordarshan centre located on National Highway 16 at village Bade Marenga, about 13 km from Jadalpur and killed three CAF Jawans and injuring two other Maoist insurgents fired at Chhattiisgarh Armed Forces Camp located at Sukma in which a Jawan was killed. In DD centre attack,

Maoists fired at Alexandar Ekka, constable posted at sentry duty and he died on the spot. Thereafter the insurgents entered the relay centre and sprayed bullets on constables sitting there - Silwami Ekka and Basudeo - both died instantly. Mazhar was injured critically. In Chhattisgarh armed forces camp firing located at Temelwada in Sukma district, one CAF Jawan Shyamlal Kanwar was killed.

—*The Indian Express,* May 13, 2013

First attack on a media centre by Naxals in the district.

May 13, 2013

Maoists threatened to kill at least half a dozen important BJP as well as Congress leaders in a banner put up at Paneda in Geedam area. In the banner they threatened to kill MLA Bhima Mandawi, former leader of opposition and Congress leader Mahendra Karma, BJP general secretary Chaitram Atami, Tourism Board's deputy chairman Vijay Tiwari and his son Abhilash Tiwari before ensuing poll. —*The Pioneer,* May 14, 2013

May 17, 2013

CRPF attacked Edesmata village in Bijapur district of Chhattisgarh and killed eight villagers, three of them minors, in an encounter. —*The Pioneer,* June 1, 2013

May 17, 2013

Naxal Karam Badru and Murram Maso were killed in two different encounters.

May 19, 2013

A Maoist was killed in an encounter near Hetaiknsa village in Malewada area of Kurukheda Tehsil in North Gadchiroli.

May 24, 2013

Twenty armed Maoists attacked the house of a tribal Special Police Officer (SPO) Eanhu Charan Madhi (25) at Kattakonda village at Kalimela area. He was shot after he did not head to Naxal's threat to quit his SPO job or else he would be killed.

May 25, 2013

In an ambush laid by Maoists, killing Salwa Judum founder Mahendra Karma who launched the movement to outs Maoists from Bastar in 2005. He was killed alongwith 28 (Karma's PSO died on June 1) including several senior Congress leaders from Chhattisgarh, near Jheerum Valley near Darbha Ghaati (35 km from Jagdalpur) in Bastar district of Chhattisgarh state. 40 people were injured. It was biggest ever attack on a political party-Congress. Those killed included former Rajnandgaon MLA Udai Mudliar, Congress leader of Jagdalpur Gopi Madhwani, Congress President in Chhattisgarh Nand Kumar Patel and his son were abducted by militants. Next day their dead bodies were found with bullet injuries. The convoy of 20 vehicles faced road block by way of felling trees and triggering a landmine and then Maoists sprayed bullets for about two hours. About 150-200 insurgents aged 18 to 24 years took part in the attack.

On May 13 itself Maoists had threatened to kill atleast half a dozen important leaders of Congress and BJP including Mahendra Karma. But the Security Forces/Administration did not take notice of the warning.

PM described the incident as "security failure." Militant rebels danced after trapping Mahendra Karma and Nand Kumar Patel. The *Pioneer* newspaper (May 27, 2013) wrote "the combination of savagery precision and ease with which the Maoists carried such a large-scale ambush makes mockery of the joint operation so aggressively carried out in the South Bastar for nearly three years by the central forces and the local police. The fact that no one got a whiff of the gathering of nearly 200 armed Naxals is a sad commentary on the status of intelligence network in the district. National Investigation Agency (NIA) which was investigating the Darbha attack on Parivartan Rally of Congress Party on May 25 suspected the role of local party bosses in the episode. A sitting MLA Kawasi Lakhma from Maoist dominated Konta Assembly seat in Sukma district in Chhattisgarh and his son were suspected to be a key link between the conspirators and the Maoists. Lakhma was allowed to escape by the Maoists, who killed Salwa Judum architect Mahendra Karma, Congress State Chief N.K. Patel, etc., on May 25, NIA also suspected that call details records (CDRs) of the mobile phones of those accompanying the convoy pointed out that some people from convoy were continuously updating Maoists on the movement of the cavalcade and the route taken by it. Naxals had used 30 kg of ammonium nitrate in the attack to create a crater on the road so that the convoy is slowed down and then Naxals could fire on it. —*The Pioneer,* June 4, 2013

May 28, 2013

Bihar Police and Special Task Force (STF) arrested two Maoist- Pratima and Anup Thakur from a hotel in Muzaffarpur. Both of them were members of Bihar-Jharkhand and North Chhattisgarh Area Committee.

Anup Thakur (30) is Maoist military commission member. A cache of arms and ammunition was recovered by the police from Patki Jungles in Latehar. He was arrested with his girl friend Vinita from Sanskar Hotel in Muzaffarpur. DGP Rajiv Kumar, Thakur was entrusted with the task of consolidating the stronghold of Koel-Sankh in Palamau, Garhwa, Latehar, Lohardaga, Gumla, Gaya, Aurangabad and north Chhattisgarh districts. —*The Pioneer,* May 30, 2013

June 1, 2013

An assistant commandant of 211 Bn of CRPF S.K. Das (35) was killed in a gun battle/firing at village Khallari (about 15 km from Nagri town) in Dhamtari district of Chhattisgarh.

Bihar police arrested Jitendra Kumar, an area commander, from his house in Doraha village in Arwal district.

June 3, 2013

Kurasam Mothi Bai alias Madhavi (40), CPI (Maoist) South Bastar Division Committee Secretary and wife of North Telangana Special Zonal Committee (NTSZC) secretary Chandrana and two others were nabbed by the police after a 20 km long chase on Bhadrachalam-Kothagudem main road near Palvancha town. The remaining two persons were identified by the police as A. Prudvi (22) (Prithviraj) a student of integrated MA course in Hyderabad Central University and his father A. Dharmaraju (50), a railway employee of Chirala in Prakasam district. The car carrying the trio overturned at Peddamma Thalli temple–a few km away from Palvancha (near Bhadrachalam). Madhavi was heading towards Vijaywada to undergo treatment for an ailment.

She was arrested by fluke by the Khammam police who were checking vehicles when the car in which Madhavi and two others were travelling sped away. —*The Hindu,* June 4, 2013

June 4, 2013

The Union Cabinet accepted the long pending work of installing mobile towers at 2199 locations in nine (9) states effected with Naxal menace to improve communication system at a cost of Rs. 3046 crore. Locations where mobile towers are to be installed are Andhra Pradesh, Bihar, Chhattisgarh, Jharkhand, Maharashtra, Madhya Pradesh, Odisha, UP and West Bengal.

A 17-year old Maoist cadre, Garjan Singh was arrested in Balaghat with two country made fire arms. Singh was a resident of Kauwa Behra in Chhattisgarh's Rajnandgoan. He was a member of small action team of People's Liberation Army (PLA) Guerilla unit of CPI (Maoist).

June 5, 2013

Prime Minister Manmohan Singh while addressing a Chief Minister's conference in Delhi termed Lelf Wing Extremism a "very grave threat". It should be viewed in a holistic manner. He further stated that centre adopted a two-pronged strategy to deal with LWE. conducting proactive and sustained operations against Naxals and addressing issues of development and governance in the Maoist-affected areas. —*The Hindu,* June 5, 2013

PM also urged states to join hands against Naxals. The nine (9) states fighting Naxalism agreed that each one of them needed to follow the Andhra Pradesh model of anti-Naxal operations and build and strengthen their police's capabilities.

The Chief Ministers of Chhattisgarh, Andhra Pradesh, Maharashtra, Bihar and Orissa, Governor of Jharkhand and representatives of Madhya Pradesh, West Bengal and UP met at the end of CM's conference and promised to help each other in their anti-Naxal operations. The meeting wanted of making collective efforts to curb financing of Maoists by intervening in the tendu leave business which is a major source of funds, through extortions for the rebels. States also agreed to crack down in illegal mining which is another major source of income. —*The Indian Express,* June 6, 2013

June 6, 2013

Anup Thakur alias Subhash Thakur alias Tarun, a member of military commission of People's Liberation Guerilla Army (PLGA) who was arrested from Sanskar Hotel in Muzaffarpur (Bihar) on May 28 who is also a member of Bihar-Jharkhand North Chhattisgarh Special Area Committee of CPI (Maoist) admitted to have undergone training for the job of stitching a bomb inside the body. He underwent this training for this job with the Maoist cadre from Andhra Pradesh. He confessed to have been responsible for stitching a bomb inside the body of a CRPF Jawan who was killed at Katiya village of Jharkhand on January 7, 2013. Eleven security personnel were killed in the two day encounter between PLGA and CRPF. Bodies of four policemen were retrieved two days later. 4 villagers including a minor were killed when an improvised explosive device (IED) went off when they lifted the boy of Baijnath Kisku of CRPF's112 Bn on January 9. Two days later, an IED consisting of gelatin sticks, a detonator and a battery in a container was found inside the body of the other Jawan, Babulal Patel, and defused. Thakur confessed his role in 24 incidents of Maoist violence.

—*The Hindu,* June 7, 2013 Report by Anumeha Yadav

June 6, 2013

Bhursu Salam (30) who was involved in fatal attack on a sub-Inspector Shankar Lal Sahu in Bayanar, is a resident of Rengagodi village under Bayanar police station, Kondagon was arrested in a search operation in the jungles of Bayanar, Mungwal, Badko, Kunjung and Adnar. Salam used to work for Bayanar dalam.

June 6, 2013

A member of Adnar militia, Asman (20) resident of Adnar itself was arrested from his house on a tip off.

June 8, 2013

The Andhra Pradesh police conducted house-to-house search at Gutthikonda and Vemagiri villages to check if any Maoist sympathiser(s) is staying there after the Chhattisgarh incident of May 25, 2013. Police had already been keeping a close watch on the forest areas in Palnadu since there was a time when Maoists had made Gutthikonda, Julakallu and other surrounding villages their hideouts and also meeting points whenever the heat was turned on them by the police in Nallamala Hills.

June 11, 2013

Union Home Minister Sushil Kumar Shinde held Maoists as terrorists and underlined the way the Red ultras had killed innocent people in Chhattisgarh on May 25 showing the terror face of Naxal movement. "A person was fired bullets 74 times (on Karma's body) - he died in the attack – and stabbed 75 times. Can you say it is a simple thing ? Is it not terror ? It is a terror act", he said.

June 11, 2013

The Maoists have threatened BBC reporter and author Subhrangsu Chowdhury in Kolkata for his writings which they consider to be objectionable. The Maoists have cautioned

Chowdhury for an article in BBC Hindi – Master ki hat Naxlon ki Kaman (Head Master to Military Mastermind) – where he said the change of guard in the CPI (Maoist) in Dandkaranya is one of main reasons for the brutal attack in South Bastar on May 25.

June 11, 2013

The Global Peace Index (GPI) 2013 which was released in Mumbai has ranked India among the 25 least peaceful nations to live in. The country was placed 141 among 162 nations having lost more than two lives inaday or a staggering 799 persons to internal conflicts in 2012.

June 11, 2013

Maoists in Raipur defended the May 25 ambush in Bastar district and detailed why they attacked senior Congress leader Vidya Charan Shukla who died on June 11, 2013 in a Gurgaon hospital of wounds sustained in the attack. They mailed a 4-page document to 'the *Hindu*' newspaper and wrote four lines about V.C. Shukla saying he was a people's enemy who had acted as a loyal servant of imperialists, comprador bureaucratic bourgeoise, landlords and had played a key role in formulating and implementing exploitative government policies. The statement was issued by CPI (Maoist) state committee.

June 11, 2013

Two Maoists were arrested from Marudbaka village under Awapalli police station are in Bijapur district of Chhattisgarh. The arrested Maoists were identified as Gatpalli Narraiya (40) and Kunjam Lachhu (20), members of the Awapalli Jan Militia Group.

June 11, 2013

A statement on June 11, 2013 night came for the first time denying links with social activist and paediatrician Binayak Sen. The state wing of Dandakaranya Special Zonal Committee (DKSZC) called the book *"Let's call him Vasu"* by Journalist Shubranshu Choudhury 'a pack of lies, half-truths and scattered information.' The statement also stated 'even the disseminated information is distorted,... and true lies, especially, the episode on Dr. Binayak Sen and the so called relationship between Jeet and Mukti (Guha Niyogi) and our party." The party also reputed the allegation that it has taken money from Essar Steel as claimed in the book.

June 11, 2013

In a programme called Manomilan (Meeting of hearts) at Gadchiroli Police Headquarters under the initiative called 'Campaign Navjeevan', twenty eight extremists from different Naxal dalams in Gadchiroli and Chhattisgarh border areas surrendered before Gadchiroli police.

Gadchiroli Superintendent of Police (SP) Mohammad Suvez Haque, Deputy Inspector General of Gadchiroli range Ravindra Kadam and Aheri Additional SP Rahul Shreerame visited the families of Senior Naxal leaders, including that of Korchi Area Secretary of CPI (Maoist) Gopi alias Niringsay Madavi and Pahad Singh, the Divisional Committee Member of South Gadchiroli division of CPI (Maoist).

June 12, 2013

Vice President of steel major 'Lloyds Metals and Engineers', a Hyderabad-based mining contractor and a local policeman were killed by the Maoists in the jungles near Nanded village of Gadchiroli in Maharashtra. A message on a page of a register was found near the body of Lloyds Vice President Jaspal Singh Dhillon. Contractor P.A. Mallikarjun Reddy and Patil Rajesh Sadmake were the other two that were killed by CPI (Maoists) who claimed responsibility for the murders as part of their ongoing struggle to save the forests and land of tribals. The pamphlet left by Naxals near the bodies also stated "The government is trying to start mining in Surajagad and Damkodvadavi hills in Gatta. This is our reply to the 'Jan Virodhi' (Anti People) policies of the government. Dhillon Singh, Mallikarjun and Surajagad Patil have been punished as per the law of the People's government. Anyone who indulges in anti-people activities will be given the same punishment. We will fight against those who are hell bent on displacing Adivasi Janta (tribals) for mining."

June 12, 2013

Inderjeet alias Kapil Yadav, a close associate of CPI (Maoist) Central Committee member Arvindji and his associates had an encounter with the security forces near Kumandih railway station in Latehar (Jharkhand). Four Naxals were injured including Inderjeet who quietly slipped to Patna for treatment of his injuries. One woman Naxal was killed in Narayanpur district of Chhattisgarh, another woman comrade was liquidated in Bijapur.

June 13, 2013

150 Maoists gunfired 13331 up Dhanbad-Patna Intercity Express for about one and a half hours around 1 pm at Mananpur (Jamui). One RPF Jawan Sukanta Debnath was killed in the Maoist attack alongwith 1 Bihar police Jawan and a passenger. Maoist stopped the train at Bhalui Halt at a place about 175 km from Patna and then fired at it. Sukanta was a native of West Bengal.

June 14, 2013

Six of the fifteen men - including former Special Police Officers (SPO) Kicche Nanda and Kawasi Mangalram – accused of raping six tribal women during Salwa Judum compaign in June 2009 in South Chhattisgarh were acquitted by Dantewads Sessions Court Judge A.K. Beck after the women turned hostile and refused to recognise their alleged rapists. In June 2009, six girls from Samsetti and other villages had filed rape charges against nine SPOs and three Salwa Judum leaders whose names are Kartam Surya, Kovasi Mangal Ram and Kichche Nanda. Kartam Surya were killed by the Maoists in February 2012.

June 14, 2013

In view of the renewed threat of Maoists in West Bengal, the centre approved six additional companies of Central Armed Police Forces (CAPF). After the death of Polit Bureau member K. Koteshwara Rao in an encounter, Maoists have been trying to re-group in the state.

June 15, 2013

Maoist victims kin Monika Mahto and Kumkum Singh Sardar are contesting Panchayat Polls as Trinamool Congress candidates from Purulia, West Bengal. Monika's husband Rajan Mahato, a Trinamool Congress leader was killed by Maoist at Ghatberia on July 29, 2010 and Kumkum's father Ajit Singh Sardar and his son Banku Singh Sardar were abducted and killed by Maoist in Khumtar village.

June 18, 2013

Inderjeet alias Kapil Yadav, who planted bombs in the abdomens of slain CRPF Jawans in the January 7, 2013 Latehar encounter that killed 11 security personnel was arrested in Patna from a hospital. He was operations commander of the Eastern Regional Bureau Company of CPI (Maoist) and has been active in Koel Sankh area of Jharkhand and bordering areas of Gaya in Bihar.

June 20, 2013

Maoists allegedly put up some posters at Benageria village in Jhargrame police station (West Bengal) area sounding a caution for the State Minister Sukumar Hansda and Trinamool Congress leader Gourango Pradhan for buring alive an 80 year old woman Sabitri Sarkar. The poster said "The leaders who are responsible for the death of this 80 year old woman will be brought to justice at the people's court." But Jhargram SP Bharati Ghosh said "This is the work of some miscreants and not Maoists."

—*Times of India*, Kolkata June 21, 2013

June 23, 2013

Residents of Kuwari village (130 km from Ranchi) in Jharkhand's Gumla district submitted a statement to Gumla police on June 22 denying the report that six children were forcibly taken away by Maoists for conscription. The report to this effect had appeared on June 21 on the front page of a Hindi daily *'Prabhat Khabar'*. In an exclusive interview to 'the *Hindu*' Nakulji, Maoist Commander of the east Koel Sankh Zonal Committee – spread over Gumla, Lohardaga, Latehar districts – too denied the allegation stating "We do not forcibly recruit anyone, specially children and we cannot. If we did that, those who join will become a risk to the lives of other cadres by not following party discipline. There are some incidents in which adolescents join the party because they are drawn to what they see around them, even if their parents may not be supportive of their decision." All the children had gone to ferry the luggage and bag packs but returned to the village. Few children had actually accompanied the party cadre after they held a meeting in the village.

June 23, 2013

Police and Maoists exchanged fire near Murgel in Gadchiroli district of Maharashtra. Explosives, detonators were seized from the spot. There were no casualites.

June 25, 2013

The Odisha police arrested two Maoists from Malkangiri. They were suspected to be part of the group that ambushed the Chhattisgarh Congress leader's convoy.

June 24, 2013

In an anti-Naxal operation that began near Kumandih village of Latehar district of Jharkhand on June 24, 2013 and lasted till 26th June, there was exchange of gunfire. Maoists fired on the personnel of CRPF and Jharkhand Jaguar. None was hurt.

June 27, 2013

Four Maoists gunned down two police constables Rajreddy, Pocham Gaddewar in a marked in Maharashtra's Gadchiroli district. Constable's wife Ramadevi was also injured.

June 27, 2013

Bombay High Court granted bail to Ms Sheetal Sathe an activist of radical music group Kabil Kala Manch (KKM) and an alleged Naxal sympathiser on humanitarian grounds as she was expecting her baby next month. Ms. Sathe and her husband Sachin Mali, both belonging to KKM were underground for two years. They had surrendered at Mantralaya on April 2, 2013.

June 30, 2013

Two landmines were spotted in Madhupur under Lalgarh police station in West Bengal.

July 2, 2013

One hundred odd Maoists ambushed and killed Pakur Supdt. of Police in the forests in Jamia village in Jharkhand's Dumka district. 4 policemen were also killed. These policemen were travelling in a convoy of three Sports Utility Vehicles (SUVs) through dense forests of Jamia village. Police Supdt. Amarjeet Balihar, an adivasi, was passing through Kathikund forest in Pakur (Jharkhand) when Maoists surrounded his vehicle in Kathikund near Amrapada in the afternoon and began firing indiscriminately. CPI (Maoist) spokesperson Gopal issued an statement earlier on June 29, 2013 after Latehar district encounter of June 24 threatening that attacks will be intensified if the government did not call off "Operation Greenhunt". Four other policemen killed were identified as Ashok Srivastava, Manoj Hembron. Chandan Thapa and Rajiv Sharma. The injured were Bablu Murmu and Santosh Mandal.

July 2, 2013

Naxals killed Arjun Petta Madavi suspecting him to be a police informer. His body was found near Kalhed village in Sironcha division of Gadchiroli district of Maharashtra.

July 2, 2013

The spouses of slain Maoist Cherukuri Raj Kumar alias Azad and Journalist Hem Chandra Pandey, Mrs. K. Padma and Mrs. Babita accused CBI of deliberately delaying submission of all records in a court in Adilabad related to its final report on July 2, 2010 encounter.

July 2, 2013

Maoists thrashed two former members of the party's militia near Balapan village in Vishakhapatnam. This followed looting of the house of a former Mandal Parishad Territorial Constituency member Dora Chittibabu in the same village.

July 3, 2013

A container containing 25 kilo explosives was found in Jhargram's Jamaria.

July 4, 2013

Former Maoist leader Ghanti Prasadam was seriously hit when unidentified assailants fired at him outside a hospital in Nellore. The attackers pumped three bullets into his chest and stabbed him several times. Ghanti Prasadam, son of a farmer from Srikakulam, graduated from Bobbili college was arrested by Andhra police alongwith five others at Aurangabad in May 2006 for allegedly hatching a conspiracy against the government but was acquitted in August 2010 for want of evidence.

Maoist who killed Supdt. of Police of Pakur (Jharkhand) district on July 2 triggered more than 10 explosions in the forests of Kumundih in Latehar on July 4 and 5.

July 5, 2013

Dr. Binayak Sen was refused permission to participate in an international seminar on healthcare in conflict areas in Kathmandu by a Raipur court. The court order said "the application is not bonafide".

July 7, 2013

Six Maoist women were killed in an encounter with Gadchiroli police's C-60 commandos alongwith a section of COBRA commandos. Two bodies were recovered from Bade river on the bank of which encounter took place in jungles of Sewari in Etapalli division. The six women Maoists killed were probably part of platoon 3 and Kasansoor Dalam.

July 8, 2013

Maoist Shambhu Yadav was arrested at Dhamni village in Bihar's Aurangabad district.

Chhattisgarh High Court rejected bail to tribal teacher Soni Sori for having linkage with Maoist activists. She was arrested on October 4, 2011 in New Delhi. She was allegedly working as a courier for Essar Group.

July 9, 2013

The Supdt. of Police, Bastar Mayank Srivastava was held responsible for May 25, 2013. An internal enquiry held him 'acting irresponsibly' in having shifted additional forces to other districts.

July 14, 2013

A 45-year old Latehar women Jasmatiya Devi lost her right foot as she stepped on an Improvised Explosive Device planted by Maoists. The incident took place near her village in Latehar's Manika block.

July 16, 2013

Police gunned down a Maoist in the forest of Gorna Pujaripara village under Bijapur police station limits.

A former woman ultra carrying a cash reward of Rs. 15000 on her head was arrested in Chhattisgarh's Bilaspur district. The woman Kamla Gond had participated in various Naxal attacks in Balaghat district.

July 17, 2013

About 50 Naxals attempted to explode a bridge over Pilaru river by exploding bombs below the structure. Three Jawans of Special Auxiliary Police (SAP) and two private security guards were killed under Goh police station in Aurangabad district of Bihar. The toll later rose to six. The driver of a bus in which police reinforcement was being moved to the spot from Koh in Gaya district also died.

A Naxal carrying a reward of Rs. 5000 was arrested from Mungwal village under Bayanar police station limits of district Kondagaon in Chhattisgarh. The Naxal Hinsaram Muriya is a member of CPI Maoist – Bayanar Dalam.

July 19, 2013

Three Maoists were killed in an encounter with anti-Maoist force-Special Operation Group and Rayagada district police inside Tureighati forest near Kirambadunguri village in Orissa.

July 21, 2013

Constable Dhansai Sori, posted with Benoor police station was abducted by Maoists from Narayanpur district of Chhattisgarh alongwith his friend Ghyasiram.

July 22, 2013

Two villagers were brutally beheaded in Gumla by Maoist's splinter group – Pahari Cheeta.

July 23, 2013

Maoists killed six cadre of People's Liberation Front of India (PLFI) in Murhu Block of Khunti district of Jharkhand. Their bodies were recovered from Burudih-Namsilli jungles. (PLFI were part of earlier Maoist Communist Centre but now it has become almost a criminal gang).

July 27, 2013

State Bank of India, Jharkhand officials – Branch Manager Pramod Kumar, Field Officer Anup Kumar Lal and accountant A. Karketa – were kidnapped by suspected Naxals while they were heading towards Ranchi from Panki in a car. They were abducted in Palamau district of Jharkhand. Branch Manager Pramod Kumar managed to escape on July 27/28 and reached Herhanj police station in adjoining Latehar district. The driver of the vehicle was released by Naxals.

July 28, 2013

The body of police constable Dhansai Sori (25) who was abducted by Maoists on July 21 from Narayanpur district was recovered from dense forest area of Maharabeda village between Jhara and Dhaudai police stations. His friend Ghyasiram who was also abducted alongwith him was released later.

July 28, 2013

Anil Purti (25) one of the two PLFI cadres who escaped Maoist's attack on July 23 in Khunti district's Murhu block which left six of the dead, surrendered at Ranchi's Rajendra Institute of Medical Sciences. Anil Purti hails from Buruma village in Murhu and had suffered two bullet injuries. Anil said "the area where the attack took place is controlled by the CPI (Maoist). Ram Mohan is the area commander. The organisation decided to try and drive them out. Our mission was to lay the ground work for it there, by concentrating on Namsilih village. We were there to talk to the villagers to draw them to the PLFI. We had visited the village in the evening. It was our first night of camping in the area." (See ! What excellent intelligence Maoist could get. Within hours they struck).

July 29, 2013

A rifle seized from suspected Maoist courier Anil Kumar Yadav and arms supplier Prafulla Kumar Malakar, both residents of Bihar, in Hazaribagh on August 29, 2012 was confirmed by the National Investigation Agency that the M-16 assault refle recovered in Jharkhand is genuine and standard issue of American military. It was manufactured in 1960s.

July 31, 2013

Paltu Sen, a member of the Central Committee of CPI (ML) New Democracy and State Secretary of the West Bengal unit passed away in West Bengal. The revolutionary trade unionist was also All-India President of Indian Federation of Trade Unions.

July 31, 2013

Maoist 'Sub-Zonal Commander' Niraj Yadav and 'Area Commander' Baleshwar Yadav were killed by rival faction Tritiya Prastuti Committee (TPC) in the forest of Jharkhand's Chatra district. Bodies of these two self-styled commanders were recovered from the jungles of Chatra's Pratapur block on August 1, 2013. Under the Gerua bridge. They had allegedly been abducted by the TSPC alongwith four others from Parasachuan village in Bihar's Gaya district on July 31.

July 31, 2013

Maoists killed Sumar Usendi, former Zila Panchayat member and a cousin of forest minister Vikram Usendi in Solangi village of Kanker district.

Index

R